Gifts 2

How People with Down Syndrome Enrich the World

Edited by Kathryn Lynard Soper

Foreword by Madeleine Will

Woodbine House   2009

All rights reserved under International and Pan-American copyright conventions. Published in the United States of America by Woodbine House, Inc., 6510 Bells Mill Rd., Bethesda, MD 20817. 800-843-7323. www.woodbinehouse.com

Cover photo of the Riley Family by Crystal DelaHoz of Love, Me Photography

Library of Congress Cataloging-in-Publication Data

Gifts 2 : how people with Down syndrome enrich the world / edited by Kathryn Lynard Soper.
-- 1st ed.
   p. cm.
 ISBN 978-1-890627-96-6
 1. Down syndrome--Patients. 2. Children with mental disabilities. I. Soper, Kathryn Lynard. II. Title: Gifts two.
 RJ506.D68G54 2009
 362.198'92858842--dc22

                                         2009023578

Manufactured in the United States of America

10   9   8   7   6   5   4   3   2   1

Dedication

• • •

In loving memory of
Melissa Riggio

Contents

● ● ●

●

THE GIFT OF AWARENESS

THE GIFT OF COURAGE

●

THE GIFT OF JOY

Acknowledgements

● ● ●

RALPH WALDO EMERSON said, "The only true gift is a portion of yourself." This anthology is the product of many true gifts, generously offered by individuals and families in order to make the world a better place for people with Down syndrome.

I thank the 76 contributing authors to this anthology, as well as the individuals with Down syndrome featured in their stories. I applaud them for being agents of positive change, and I am grateful for their encouragement and cooperation throughout the publication process.

I thank my assistants: Jessica Capitani, who provided much-needed help in managing essay submissions, and Rebecca Phong, who skillfully compiled the photo submissions. Their many hours of diligent effort are much appreciated.

I thank my agent, Kate Epstein, and the staff of Woodbine House for making the business of this publication a pleasure. Extra thanks to Nancy Gray Paul and Susan Stokes for their valuable editorial assistance.

I thank the 63 mothers who contributed to the first volume of *Gifts*, and the thousands of readers who have cherished that volume and shared it with others. Their enthusiasm provided the foundation for *Gifts 2*.

I thank my family for their continuing love and support. I especially thank my husband, Reed, for his rich contributions of time and energy which made the completion of this volume possible. And finally, I thank my son Thomas for being its inspiration.

Foreword

● ● ●

THERE IS NO WAY to underestimate the power of personal narrative in attempting to convey an authentic message. Data, research findings—they are important, too. But a personal story lingers in the reader's mind and heart.

Over the past decade more and more studies have documented important aspects of the lives of people with Down syndrome in their families and in their communities. These studies reveal that people with Down syndrome face obstacles but that assistance and support is often available to them and that the path to productivity and independence is becoming wider and brighter. Studies also indicate that among parents of children with Down syndrome there is a lower divorce rate than among those who do not have a child with Down syndrome, and, interestingly, siblings of children with Down syndrome affirm again and again that having a brother or sister with Down syndrome has enriched their lives.

Part of the cultural archive of information we have compiled from the experiences of countless individuals with Down syndrome and their families over past decades and several generations, these research findings, these facts, are often expressed in the dry, detached language of scholarship. In contrast, this volume of personal stories, which validate research findings, catapults us into a world that is deeply authentic and poignant, full of experiences that are carefully drawn and lovingly articulated in the unique voice of each author. The narratives present life slices that, when taken as a whole, reveal the rich, layered, and meaningful reality that many of us recognize as life in the Down syndrome community. One can't help but be struck by the use of images of light in the stories—tunnel, open eyes, vision, seeing, for example. These words stand in stark contradistinction to other words like "defect" and "burden" that permeate our society and which we are determined to sever from our children by shining light on our reality.

As the words of the great hymn, perhaps the greatest of all hymns, tell us—"I was blind but now I see." Oh yes, the message is clear and persuasive: the challenges are real but so are the gifts—the gifts of acceptance, awareness, friendship, courage, and joy.

Madeleine Will
Director, National Policy Center
National Down Syndrome Society

Introduction

• • •

Gifts to Open

SUMMER, 2008. Halfway through the "New Parents' Survival" workshop at the National Down Syndrome Congress convention in Boston, we paused for a question-and-answer session. Almost immediately, a woman with a young baby in her arms stood up.

"I don't have a question," she said, "but I was hoping I could speak for just a moment."

I exchanged glances with Jennifer Graf Groneberg, my co-presenter for the workshop. She looked as curious as I was. "Sure, go ahead," I told the woman.

She took a deep breath. "This is Grace," she said, holding her baby a little higher so we could better see. "I just wanted you to know that if I hadn't read your book, my daughter wouldn't have been born."

The room grew quiet and still, and a lump rose in my throat. "Please tell us more," I encouraged the mother. She went on to explain that when she received a prenatal diagnosis of Down syndrome for her first-born child, she and her husband had reluctantly decided that abortion was their best option. But then she read *Gifts: Mothers Reflect on How Children with Down Syndrome Enrich Their Lives.* She was touched and transformed by the stories in the book, true stories of ordinary women finding joy and purpose in mothering children with Down syndrome. Together with her husband, she decided to continue her pregnancy. And the result was baby Grace, a beautiful little girl with bright eyes and pink cheeks.

It was difficult to continue the presentation after such an emotional exchange. Since the publication of *Gifts* the previous year I'd received a great deal of positive and poignant feedback. But I'd never before experienced such tender and dramatic confirmation of the power of its stories. Sixty-three mothers of children with Down syndrome took the time, energy, and risk to share their experiences with the world. As a result, the world changed—and not only within the walls of Grace's loving home. The full impact of *Gifts* cannot be measured, but it's clear the collection has brought comfort, knowledge, and healing to many, and is changing minds and hearts for the better.

In this spirit, I'm pleased to present *Gifts 2,* a companion volume of stories written by a wide variety of people whose lives have been touched by an individual with Down syndrome. Not only do we hear from members of immediate and extended families, but also from neighbors, doctors, teachers, coaches, therapists, and friends. The individuals with Down syndrome highlighted in their stories range in age from infancy to adulthood, providing a colorful spectrum of experiences. And as in the first volume of *Gifts*, the perspectives shared are rich with emotion, insight, candor, and humor.

As I've edited this collection, I've been impressed both by the uniqueness of each story, and by the thematic threads that knit the stories together in meaning and purpose. We might not expect to find common elements in the differing stories of a wrestling coach and a grandmother, or a speech pathologist and a neighborhood friend, or a genetic counselor and a doting aunt. But we do. Again and again, as the authors stand up to "speak for just a moment," they describe the positive change sparked and nourished by their relationship with an individual with Down syndrome. They reveal the gifts discovered in these relationships: acceptance, awareness, courage, friendship, and joy. They discover new definitions for words like *perfect* and *success*, and they emphasize that in their caregiving roles with people with Down syndrome, they learn more than they teach, and receive more than they give. As story links to story, the separate voices of the authors combine to form a vibrant chorus of celebration and gratitude.

My son Thomas, who has Down syndrome, recently turned three years old and began preschool. As the bright yellow school bus stopped in front of our home, collected my little boy, then drove slowly away, I was overcome by bittersweet emotion that has lingered on, enveloping me even in this very moment. How thankful I am that Thomas is my son. How amazed I am that his first three years have passed so quickly. I'm proud of him for taking a significant step toward independence. But I worry about sending him out into a world that offers more opportunities than ever to people with Down syndrome, yet remains steeped in doubt regarding their value and capacity as human beings.

That's why books like this one matter so much. I believe the chorus of voices arising from its pages will strike a chord in the lives of many, making the world a more welcoming place for my son and for all children whom society classifies outside the bounds of "normal." I don't believe any reader can come away from this volume without increased esteem and respect for individuals with Down syndrome and the contributions they make, both in their homes and in society at large. Yes, these stories prove that people with Down syndrome enrich their families beyond measure. But just as importantly, these individuals enrich the world. A world belonging to all human beings, no matter what their chromosomal configurations may be. A world that has yet to fully appreciate people with Down syndrome, and has only just begun to open their priceless gifts.

Kathryn Lynard Soper
South Jordan, Utah

THE GIFT OF ACCEPTANCE

Eleanor Nipe, Evan Anderssen, Eli Anderssen, and Kate Roberson

1.
Family Ties

by Deborah Nipe

COLORFUL CHRISTMAS LIGHTS sparkled in the windows of the cottages of Whitten Village as my friends and I drove through the gate. We were a typical group of college students, excited by the prospect of Christmas vacation only a few days away. Whitten Village was a residential facility for adults and children with developmental disabilities, and with all good intentions—it was the Sixties, after all, and we all wanted to save the world—we had come to sing carols and deliver holiday treats. My roommate Mary and I were a little nervous, since as freshmen it was our first time being part of this annual event.

As we were led through the facility, stopping at several places to sing carols, we experienced a variety of reactions to our presence. Some of the residents smiled shyly and clapped their hands to the music. Others seemed barely aware that we were there. But then we were taken to the cottages where the children who had Down syndrome lived, and the mood changed completely! One cottage was full of little girls, all with the same short haircut and bright red nightgowns. They were so happy to have us there, and their smiling faces glowed in the lights of the Christmas tree. Mary and I both had long hair then, and the children came closer to touch it, and put their small hands gently on our faces. They loved it when we sang "Jingle Bells" for them, and were delighted with our gifts of candy canes and homemade cookies. When it was time to end our visit, we reluctantly returned to campus and prepared to go home to our families for the holidays. But these precious children would spend Christmas with their caregivers.

Fast forward about forty years, to a phone call from my daughter, telling me that the doctors' suspicions were indeed correct, and that the son that she and her husband were expecting did have Down syndrome. We already knew from a routine ultrasound that the baby had a serious heart defect, which the doctors said was cause to suspect Down syndrome, pending further testing. For some reason I hadn't been overly worried about the heart issue, since I knew that remarkable surgery could be performed to correct these defects. But Down syndrome? I had no idea what to expect with that diagnosis.

I had waited impatiently for my daughter's call, and when it came I could tell from the sound of her voice that they had not received the news they wanted. I tried to be calm while she grieved. She cried for the baby growing inside her, and she cried for her first child, who would only be 13 months old when this new sibling arrived. When our conversation ended I wept, not only about my grandchild's diagnosis, but also because it was very hard to see my child in pain and be helpless to fix it. I wondered how this baby would change our lives, and whether our family would be able to love and accept him with whatever challenges he might bring. And I remembered the little girls in their red gowns, and wondered if this was what the future would be like for my grandson.

After the initial shock of the diagnosis, I became a woman obsessed. I couldn't read enough about Down syndrome. One of the first things someone shared with me was "Welcome to Holland" by Emily Kingsley, which I thought was a beautiful analogy. Through a Down syndrome list-serve group I discovered articles by Dr. Len Leshin, Michael Bailey, and others, who wrote from personal experience about having a child with Down syndrome. I talked to teachers who work with children with special needs in public schools, and therapists who work with them at home. Thankfully, one thing I kept hearing from parents of children with Down syndrome was that their children were more like other family members than different. I was comforted by that, and began to look forward to the birth of my third grandchild and to being able to watch him grow.

Evan arrived a month early, but his birth was fairly uneventful. I saw him when he was about five minutes old and he was beautiful. He looked a little like his big brother, Eli. I was so proud of my daughter and her husband and their knowledge of Evan's condition. The questions they asked the doctors showed that they had prepared themselves well for possible problems. But Evan surprised everybody and had none of the issues they had worried about! He stayed a few extra days in the hospital and then his parents were able to take him home.

The first six months of Evan's life were just like the first months of any baby's life. The heart defect really caused no symptoms during this time, and when the doctors decided it was time to correct it, we traveled to Charleston to have this issue addressed. This trip was a team effort, with my son John and his wife, Amy, taking care of Evan's older brother, Eli, who was 21 months old. My sister took charge of the preschool we own together so that I could be with Evan and his parents. Evan's grandfather traveled to Charleston from another state. Evan's sister Brittany, a college student in Charleston, was at the hospital with us. During the surgery, Evan's extended family and our friends kept in touch by phone and email, and my nephew (also a college student in Charleston) came to sit with us while we waited. Already, Evan was an important member of our family. Together we rejoiced when the surgery was successful, and we gratefully returned home.

With Evan's health stabilized, we could relax and move on with the business of getting to know this little person who had already become such an important part of our family. I watched in amazement as I saw his parents treat him just like his brother Eli. His Daddy rolled on the floor with him, lifting him high in the air and "airplaning" him on his legs, and I knew his Dad was thinking of the day Evan could go with him as he hikes the trails and cycles up the mountain. His mother took him everywhere and kept him close to her in the kitchen while she made breakfast, so that he could "help." They talked to him, and sang to him, and read to him, and took him to the zoo and to the park and to the mountains to pick apples. As a result, Evan's personality started to shine through, and much to my delight I saw traces of his parents and brother clearly evident in him. Before he could walk, when he held onto his easel with one arm and used a marker with the other, I saw in him his mother, who is studying to be an art teacher. When he pushed the kitchen stool over to the sink and climbed up, I knew he had been watching Eli, who has been helping in the kitchen since he could walk.

I confess, all that time I was watching anxiously to see if Evan's personality would reveal any likeness to his grandparents and extended family, and I wasn't disappointed. Evan's household includes two dogs that he loves, and when one of his first words was "woof," I thought, *Oh, he's going to be an animal lover like me.*

When I noticed that music makes him stop dead in his tracks, cock his head, and listen intently, I thought, *Oh good, he's going to be musically gifted like his Uncle John and his Grandpa and his great-grandmothers.*

When we took him to the bookstore and he greeted everyone with a smile and a big "Hi!" he reminded me of his paternal grandparents, who are both friendly and outgoing and at ease in groups of people.

When I picked him up and he leaned his head into mine and patted my shoulder, I thought of his great-grandfather Pop, who is kind and gentle and soft-spoken.

When I see Evan climb into the overstuffed reading chair and pore over his favorite books, I think of my mother, whose favorite spot in the house was the kitchen table. She always had a tall stack of library books at home and spent hours each week reading biographies and books about politics. Her house, like Evan's, still has books in every room.

This week I traveled to my daughter's home to celebrate Christmas day with her family. They live in a wonderful house in the woods, on the side of a mountain. As I came in the front door, the twinkling of the tree lights, the sight of the stockings hung on the stair railing, and the delicious aroma of Christmas dinner warmed my heart. Three little boys (Evan became a big brother to Callum last year!) played near the tree, in the midst of a mountain of wrapping paper and ribbon and new toys.

After dinner and more gifts, I stole a quiet moment with Evan. As he proudly showed me how his new toy worked, I thought of those little girls in their red gowns many Christmases ago. I wonder about their families and the circumstances that prevented them from keeping their children at home. How different Evan's life is from theirs. He lives in his own home and shares bunk beds with his big brother, with his little brother in a crib nearby. He is surrounded every day by a family that loves and supports him. He has a large extended family of grandparents, great-grandparents, aunts, uncles, and cousins who see him not as a child with a disability, but just as our Evan—and he can identify each of us by name. He is part of our family.

And those wise parents who shared their experiences of living with children with Down syndrome were right—he *is* more like us than different.

●　●　●

Deborah lives in South Carolina, where she and her sister operate a preschool in a beautiful old Victorian house. She loves reading, painting furniture, and spending time with her grandchildren, Eleanor, Eli, Evan, and Callum.

Peyton Burgener with his big sister Ashley Henna

2.

From Weird to Wonderful

By Ashley Henna

"ASH, ASH." THAT'S what I heard from the little voice on the other end of the phone. My mom had put the phone to his ear, and he knew that it was me, his big sister Ashley, talking to him. His greeting gave me a big smile.

Actually, I've always got a big reason to smile. He's got big blue eyes, the longest eyelashes I've ever seen, and untamed blonde hair that sticks out in eighty directions. His belly is huge and his laugh is contagious. His smile makes my heart melt. People talk about how cute he is, and I'm the first to agree. He's a stud. He's my little brother Peyton, and he has Down syndrome.

When my mom told me on that snowy February day two and a half years ago that I would be a big sister for the third time, I was less than thrilled with the news. I would be twenty-one years old when the baby was born, a year older than my mom was when she had me. At a time when my friends were welcoming nieces and nephews or getting married and starting their own families, my family's situation was definitely not typical. I was the only one among my circle of friends who had divorced parents and remarried parents. It made me feel even more self-conscious to have expectant parents!

I was angry and embarrassed with the whole situation. I could seriously be this kid's mom, yet I'd be its sister? It was all just too weird for me! Plus, since I was so much older than the new baby, would it even know me? Doubtful. I was going to college two hours away from home, and as soon as I graduated my plan was to move to LA. A new sibling definitely didn't fit into my plan, and I definitely wasn't going to change my plans to make it fit.

To top it off, I didn't even know what to do with a baby. Sure, they're cute to look at, but what do you say to a newborn? It certainly can't talk back! Which way is the right way to hold it? With my clumsiness, I was almost sure that I'd drop it! And having to change a diaper? Disgusting! I had never been a babysitter, and I obviously didn't know the first thing about a baby. And I didn't especially care to learn.

Peyton was born on September 15, 2006, just three days before my twenty-first birthday. When I arrived home for the weekend, I went to the hospital to meet the new little guy. As I (reluctantly) held him for the first time, to my surprise, this day-old little baby grabbed my finger. He had me. I was done. Me, a girl who had no idea what to do with a baby, was putty in his little hand. From that second on, my whole life was different. Instantly my embarrassment, resentment, and disinterest transformed into a strong desire to be with my tiny brother every single day.

When Peyton was a week and a half old, my mom called to tell me that he had Down syndrome. I was upset at first, but after reading tons of information and asking a million questions, I knew that

Peyton would still be able to do anything everyone else could do…
he just might have to work a bit harder at it. In my mind I had made
a commitment to be the best sister that I could be for him, no matter
how much older I was or how far away I lived.

The older Peyton has gotten, the more I have wanted to be
around him. When the time came for me to make my official decision to move to LA, I changed my plan and opted to stay closer to
home. I now live in St. Louis, which is only an hour away. I am the
intern at the Down Syndrome Association here, where I have gotten
to know some great people who have become very important in my
life. I see Peyton at least once a week, and I couldn't be happier. Each
and every time that I see him, he has learned something new or has
gotten better at things that he has been working on. He's learning
new animal sounds, new words, and new sign language gestures.
He's crawling, pulling up on furniture, and getting closer and closer
to walking. I'm always so excited and proud to see all of the new
"tricks" he has learned.

It's so hard to believe that two years ago I didn't particularly
want this little guy in my life, but now I can't even imagine my life
without him. People ask me, "Isn't it weird having a brother who's
twenty-one years younger than you?" But even my slightest thoughts
along those lines are immediately squelched by the idea of how awesome it is when Peyton reaches for me every time I see him. Or how
every time I come home or come downstairs in the morning, he is
the first one to greet me with that big, beautiful smile of his. Or how
when I hang him upside down or tickle him, his laugh makes me
laugh even harder. Or how exciting it was when I first taught him
that a cow says "moo." Or how one of his first words was "Ash" and
he excitedly repeats it and points when he sees me. Or—my favorite—how just the other day he crawled over to me and pulled himself
up to give me a hug.

None of that is weird to me. Instead, it's wonderful.

● ● ●

Ashley was born and raised in Vandalia, Illinois, and is a 2008 graduate from Southern Illinois University Carbondale's advertising program. She currently lives in St. Louis and spends most of her free time at the Down Syndrome Association. She enjoys photography, movies, traveling, Wii, and spending time with her family and friends. She is more proud of her best buddy and brother, Peyton, every day. He has now learned to walk!

Betty and Jeff Schmidt

3.

Paving Roads

By Betty Schmidt

WHEN OUR SON Jeff was born, my husband said to his father, Jeff's grandfather, "Well, Dad, he'll never be a rocket scientist."

His father responded, "Well, Son, you never became president of the United States, but I love you for who you are."

Wise words from an eighty-year-old man who saw his only grandson as pretty near perfect. If he had hopes for a Rhodes scholar, no one knew it. He felt he'd received the greatest gift in his grandson, Jeff, and went on to mentor the little boy just as he'd taught his own son.

Jeff has grown up on the same plot of land where his grandfather was raised. "Gha," as Jeff called his grandfather as soon as he could utter sounds, arrived on his riding mower each clear morning during spring and summer. He sat Jeff between his legs and took him on a journey around the farm's open spaces, circling and threading their way between the orchard trees and the expansive lawns. When planting time came in the spring, Jeff sat up on the tall tractor with his Gha and watched the pattern going up and down the spaced rows, learning over the years how to steer the giant machine.

As a result of their plentiful time together, Jeff developed roots that go deep into the soil on these 250 acres, and his life displays the rich fruits of his grandfather's teachings: good manners, hard work, endurance, bravery, and, most of all, respect for all living things. On a big farm like ours, it's not unusual to wake up in the morning to new dogs or cats that people have dropped off in the middle of the night. These cast-offs are usually emaciated and starving, sometimes pregnant. Due to abuse, many are afraid of any human involvement, and the most we can do is offer them, from a distance, a bowl of food and a pan of water. At present, Jeff has five dogs he loves and cares for. They're a mixed lot, not one with a full breed, but they're perfect to Jeff. He accepts them like he accepts humans who aren't perfect.

Jeff's talent for acceptance was obvious from a young age. When he was eight years old, he was diagnosed with a malignant brain tumor. At the hospital for his daily radiation treatment one morning, we passed a woman in the hall talking to her doctor and crying. She told him she was giving up because it was just too hard; the therapy was making her suffer too much. After we spent a little time with our own doctor, discussing Jeff's therapy, we walked to the big waiting room at the end of the hall, where we saw the same tearful patient we'd overheard in the hall just minutes before. Her head hung, her shoulders sagged with dejection.

Jeff recognized her, and before we could stop him, he jumped down from his chair, ran across the room, and wrapped his arms around the sad woman. When she saw that sweet smile on our son's face, she sat straighter in her chair and announced to everyone in the waiting room, "If that little bald boy can have a smile on his face for everybody, I certainly don't need to feel sorry for myself."

Jeff has been making friends with strangers ever since. They don't have to be any certain color or race. They don't have to talk or walk. In fact he likes people in wheelchairs best of all, probably because he loves opportunities to help. Once in a grocery store he spotted an elderly lady in a wheelchair trying to balance a cake on her lap. He ran to her and caught the cake before it fell. She sized Jeff up with a critical gaze and ordered, "Follow me, young man." Jeff dutifully followed the wheelchair to the front of the store where she then directed him to give the cake to a waiting companion. "Thank you, young man," she said. "You were a big help." She'd obviously mistaken Jeff for an employee, but he was as happy as if he'd just won a prize.

Jeff has the uncanny ability to spot less obvious kinds of trouble as well. When a new student entered his high school homeroom, afraid and shy, Jeff was the first to walk across the room and shake his hand, like a true gentleman. Jeff's empathy has also been evident at church. At one time, we had a pastor who suffered some emotional wounds that few church members knew of. One Sunday, he unexpectedly knelt beside the podium, head bowed in prayer. While everyone else's heads were bowed and eyes closed, Jeff slipped quietly out of his seat and went up and kneeled beside the minister. It was an awesome moment for us all.

My son's willingness to help others isn't limited to outsiders. When I go on trips, my bags go into my car as soon as I have them packed. On my arrival home, I never carry anything inside. Jeff unpacks the bags as well, returning everything to its proper place. And then he presents me with something to drink. That's his special way of making people feel welcome.

At age sixteen, Jeff extended his friendly outreach to a large group of teenagers at a multi-state youth camp. Jeff accomplished more that week than some of his typical peers. His first big achievement took place several hundred yards offshore, in the camp's expansive lake, where a huge inflated iceberg rose out of the water. With the help of two of the bigger boys, Jeff was able to climb to the top of the towering obstacle and jump the fourteen feet into the water. I noticed quite a few of the students backtracking their steps down the spaced footholds, and I didn't blame them—the height looked dizzying to me. Then I, along with everyone else in the water, watched Jeff ascend the iceberg a second time, this time without help and with grim determination on his face. When he made it to the top, he looked down at everyone and proudly waved before jumping into the water. The next trip up to the top was quicker and easier, and he did it alone, spurred on by the applause of the campers and counselors.

The campers were divided into groups, each having a different colored flag. Throughout the week's activities, points were awarded according to each group's showing in the sporting events and games. Jeff was in the Green Group, whose members included him in everything and made accommodations for him when necessary. One evening, with two boys helping him pull a ground-mounted, giant slingshot, Jeff shot the ball across the field and scored. To celebrate his victory, the group tied the green flag around his shoulders and ran with him across the open campground, flag flying in the breeze. I didn't witness this event, and was surprised the next morning by a video replay on the immense onstage screen. As the auditorium broke into thunderous applause, I cried.

There were other heroic moments that week. The camp's youth pastor asked if Jeff could say the opening prayer for worship service one night. I told him it was fine with me, but warned him no one would be able to understand Jeff because of his poor language skills. That night in the auditorium I watched as Jeff walked to the front of the packed building, took the microphone, and delivered the prayer. Indeed, no one including me understood his words, but the impact was profound. We'll never know if Jeff's speech would be better today had he not undergone intense radiation therapy years earlier. But clearly, the therapy didn't rob him of his bravery, strong will, and tender spirit. After the "Amen," which I did understand, he quietly returned to his seat, head bowed. After sitting down he signed to me, "Good boy." And I gave him a thumbs up.

When the week of camp drew to a close, I thanked our youth pastor for what I considered the sacrifice he'd made for my son. He'd

slept near Jeff in the boy's dorm, guarded him loyally, guided his activities all week, and gave his time unselfishly. He wanted no thanks
for any of this, however, and insisted that it was he who'd benefited
the most. "I've learned more from Jeff this past week than he could
ever learn from me," he said. "I watched him accomplish so much
and knew how hard it was for him, doing things the rest of us take
for granted." He then explained what an opportunity he considered
it for the other students to have Jeff in the group. "He learns from
them, and they learn from him," he said.

I already knew the truth of that statement very well.

The road we live on was once just a dirt trail that Jeff's grand-
dad walked every day. It's now paved. Most of the roads around us
have been blacktopped over the years, but here in this rural, wooded
countryside, some back roads remain dirt or graveled. They may always be so. Yet a mile from the boundaries of our farm, large, mod-
ern subdivisions stand, where city folks come to get away from the
hectic metropolis. Things change. Roads get paved. New houses
spring up.

Our son has helped pave roads. He's shown a family and a community what a person with Down syndrome is capable of. We like
to think he's made the roads a little easier to tread for those coming
after him. But just as importantly, he's made the journey gentler for
those who walk alongside him.

Jeff's grandfather passed away two years ago. His grandmother died just days before I finished writing this essay, shortly after
her ninety-sixth birthday. Jeff helped take care of his "Granny" in
her last years, with the tenderness and gentleness he reserves for old
people. He ran from the school bus in the afternoons to her bedside,
helped push her wheelchair out to the deck on sunny days, and let
her watch him blow bubbles into the air. He made sure we didn't forget her medicines. He played dominoes with her most every evening
and even let her win sometimes.

In these and many other ways, my son makes me proud: taking
care of those he loves, respecting life, helping wherever there's a need,
and working hard with strong determination. But I'm not surprised
he's become such an exceptional man.

His grandfather showed him how.

●   ●   ●

Betty is a former editorial assistant and court reporter who now spends her days as a freelance writer and editor. She lives with her husband and Jeff on a large farm in Tennessee. She maintains a website for her writing at http://bettyannschmidt.com, and one devoted to her journey with her son with special needs called Simply Special at http://simplyspecial.homestead.com.

Larkin Armstrong

4.

This Walker Doesn't Match My Drapes!

By Amy Armstrong

LARKIN'S PHYSICAL THERAPIST came by this week and left us something new: a reverse walker. Three-year-old Larkin has balance problems due to multiple health issues, and until recently she has struggled to walk with confidence. But now she stands in front of the walker, grips the handrests, and uses it to balance herself as she moves along. She is stylin' with her new ride.

I have passed the walker many times during the night and day. I stare at it. It's a fancy gold color, which of course draws attention, but my stare isn't one of admiration—it's the kind of stare you give something you aren't quite sure about. At night, when I pass the walker while going from room to room, I almost expect a cartoonish exchange of "BOO" between us. But the walker remains quiet, and I remain quiet as I try to accept its presence. The walker is a new addition to the family. An expected addition, but it still takes some getting used to. Kind of like a baby. You bring it home, and you stare.

On October 4th, 2005, Larkin Murphy Armstrong was born and the person I was, died. This kind of death had happened once before, to some extent. Larkin's older brother, Chase, was born ten years earlier, and from that point on I knew I'd no longer be sleeping in, running out the door for a quick lunch, or a quick anything for that matter. Self-focus was replaced by the little being in the bassinette, who filled my every thought, deed, and action. But while the change felt extreme, it was nothing compared to what would come in the future. At the time I saw the world through the blue eyes of my typical son and never really thought about those who are "different."

Then came Larkin.

She emerged hands-first, red-faced and ANGRY. I knew well the old saying that children born hands-first are leaders. After receiving Larkin's diagnosis of trisomy 21, I questioned that old saying. When Larkin was five months old and we were given the devastating additional news of Infantile Spasms, I threw that saying out the window. Then in August of 2007, when the doctors in St. Louis delivered a final crushing blow of Lennox-Gastaut seizures, I went outside with a can of gasoline and started a fire. I burned not only that saying about hands-first leaders, but also the poem "Welcome to Holland" and my copies of *What to Expect When You're Expecting* and *What to Expect: The Toddler Years.*

It was a good fire, although I'm sure the neighbors considered calling someone to take me away. Imagine a fire blazing next to a mother with gas can in hand, devastated, insane from grief and so very helpless, muttering under her breath every single curse against the universe. As a mother I was supposed to protect this child and *fix* all her problems. Instead, I felt broken and completely powerless. I made many visits to hospitals and heard doctors tell me things I *didn't want to hear*. I cried, thinking I could never be a good enough mother. I threw fits, thinking I did not want to have to be enough. I found myself standing in new shoes that didn't fit, and suffered terrible growing pains from trying to walk in them. My raw emotions became blisters that wouldn't heal.

I continued to wear the shoes, though, because I didn't have a choice. Eventually my blisters gently healed into tender spots. And over time, I found the shoes balanced me and kept me grounded. One morning, Larkin was in my arms drinking her bottle, and I relaxed into the moment and locked eyes with her. The pure love in her eyes flooded over me. I realized I needed to have that very same look in my eye. When I look at people, I need to have that same open, loving, nonjudgmental gaze. I began to cry with that knowledge. Then, as we sat there staring at each other, Larkin suddenly dissolved into giggles. This was a supreme treat—because of Larkin's seizures, she rarely even smiled. Together, she and I rode the giggle wave until our faces hurt. It was then I realized that while my new shoes were painful to wear at first, with experience they made me softer and more vulnerable. They made me safe. Safe, because I was coming to understand what truly mattered in life.

Larkin's new walker is a lot like my new shoes: its presence is unwelcome, and it brings into our home many raw emotions. Grandmas use walkers; children are not supposed to need them. Children are supposed to be able to crawl, walk, and smile about it as we snap photos to capture the blissful moments. This thing isn't supposed to be in my house. *It doesn't match my drapes!*

But it does match our path. And so I will accept it. Just as Larkin is helping me walk in different footwear, she herself is learning to walk with the help of this shiny new golden item. It's a hoot to watch her moving with it. It will be a long time before she is able to walk alone, but the day will come. In the meantime, we will snap pictures of the blissful event as she smiles. And if I'm worried about the walker clashing with my home décor, perhaps I just need to shop.

Little epiphanies like this make me realize that Larkin *is* a leader. She is leading us along the path to enlightenment. Leading us to acceptance. Leading us to growth. Prompting us to stop, listen, feel, absorb, and *enjoy* the little things we could easily take for granted. I now have to believe those who say that people born hands-first are leaders. October 4, 2005 brought a wonderful birth for Larkin, and an even more wonderful death for me. I do not miss the person I was. New shoes, new walker, new drapes lead to a new, better life.

● ● ●

Momologist™ Amy is a mother of two children and the founder of Larkin's Place, a nonprofit partnership with the Champaign County YMCA creating a supportive recreational environment for families raising loved ones with special needs. Amy hopes that Larkin's Place at the Y will provide a loving platform for all community members to be connected to those who have challenges. She lives with her husband, Andy, and their children in Champaign, Illinois. To follow Larkin's journey, visit www.larkinsplace.com

Keith Smalley and Carter Vaughan, Carter and Paw-pop,
rest after opening presents—Christmas, 2007

5.

Carter's Motto

By Keith E. Smalley

THROUGHOUT THE SUMMER and fall of 2003, I anxiously awaited the birth of my first grandchild. At the time I was making the transition from being the father of children to being the father of adults. As a father, my motto was "Fail to plan, plan to fail," and my wife, Susan, and I had worked hard to make good decisions with regard to our children's development. We successfully executed the goal of providing a college education for them, as well as trying to give them a good moral upbringing, and for this effort we have been blessed with three hardworking, conscientious children. My motto also served me well as I worked to support our family financially over the years, and provide for the financial requirements of retirement. Now, as a father of adults, those responsibilities would fall on my daughter and son-in-law in the upbringing of their child. My role would be to provide support but mainly to sit back and enjoy.

Except for experiencing some intense and persistent morning sickness, my daughter Jennifer had a fairly normal pregnancy at first. But in early 2004 she had some high blood pressure issues, and in March went to the hospital for cardiac fetal monitoring. An ultrasound exam showed a sizable hole in my grandson's heart. Seeing that the baby was in trouble, the doctors decided that they would deliver the baby by caesarian section immediately. About five o'clock in the evening of March 4th, Carter James Vaughan was born via c-section and was immediately taken to the neonatal care unit. When I arrived at the hospital shortly thereafter, I learned the doctors were conducting tests to confirm the suspicion that Carter had Down syndrome in addition to his heart issues. The test results were positive.

I knew next to nothing about Down syndrome, but my mind, in its analytical fashion, put the diagnosis on the back burner. Carter had heart problems, and having only one wall in the heart (two chambers instead of four) sounded pretty life threatening to me. My first concerns were for Jennifer, who was understandably distraught when I entered her hospital room. She saw Carter briefly at birth, but would not be able to visit the NICU for 24 hours because of medication she was receiving for high blood pressure. "It feels like he's not even mine," she said. They'd had no time to bond and she feared his condition was worse than she was being told. I assured her that I would bring back the truth.

After spending some time with Jennifer, I went to see Carter for myself. When I entered the unit I felt an immediate calming of my fears. Clearly, Carter had the best care possible. His color was good, and he was obviously a fighter because he was breathing without assistance. Although God and I had been having a continuous conversation over the previous six hours, I finally took time to thank him for all of these blessings. One of those blessings was that Carter was born in the year that he was. Had he been born twenty years earlier, the mountain ahead of him would have been much steeper and higher. I knew that historically children with Down syndrome had been institutionalized, but I knew this would not be the case with Carter. I also knew that medical advances had allowed people with much more life threatening conditions than Carter's to live a perfectly normal life. These were facts, and this was what I reported back to Jennifer. Although it did not remove all her concerns, I felt she was able to manage the twenty-four-hour separation a little better with my truthful assurances.

Over the next six months, Carter endured heart surgery to repair the hole in his heart, and bowel surgery to eliminate the effects of Hirschsprung's disease. Before the heart surgery, he would eat normally until he had no more energy and then take the remainder of his food through a tube inserted in his nose and down his throat. Throughout all of this, Carter not only survived, but, in my opinion, enjoyed life. He was responsive and pleasant, bright-eyed and alert to his surroundings. I marveled at his resilience after all his short life had dealt him. The trivial things that upset me on a daily basis paled in comparison to what Carter had been through.

At this time I had done enough research to know what causes Down syndrome but had not delved far enough into the subject to have expectations about Carter's development. Carter would set his own pace; that was something I had to accept. I sensed that his positive approach to life would enable him to overcome any obstacle that having Down syndrome might present. Even at a very young age, he faced challenges with an optimistic, "can-do" attitude. But he definitely had a mind of his own. One day I watched as his therapist attempted to get him to twist his body to reach for an object. Carter was capable of doing so, but refused to give in to the therapist's request. She finally gave up. When she had left the house after that session, Carter performed the task perfectly.

By the time Carter reached his first birthday, he recognized me by sight and sound, and would seek me out for interaction. We had a ritual where he would cough, I would express my concern for his cough, and he would force more coughs to gain more concern. This little game brought me comfort when Carter was eighteen months old and was hospitalized to have his tonsils and adenoids removed and ear tubes inserted. I joined Jen, Jim, and Carter at the hospital as they awaited the surgery, which would be a piece of cake compared to what Carter had already endured. With his perfectly functioning heart and bowel system, I knew the outcome would be positive—I just wanted to be there because it inspires me to see how he deals with adversity in such a positive manner. Carter had received his anesthesia prep but was alert enough to give me a cough when I walked in the room. After he left the operating room and was being held by Jen in the recovery room he again greeted me with a cough as I came up to them. Although delighted, I was careful not to encourage further coughing at that time.

My special relationship with Carter has continued to grow over the four years of his life. His playfulness makes me feel like a kid again, and his spontaneity continually teaches me the limitations of my old motto, "fail to plan, plan to fail." The nights before I visit him, I sometimes can't sleep due to happy anticipation of what he might share with me. Every day—and sometimes every minute—is a new adventure, and very little of his development is "normal." Instead of crawling, his early form of motoring was sliding on his rear end while using his hands and feet to propel himself forward, with a very rhythmic motion. In this fashion he could move across the room fast enough that I would need to run to keep up. When I took him in to work to meet my coworkers, he slid on his behind into the Principal's office and closed the door. She was quite surprised to have Carter join her meeting with the Assistant Superintendent!

When Carter finally decided that walking would be advantageous, he stood up in the middle of the room without holding onto anything and took off. He's never looked back. When he enters a place he has never been before, you can see him taking in all the potential this new environment has in store for him. He will explore every nook and cranny until he has gotten every bit of enjoyment and knowledge from the experience that he can. It is truly a joy to take him places because he is so perceptive and helps me notice things I would otherwise miss. For example, one afternoon we took Carter and his younger brother to see a *Sesame Street Live* performance. When we entered the building, he immediately let go of my hand and went running through the crowd. Having never experienced this behavior from him before, I panicked when he disappeared from view. But I quickly forgave him when I found him sitting in front of life-sized cardboard cutouts of the Sesame Street characters. Although Carter was four feet shorter than me, he saw them and I did not!

When Carter was born, I didn't yet have a plan for the rest of my life beyond covering the financial demands of retirement. Thanks to him, I've made a different kind of plan than I would have otherwise. After a career in business, which included managing a plant with a hundred employees, I have taken a job as a custodian in a small public school for fourth and fifth graders. The district practices inclusion in all of its facilities, so I get to interact with all kinds of children. I call this my transition into retirement. One of my hopes in taking this new job was to gain some tools that would help me help Carter deal with his challenges, but it seems even more likely that he'll be helping me with mine. Indeed, I've often wondered which one of us is more challenged.

I have Carter to thank for the positive change in my perspective, and for the many joys he brings me every day. He has taught me that it is possible for everything to work out even without careful planning. Instead of always trying to *make* things happen, I have learned from Carter to have the confidence to sit back sometimes and *let* things happen. I believe it is this "live in the moment" approach that will make the rest of my life meaningful. In fact, if I were to pick a new motto it would be, "Some of the best things in life aren't planned."

● ● ●

Keith and Susan were married in 1973 and together have three children. Carter is the oldest of their three grandchildren. Keith graduated with a degree in Forestry and received a commission as a 2nd Lieutenant in the United States Army while at Pennsylvania State University. He was trained as a helicopter pilot while in the military. After leaving the military, Keith held multiple leadership positions in business before becoming employed by the Lewisburg, Pennsylvania, school district.

Patricia Bauer and Margaret Muller

6.
It Is Just Part of Me

By Margaret Muller

Introductory note: *When my kids were in middle school, they participated in a schoolwide effort called the "Worthwhile Life Project." As part of the project, they had to write an essay. My daughter Margaret decided to write about having Down syndrome, and went through many drafts. She wrote that Down syndrome is a genetic condition, and that it has not stopped her from having a worthwhile life.*

Her essay, which follows, challenged some people's preconceptions. When she delivered it to classes around the school, some kids teared up. Teachers, too. Eventually, it was published in the Washington Post's *Health Section.*

Now that Margaret is 25, she's living out the dreams she had then. She's still challenging people's preconceptions, and she's still working at having a worthwhile life. Her dad and I couldn't be prouder.

                                          —*Patricia E. Bauer*

TODAY I'D LIKE to tell you about Down syndrome. My purpose for talking about this is to be able to say, "Yes, I have Down Syndrome. Sometimes I have to work harder to learn things, but in many ways I am just like everyone else." I would like to tell people that having Down syndrome does not keep me from doing the things I need to do or want to do. I just have to work harder.

Down syndrome is a condition and not a disease. You cannot catch Down syndrome like you can catch a cold or virus. It is something you are just born with—like blond hair and blue eyes. If you have Down syndrome when you are born, you will have it your whole life.

People without Down syndrome have 46 chromosomes, which carry all the genetic information about a person, in each of their cells. People with Down syndrome have one extra chromosome. So a person with Down syndrome has a total of 47 chromosomes in each cell. Doctors and experts are not really sure what causes it, but they say it occurs in about 1 of every 700 babies. This happens randomly, like flipping a coin or winning the lottery.

Everyone with Down syndrome is a totally unique person. The extra chromosome makes it harder for me to learn. Sometimes I need someone to say, "Settle down and get busy!"

Even though I have one extra chromosome, the rest of my chromosomes carry information from generation to generation just like yours. Chromosomes control certain genetic characteristics, like eye color, skin color, height, and some abilities like music, art, or math.

For example, I get my blue eyes from my father, my fair skin and freckles from my mother, my blond hair from my grandmother, my long thin feet from both my mom and my dad, and my need to wear glasses from both my grandparents and my parents. I like to concentrate on the ways that I am like everyone else.

I am very lucky to be alive today rather than 50 years or even 20 years ago, because back then the doctors and experts believed that people with Down syndrome were not capable of learning. But now we know that people with Down syndrome are capable of doing many different things.

I personally am doing things that some people didn't think I could do. When I was born, somebody told my mom that it was too bad that I was named "Margaret" because I would never even be able to say my name. That person might never have expected that I could win four medals in Special Olympics swimming, be a green belt in karate, cook a pizza, read a novel, run half a mile, or get up in front of the class and give a speech! With a lot of hard work and encouragement, I have been able to do all these things.

I am not sad about the fact that I have Down syndrome. It is just part of me. I have a great brother (most of the time), and parents who love me a lot. I have wonderful friends who enjoy hanging out and having fun with me. I have teachers who help me keep on learning new things. I am glad to be a student at Lincoln Middle School, because it is a great school and almost everyone is really nice. Down syndrome has not stopped me from having a worthwhile life.

● ● ●

Margaret is a graduate of the Riverview School in East Sandwich, Massachusetts, and Project Forward at Cape Cod Community College in Hyannis, Massachusetts. Her mother, Patricia E. Bauer, is a journalist and the editor of www.patriciaebauer.com, a website of news and commentary on issues related to disability.

Jennifer McLeland, Ellen Stumbo, Nichole Stumbo, Ellie Stumbo

7.
Not A Mistake

By Ellen Armendariz Stumbo

I WAS SITTING in the family room watching TV and stroking my pregnant belly when my husband, Andy, walked into the room. Ten minutes before, he had answered a knock at the door. When I looked up and saw his dumbfounded expression, I knew instinctively that something was wrong.

"Jennifer has Down syndrome," he finally said.

"What!"

"The doctor suspected Down syndrome and did some blood work. The test results came back positive."

I didn't know what to say and I certainly didn't know what to think. Jennifer, the newborn daughter of our dear friends, Bill and Kristin, had Down syndrome. Andy and I were also expecting a girl, and Kristin and I had dreams of our daughters growing up together and being best friends.

"But…are they sure?" I asked Andy. "I mean, how is this possible?" Just three weeks before, he and I had stood in the small hospital room holding that precious, beautiful baby, and gazed into her sweet face. There was plenty of joy and laughter as the brand new parents showed off their daughter. We were delighted. Our friends had a baby girl!

That scene replayed in my mind as I tried to understand this unimaginable tragedy our friends were facing. Jennifer was such a beautiful baby—was it really possible that she had Down syndrome? Wouldn't such a baby be…well, not beautiful?

The diagnosis had to be a mistake, it just had to be a mistake. Why was this happening to our friends, and how would they ever survive? Were they devastated? Were they scared? Were they embarrassed to tell people? Would they still show off their daughter, take her out in public? How would other people look at them and their baby?

In my helplessness, I reminded myself that there were no better parents for a child with Down syndrome than Bill and Kristin. Both of them were full of love and acceptance. I was also comforted by the fact that they had friends who would walk this road with them, two close friends who also had a daughter with Down syndrome. But there was one question that I could not get out of my head: What if *my* baby girl was born with Down syndrome? *Oh my God, I could never have a child with Down syndrome, please let my child be healthy.*

The next time I saw Kristin, I felt uncomfortable. I didn't know how to act around her. I asked how Jennifer was doing and what life was like with a brand new baby, and I told her how excited I was to have our baby girl born in a few months. I was not going to bring up Down syndrome. I am ashamed to say that I never once asked about my friend's feelings. Andy, on the other hand, had multiple conversations with Bill. Bill shared that one of the most frustrating things for him was when people would say, "I'm sorry." Bill and Kristin weren't sorry and didn't want others to feel sorry for them. When Andy told me this, I realized that I did feel sorry for them, and that my attitude needed to change. Jennifer would still be our daughter's best friend, Down syndrome or not.

Our daughter Ellie was born in August, just three months after Jennifer. Often Ellie and Jennifer reached milestones like rolling, sitting, and crawling around the same time. My daughter was four months when she rolled over and Jennifer was seven months, the time when most "typical" children are sitting on their own. It never occurred to me that seeing this contrast might have been hard for Kristin. How consumed I was with my perfect baby and my perfect life!

When Jennifer was fifteen months old, Kristin took a part-time job and needed to find someone to take care of her daughter. I happily volunteered to have Jennifer come to our house. I was so excited, knowing it would be good for Ellie to have a playmate. Little did I know that Jennifer was coming to our house because *I* needed *her*.

Over the following months, Kristin and I became closer friends and she started sharing more of her thoughts and feelings about having a daughter with Down syndrome. I became better able to see things through her eyes and join in the celebration as her daughter reached milestones. We cheered when Jennifer was standing on her own, whooped when she was able to sign, and bragged about the simple words she was able to say. Most importantly, I got to see how beautiful life can be with a child who has an extra chromosome. Jennifer had Down syndrome, sure, but the diagnosis was such a small part of who she was. Jennifer was perfect, exactly how she was intended to be. And in only a few short months, I fell in love with her. That year, in our Christmas letter I wrote, "I love that little girl almost as much as if she was mine." And I meant every word.

Shortly after the holidays, we decided to try for another baby. It did not take very long for me to get pregnant again, but for some reason it seemed to be a complicated pregnancy. During an ultrasound exam at nineteen weeks, I felt the need to ask if our baby's heart was okay. The technician didn't say much, other than confirming that four chambers were visible. A few minutes later, back in the examination room, my midwife said that they had found some fluid around the heart, and I needed to have a level II ultrasound. I walked out of the clinic crying that day. I felt utterly helpless as I shared the news with Andy over the phone. The next day we had to fly to Florida for a conference, and the ultrasound would have to wait a week. A week seemed like an eternity.

Our first night in Florida I woke up in the middle of the night with an unexplained and overwhelming sense that our baby was going to have Down syndrome. With a heavy heart I prayed, *Not Down syndrome, Lord please! It's okay for our friends but not for us.* I locked myself in the bathroom and let the tears come. I was not like Bill and Kristin; I could never have a child with a disability. The delays, the therapies, and other people's perceptions were too much for me to handle.

The next morning I was still very upset. "What if our baby has Down's?" I asked Andy.

"Why do you ask that?" he replied, confused.

"I…" My voice broke as I struggled with my emotions. "I had a dream about it," I finally said, as tears streamed down my face.

Andy was thoughtful for a while, then he reached out and held my hand, "If it comes to be, then we will walk down that road, and you and I know that we will not walk it alone."

I fell into his arms and cried. He was right. Bill, Kristin, and Jennifer would walk with us every step of the way.

When we went to have the level II ultrasound, we were overjoyed to hear that the fluid around the baby's heart was gone. The doctor said not to worry about anything, our baby girl was perfectly healthy and an amniocentesis would not be necessary. We felt relieved to know that everything was okay.

But then, two weeks later, we went to my regular prenatal checkup. "How are you guys feeling about the level II ultrasound?" my midwife asked.

"We feel great," I responded.

She looked confused. "Didn't they tell you?"

"All they told us is that the fluid around the heart is gone," Andy replied.

The midwife paused, took a deep breath, and looked from Andy to me. The concern in her face threw me into panic. I feared she'd say those words that had only been spoken in the sharing of my dream. It was only a dream. It had to be only a dream.

"Your baby might have Down syndrome," she finally said.

My heart sank. I swallowed hard and looked at Andy. It struck me that despite this news, his eyes were peaceful. The only thing I knew for sure was that this was our baby girl and we would love her, even if she had an extra chromosome. All I could muster in reply to the midwife was, "It will be okay if she does."

As Andy and I drove home, we decided that since there was only a possibility of Down syndrome and not a definite diagnosis, we wouldn't share this information with anyone except two people: Bill and Kristin. When we did, they helped us process our feelings and assured us that they would journey alongside us. Our close friends were becoming our family.

Nichole was born on October 2, 2007, after a smooth and quick labor and delivery. And yes, Nichole was born with Down syndrome. As soon as she was placed on my tummy, I thought *she looks like Jennifer*. Several nurses told us how lucky our daughter was, for they had never seen such love and acceptance from parents who had a baby diagnosed with Down syndrome. I had fooled them all. They didn't know that when I looked at Nichole's face, all I saw was Down syndrome. I couldn't see my baby.

Back at home with Nichole, I was a depressed mess. My life had been destroyed and the shattered pieces lay scattered around me. My vision blurred from the constant tears; I couldn't even begin to put together a façade. I was in a deep and ugly hole, feeling as if warmth and light had vanished forever, and leaving me to slowly die inside. I prayed and I prayed that I would wake up from the nightmare to find out that I had a "normal" baby girl.

Exactly a week after Nichole was born, her doctor called to confirm her diagnosis: trisomy 21. I called Andy and he came home from work early. We sat in the living room and I cried while we held each other. I thought I was ready to love a child with Down syndrome; I thought I would be able to handle it. Why was this happening to us? It had to be a mistake, it just had to be a mistake!

The doorbell rang. Andy opened the door wide and a beautiful and spunky little girl walked in, wearing one of her huge smiles. She waved both arms at us and said, "Hi!" It was Jennifer, and despite my great sadness, she had just made me smile.

Our friends stayed to visit for the evening. I couldn't take my eyes off Jennifer that night. I couldn't help but imagine our new life with a child with Down syndrome. And what I imagined was beautiful! I saw love, joy, and peace bundled in a baby. I saw great celebration of even the smallest of accomplishments. I imagined Nichole as a little girl running to me, offering a hug and a kiss, playing with her sister, and bringing laughter into our family. And that was only the beginning. My heart was pounding hard, fully engaged and overflowing with joyful dreams for the future. I was ready to embark on this new adventure.

By the end of the evening, I knew I could be done with my tears of sadness. As I looked into Jennifer's eyes, I knew beyond any doubt that everything would be okay. That life with Nichole would be surprisingly rich in all aspects. That I had so much to look forward to.

Today, nineteen months later, I am even more convinced that Nichole is absolutely perfect. I would not have her any other way. Because of her, I have basked in love, joy, kindness, gentleness, peace, and goodness. Nothing about my daughter is a mistake. God does not make mistakes.

● ● ●

Ellen shares life with her husband, Andy, and two daughters. She is greatly involved in her church, where her husband is an associate pastor. Ellen's passion to promote Down syndrome awareness keeps her busy speaking at schools, mothers' groups, and churches. She and her husband plan to have more biological children. Ellen keeps a family blog where she openly shares her heart as she faces the challenges of being a wife, mother, and advocate: www.elliestumbo.blogspot.com.

Patrick Foraker and Caroline Foraker

8.

Learning to Fly

By Beth Foraker

JULY 1, 1999: The day my husband and I celebrated our tenth wedding anniversary, and the day our third child, Patrick, was born with Down syndrome. After we heard the diagnosis, I looked at my husband and said, "This isn't what I had planned ten years ago for today. How about you?"

I wasn't completely surprised by the diagnosis, though. Although all prenatal tests and screenings showed otherwise, I'd known in my heart that Patrick had Down syndrome. As I labored in childbirth, my mantra was, "Please let me remember this experience, and please let him be okay." I really wanted to be fully present in that moment of birth. With this unusual intuition, I somehow *knew* that my life was changing forever. I was desperate to be aware, to notice, to pay attention as the change unfolded.

In the instant Patrick was placed on my tummy, a wave of familiarity washed over me that I had not felt upon meeting my other two children for the first time. It felt like someone whispering to me: "This is Patrick and he has Down syndrome. He is *exactly* as he should be." I was immediately at peace, yet simultaneously scared to death. I had no knowledge of people with disabilities; I just knew their lives seemed hard, much harder than ours. I urgently wanted to circle the wagons and protect this baby like no other.

Little did I know that he would need no protecting.

Patrick wasn't blessed with a heart that had all of its chambers intact. At nine weeks of age, he had to have his custom built by a very adept surgeon. At two, he was diagnosed with leukemia. His oncologists custom fitted him with an individualized chemo regime that would last him until the month before kindergarten. Through all of these incredibly difficult health issues, Patrick responded like the inflated dummy that rebounds with ease, popping back up after the boxer knocks it down.

At six he entered kindergarten, clumsy from three-plus years of not fully using his body and napping every day. His speech was garbled, but his mind was ready. He had friends to meet and words to write. He had work to do and places to go. There was no stopping him. But all I wanted to do was to hold him close and to protect him. In fact, I would have loved to homeschool him. I couldn't get enough of his physical presence, which was finally full of energy. I didn't think his kindergarten friends deserved to play with him. I thought it should be me instead.

Silly mommy. Did I remember nothing?

Patrick accepts his life as it unfolds. He knows how to savor the moment. He goes with the flow and follows his heart. He doesn't rage against the unfairness; he doesn't pout. He certainly doesn't ask, "Why me?" In a very cosmic way, he *gets* it, and he helps us do the same. Watching him deal with open-heart surgery as a newborn I realized just how quickly we can heal if we take our mind out of it. Watching him deal with chemo day in and day out for years, I learned that raging and fighting and feeling betrayed just don't help at all. The fastest way to heal is to nap when needed, to eat what tastes good, and to sing and dance whenever possible...oh, and to surround yourself with people you love.

I want to be real here: Patrick is not some kind of hero or angel or starry soul. He just knows at a very basic level how to live. Thanks to him, I've found acceptance of myself and my shortcomings; acceptance of my family, of my friends, and—dare I say it—even the crap in life. Everything feels so much better when I just let it *be*.

Patrick is in third grade. He's got his full head of silky blond hair back. His sparkling, denim-colored eyes are mischievous, and he continues to face new adventures. (Thankfully, they are the typical-kid kind: What should I order for hot lunch? What kind of birthday party should I have?) Yesterday, when we were getting ready to leave for school, he put on a magician's cape, ran to our backyard, and jumped onto the rope swing. He hung on and flew through the air with the cape billowing behind him, his blond hair flying in the wind. Super Patrick! Watching him fly through the air, I realized for the four billionth time that I must try to live like he does. I must grab the moment, seize the day, and morph into my super self. The moments pass. The opportunities fade. I can't think about it for long, if at all. I have to run to the backyard and just fly.

Of course, these things aren't easy to remember. I've had nine years with this boy and I still need my daily lesson that acceptance is the surest way to enjoy the precious present. But every time I forget, all I need to do is follow the little boy in the cape.

●　●　●

Beth lives in a college town with her husband, John, and their four children. The kids range in age from teenagers to toddlers with all sorts of labels sprinkled around: "gifted," "delayed," "hard-working," "social." Each of them could wear any label depending on the day! She finds bliss in the chaos and daily is grateful for the handprints, the giggles, and glimpses of grace. This story is dedicated to her husband, John, whose over-the-top love for his family makes Beth smile every day.

Amy Flege and Shelly Steere

9.

Special Surprise

By Amy Flege

WHEN I WAS a child, summertime meant playing with my many first cousins on Grandma and Grandpa's farm. Our days were like scenes from a nostalgic movie: We got to drive the tractor with Grandpa, feed the pigs, and gather the eggs from the chicken house for Grandma. We would dress up the kittens in doll clothes and play house, or go up to the hayloft and play "Little House on the Prairie." Some of us would even spend the night—we'd set up a "house" in Grandma's sewing room and sleep in it together, like a big happy family. No matter what we did, my cousin Shelly was included. Shelly has Down syndrome, and to some people he might have seemed different. But not to us. We had all been raised with him and knew what Down syndrome was. Sure, there were things he couldn't do like us, but he always ended up doing what all us kids did. He was just Shelly!

As I grew up, Shelly and I continued doing many fun things together: swimming, riding bikes, wading through the creek, riding motorcycles in the woods. When I got older, I would see him riding through town on his bike as I headed to my part-time job after school. He would stop at the corner of Main Street and wave to everyone he knew, which was just about everyone. So many people knew and loved Shelly. They would honk their horns to make sure he saw them! It was then I realized that it wasn't just me who knew how special Shelly is.

Shelly has many friends because he is so considerate of others. He works at a local secondhand store, and if he sees something that reminds him of a friend or family member, he buys it and sends it to us in the mail. Even though I've now moved away from my hometown and don't see him as often as I used to, he still sends me gifts. Knowing my husband and I are huge Minnesota Viking Fans, he sends us the best Viking memorabilia! Sometimes it's a poster or a shirt. No matter what it is, we treasure it, knowing he picked it out with pride and bought it with his own hard-earned money.

Shelly's memory for birthdays and anniversaries is amazing. We come from a huge family: twenty-three first cousins, thirty-something second cousins, many aunts and uncles. His calendar is filled out in detail with our family's important dates, and each year he sends cards for birthdays and anniversaries. I don't know how he does it, but he always remembers!

When I was pregnant with my third child, Shelly sent me the cutest little baby announcement cards he'd bought at the store where he worked. With a sweet old-fashioned baby carriage on the front, they announced the birth of a special baby. His thoughtfulness brought tears to my eyes: he knew this baby was special. And indeed, when Mayson Michele was born, not only were we blessed with her beauty, but also with her special surprise: an extra chromosome.

As soon as I saw my newborn daughter, I knew. "She has Down syndrome," I said to my husband. He questioned it at first, but I was certain. Both of us felt calm and peaceful as we admired her full head of dark hair and her big blue eyes. Some people mourn the birth of a child with Down syndrome, but not us. We never cried, or grieved the loss of a "perfect" baby like so many new parents do. We knew she was already perfect. We knew because of Shelly.

●   ●   ●

Amy resides in Iowa with her husband, Stacy, and their three children. Their youngest daughter, Mayson (2006), was born with Down syndrome. Amy enjoys being a stay-at-home mom raising her children, volunteering at their schools, and being a advocate for Down syndrome. She currently is a board member of the Hawkeye Area Down Syndrome Association. You can read more about Amy's family on her blog at http://theflegefarm.blogspot.com.

Katie and Stephanie McTaggart

10.
The "Perfect" Family

By Katie McTaggart

TWENTY-FIVE YEARS AGO, I gave birth to my second child: a beautiful girl named Stephanie. My husband and I were young and extremely naïve. Our firstborn, a "perfect" little boy, was the light of our lives. He was such a great kid; we thought we had parenting completely wired! Since Dennis had no problems, and we obviously knew what we were doing as parents, we naturally assumed that our second child wouldn't have any issues either. We were shocked beyond words when our pediatrician told us that Stephanie had Down syndrome.

Our first thoughts were of Dennis and how his sister's diagnosis might affect his life. The only information we had about families who had a disabled child was pessimistic. We were devastated to think that our "perfect" family might very possibly become a dysfunctional family overnight. We even had visions of Dennis becoming antisocial or a substance abuser. We could see no positives at this point in our lives, despite the ignorant yet well-intentioned encouragement we received from others. Many people relayed the clichés to us: "Children like this are only given to parents who can handle it," and "You must be very patient," and so on. Most of the time such statements only confused us or even angered us. We didn't feel particularly "special"; in fact, we figured there was a mistake in our receiving this monumental task of raising a child with a disability. We stayed in the "Why us" stage of grief for a very long time.

Despite our continuing bewilderment about having a child with Down syndrome, something told us that our family wasn't complete. We went on to have two more daughters: Alissa, who is five years younger than Stephanie, and Melinda, who is seven years younger than Stephanie. I often joked that Alissa and Melinda were our "consolation prizes" for having an imperfect child. Tom and I still couldn't understand why Stephanie had come to our family.

It was Dennis who first grasped the concept of why Stephanie was given to us. One day when he was a toddler, Dennis got up from his afternoon nap and found me sitting in our living room, crying. Sobbing, actually. This might've frightened other small children, but not Dennis. He gave me a hug, quietly walked over to our bookcase, and picked up the book, *Down Syndrome: Growing and Learning*, written by Siegfried M. Pueschel. He brought it over and handed it to me. Then he said, "I love Deffie," his name for Stephanie. Even at the age of two he understood his sister was special, although it took his parents longer to fully understand this.

We moved to a new neighborhood during the summer between Dennis's first and second grade years. I enrolled both Dennis and Stephanie in summer school at the same elementary school. One day, Dennis's teacher took me aside to tell me that she had some concerns about Dennis. Apparently he wasn't running and playing with the other children in his class during recess—he was following Stephanie around the playground as the protective big brother. I explained that there was no reason for concern—Dennis cherished his sister and was protecting her not out of duty or obligation, but out of love.

By this point, our grief had transformed into warm acceptance and appreciation for Stephanie. However, it has taken us over twenty years to gain a full awareness of the meaning of her birth into our family. This meaning is evident in the life choices our other children have made. Dennis decided at a very young age that his mission in life was to help others, and he's now a grown man, pursuing the career he always wanted: being a firefighter.

Dennis's commitment to serving others is impressive, and not only to me. A couple of years ago, he was in the running to be included on a firefighter "pin-up" calendar. The proceeds from the sale of the calendar were to benefit the Children's Hospital Burn Center. The night of the judging ceremony, I walked into a ballroom at the Hyatt Regency in Denver to a room full of loud, half-drunken women who had been enjoying the open bar. One of the questions asked of each contestant was, "If you are chosen to be in the calendar, what do you expect to get out of it?" Most of the "hunky," gorgeous men answered something like, "I expect to get a lot of dates." Dennis came out in full bunker gear, amid the clamor of women screaming, "Take it off!" He removed his jacket and had no shirt underneath. The crowd cheered. When asked what he expected to "get," his answer was, "I don't expect anything, I just want to help the kids." There was a sudden hush, and then a sound erupted simultaneously from all 400 women in the room: "Awww,,," Needless to say, Dennis was chosen to be in the calendar!

Alissa and Melinda have also shown clear signs of positive influence from their sister. One day when Alissa was in elementary school, I arrived with Stephanie in tow, to pick up Alissa and two of her fellow Brownies after their weekly Girl Scout meeting. We got there a bit early, so we waited quietly at the back of the room for the meeting to end. Alissa's two friends were giggling and gesturing toward Stephanie. The giggling and pointing continued when we got into my minivan to drive the girls home. I eventually pulled the van over to the curb and sternly told the girls how unkind they were being, and that their behavior not only hurt Stephanie's feelings and mine, but also Alissa's. Alissa sat silently.

After we dropped off the two girls, Alissa told me she was glad I had spoken up. She had been too shy to confront them. Not long after this incident, she stopped playing with the two of them, and as she got older she showed an increased capacity to stand apart from the crowd. Peer pressure didn't seem to be an issue for her, or for Melinda. Both of them made friends with students who weren't necessarily "cool," and joined their high school marching band, which wasn't one of the most popular groups to be involved in. They didn't feel the need to conform.

Like Dennis, both Alissa and Melinda love helping people, and they've chosen career paths that will allow them to be of service to others. When Melinda was writing her college essay, she decided to use Stephanie as the topic. At first this seemed a very difficult task. Alissa had tried to use this subject but just felt too close to it. Melinda had several false starts, but finally wrote a beautiful essay about how having a sister with a disability has enriched her life and made her a better person. She received multiple scholarship offers and has settled on attending a private university where she will major in nursing. She wants to become a neonatal nurse. Alissa hopes to become an OB/GYN nurse. They both love anything baby-related, especially babies with Down syndrome.

Even though Stephanie adds a new dimension to our family, we often observe very "typical" interactions between the four kids. These days Stephanie worships the ground Dennis walks on, but as teens they had the kind of relationship most siblings do. When Stephanie was in middle school, part of her life skills training included riding the bus. Occasionally, Dennis would see her on the public bus and say "Hello." She would look out the window and act as if he wasn't there! Then, when Stephanie started at Dennis's high school his senior year, he would stop by the special education classroom to see her, but she would ignore him every time! It was then Dennis began to realize that she was more like others her age than she was different.

Stephanie's "normal" behavior has surprised Alissa and Melinda, too. From a young age Stephanie has noticed "cute" boys, and always worked harder in school for the male teachers, which made us smile. Stephanie has also been known to flirt with her sisters' boyfriends. One benefit of this has been that we can gauge whether the boy is a "keeper" by how he responds to Stephanie. She currently has a boyfriend, who also has Down syndrome, and we love to watch them together. Charley makes Stephanie giggle and he makes her happy, which is the same type of relationship she has seen her parents share all her life, so it seems very normal to her. And on Friday nights they do what most young adults do: have fun with their friends. As a group they enjoy dances, plays, sporting events, and movies. It's the highlight of their week. Stephanie says she wants to get married someday—that would surely bring us many more valuable learning experiences.

Over the last few years, Tom and I have arrived at an awareness of just how deep Stephanie's impact on our family has been. By having this "imperfect" person among us, the dynamics of our family have been irrevocably changed for the better. We've been required to learn patience (and we're still learning!) and to come to a realization of what is really important. This has been especially significant for Dennis, Alissa, and Melinda, but Tom and I have benefitted as well. Stephanie has provided us a multitude of opportunities to "pick our battles" as parents, both with Stephanie and our other children. She has humbled the cocky people we used to be, and she has taught us to be the parents we thought we were twenty-five years ago.

A few weeks ago, we all went out for dinner on the night before Alissa was leaving town for her sophomore year of college. When the waiter came to take the drink order, Stephanie hesitated. My husband, Tom, asked her if she wanted iced tea. She shook her head, as if she didn't know what she wanted. Finally, Dennis realized what was going on. He said, "Steph, you want a beer, don't you?" She nodded and the whole table burst into laughter. We had all forgotten (except for Dennis) that Stephanie always has to have a beer with her brother. She doesn't do this with anyone else, only Dennis. Thankfully, she had her ID with her because instead she looks more like fourteen than twenty-five! When the waiter brought Steph's drink, I caught

Tom's eye and smiled. We surely don't have the perfect family life that we envisioned thirty-one years ago when we got married—but we have something even better, a home full of warm relationships between imperfect yet completely loveable people.

● ● ●

Katie lives in Colorado where she is a CPA in corporate accounting. Her family has been the focus of her life for the last thirty years, half of which were spent as a stay-at-home mom. She is extremely proud of the family she and her husband have created and she loves to share the stories of each of her four children, including Stephanie (1983), who was diagnosed with Down syndrome shortly after birth.

Gene and Brayden Lehnick

11.

Angelico

By Gene Lehnick

WHEN MY DAUGHTER-IN-LAW, Dolly, called and asked if I would write an essay about Brayden, in a flash many thoughts went through my mind. The first was that I didn't want to disappoint Dolly by telling her no. The second was that I didn't want others to know the depth of my emotions about my newest grandson. Maybe it's a macho thing that I didn't want to be thought of as a "softy." But the more I thought about it, the more I realized that sharing my experience would be a way to honor my grandson and his family.

My wife and I were very excited when Dolly and my son Jared told us they were expecting a new baby. The happy couple already had two young children: Cody, who was beginning first grade, and Kaylee, who was trying to be a grown-up three-year-old. With both children quickly moving beyond early childhood, Jared and Dolly were starting to plan for the next stages of their family's future. But before we even knew if their third baby was a boy or girl, my wife and I sensed this child would take their lives in a different direction. At the time we didn't know just how much of a change there would be.

Several weeks passed, and we learned that our new grandchild would be a boy. Dolly and Jared were getting the room ready for the upcoming arrival, and all Cody and Kaylee could talk about was their little brother "in mommy's tummy." We thought everything was going well, and began to settle into our comfort zone again. Then Jared and Dolly were given unexpected news: the AFP test indicated that the baby had a 1:22 chance of having Down syndrome. Jared and Dolly immediately had additional tests done for the baby and consulted specialists to find out more information. At that point, I was having a lot of mixed feelings. I felt helpless and anxious about their current situation, but at the same time, I admired their willingness to prepare themselves for the future.

When Jared called us to let us know that the amniocentesis had confirmed trisomy 21, we could hear the stress and worry in his voice. All we could do was listen and try to offer encouragement and support. It was so difficult to know that our children and new grandson faced untold challenges that would continue through the rest of their lives. My wife managed to say to Jared, "We'll get through this somehow— we'll figure out a way." Our voices were choked with tears and we advised that they try to rest and take time to absorb the news. As a father, I wanted to hug them both and give them comfort and strength.

When we met them the next day, I could see fatigue in both Dolly and Jared's eyes from too little sleep and too much stress. It pained me to see what they were going through. "What's the next step?" I asked.

"We have a lot of thinking and praying to do," Jared replied. In that moment I developed so much unconditional respect, admiration, and love for these two. Even now I cannot think about it without getting teary.

The doctor had told them they had a decision to make—either terminate or proceed with the pregnancy. He also informed them they only had a few days to make a decision due to legal restraints and medical concerns for late-term abortions. They immediately consulted another doctor, who pointed out that children with Down syndrome have a wide range of abilities and characteristics and that he could not predict exactly how the baby would be affected.

Both Jared and Dolly started seeking more information about Down syndrome. They spoke with spiritual advisors as well as people who had personal experience. They discussed the situation with family members they felt comfortable talking to. With aching hearts, my wife and I told them we would respect whatever decision they made but ultimately it was their choice.

After several sleepless nights for Jared and Dolly, and several days of worry for us all, Jared called to tell us their decision. "We decided to continue the pregnancy," he said. "We can't authorize the taking of a life when we don't know what God has in mind, and we don't know how Down syndrome will specifically affect our son."

I went outside and cried. These two young adults—our "kids"—had just made a very mature decision that would affect the rest of their lives, and the relief in their voices was emotionally overwhelming. Although I had many questions and realized that the road ahead might be challenging in some ways, I too was relieved that the most important decision had been made.

The next several months went by quickly. In addition to taking care of their daily responsibilities, Jared and Dolly began preparing for the baby's arrival. They learned as much as they could about Down syndrome. My wife and I kept in close contact with them, offering to help in any ways we could. During this time, I tried to imagine how we would all cope with this new little person and what we could do to give him the best life possible. I wondered if he would have physical problems or learning disabilities, and whether he would enjoy social interaction with others. I didn't know the answers, but in my heart there was no question that he would be accepted and loved.

The day finally came when Brayden arrived. When I went into the hospital room to see him and Dolly, the first word to describe him in my thoughts was "Angelico," the Spanish word for "Angel." He looked like an angel lying there, so quiet and still. His father had the biggest smile I have ever seen, his brother and sister were beaming with pride. His mother looked tired, relieved, and happy. Although Brayden was born with trisomy 21, he had no health problems, and for the moment the world seemed complete. He looked soft and sweet, and when he opened his eyes, I immediately saw characteristics similar to his brother and sister. How could he *not* fit into our family? He was so cute—as his grandmother said, "right down to his ten little toes." He was full of innocence and vulnerability, and he loved to be cuddled. Looking into his eyes, I felt as if I could see into his soul.

No one knows exactly what the future holds, but I do know Brayden Grant Lehnick will bless us all and will be loved more than words can express. His parents love him and are already working with therapists to help him develop as he grows. His brother and sister love him and are very attentive to him. I can't leave out the great grandparents, grandparents, uncles, aunts, and many cousins from California to Florida who love him, and have already made plans for him as soon as he gets a little older.

To Brayden, I'd like to say that you are an inspiration to us all. You have already enriched my life, as I'm much more aware and appreciative of the successes of those with special needs, and I know you have your own valuable contribution to make to society. Always do your best, and never forget that you have so much to offer the world. I love you, and I look forward to watching you grow and develop, my Angelico.

●　　●　　●

Gene has lived in the Fresno, California, area for many years. Before moving to California he lived in Colorado, where he graduated from Adams State College. Gene gets the most joy in spending time with his family and grandchildren. He has two sons and seven grandchildren. He dedicates his story to his youngest grandson, Brayden—his "Angelico"— and to Brayden's parents, Jared and Dolly.

Beth Duncan and Emily Duncan

12.
The Missing Piece

By Beth Duncan

SHE REACHES OUT her soft hands and strokes my face. Her face is just inches from mine. I can smell her hair, her skin, and her sweet breath. After twelve years, it is so familiar a smell to me.

"Mommy," she says as she looks into my eyes. "Mommy." She loves me—I can feel it in her touch, see it in her eyes, and hear it in her voice.

"Emily," I reply as I cup her face in my hands and look into her eyes. She has taught me this simple gesture. Its beauty brings tears to my eyes.

She can say more than "Mommy," of course. She can talk about school and about her friends and teachers; she can tell me every item that she ate for lunch and for breakfast; she can talk about our trip to Disney World over two years ago; she can tell me that her tummy hurts or that she is tired and wants to go to bed. Her knowledge is deep, although often misunderstood. Even I don't fully understand her or how she fits into my life, although I'm gradually learning.

Emily was our first child, born when I was 27 and full of idealism and hope. Her diagnosis of Down syndrome quickly initiated us into reality: life brings us events that we don't always want or expect. Twelve years and three children later, the initiation process continues. Emily consistently shows us things the other kids cannot—their "normalness" makes them unable. Being normal is really not all it's cracked up to be. In fact, being less normal has become a goal of mine, thanks to Emily.

As a child, I sensed something really special in store for my life. I was excited about the pieces of my life coming together like an intricate puzzle. Unfortunately, over time, I became influenced by the world's standards, and, like the other kids around me, tried to squeeze myself into the mold, into the wrong puzzle. I tried to wear the right clothes, hang out with the right people, go to the right parties, and join the right clubs. I forgot who I was, or who I had dreamed of becoming, and instead became more and more normal. It was easier that way, and it seemed to boost my self-esteem—I felt accepted when I was like everyone else. But over time, trying to fit in actually challenged my self-esteem. I couldn't stand up to the pressure of trying to be what I was not. Hidden underneath the person I'd become was the real me waiting to be discovered, but I didn't know how to find her.

Enter Emily. For years I couldn't figure out how she fit into the puzzle of my life. Sometimes she seemed like a piece to a whole different puzzle, mistakenly put in my box. I saw "normal" little girls all around me, and thought they would fit so much better. But as I mature and grow, the Emily piece is beginning to fit perfectly into place, the place it had belonged all along. I imagine some day when I see the whole puzzle put together, I'll be in awe, fully realizing the contribution of my firstborn not only to my life, but to the lives of many others as well.

Recently, I watched Emily walk down the school bus aisle. She was coming home from school, and I had stepped up into the bus to talk to the driver. Emily wasn't cool or suave, as normal kids would act on the bus. In fact, her pants were pulled up way too high, above her waistline. A long bunch of her silky blond hair hung in front of her glasses, which were smudgy from her day at school. Her pale pink shirt was dirty too. She didn't care. She was focused on her routine—hugging and saying goodbye to all of the other kids with special needs and their helpers on the bus. She smiled and giggled as she interacted with them. It didn't matter in the least what they looked like, smelled like, or acted like. Their value to her did not depend on anything external. Unlike myself as a twelve-year-old, fitting in didn't matter to Emily. Being cool didn't matter either; having the right clothes or right mannerisms was insignificant to her. All that mattered was reaching out to others and connecting with them in a meaningful way.

She is who she is. She is beautifully herself. She doesn't try to be what she's not.

I can't say I've totally come to terms with this quality that Emily has in such pure form. She is putting together her own puzzle with simple precision and grace. She will not try to squeeze into someone else's puzzle—for her that would make no sense. At times I wish she would try to fit in more, play the right part, and wear the appropriate mask, as "normal" people do. It doesn't always work to be real. But I've learned that if Emily is forced to play the part, she rebels. She is driven to be her true self.

Who is my true self? I am trying to rediscover that. Throwing off normalcy and becoming "abnormal" is my goal. To do this, I need to embrace the Emily puzzle piece, accept it for what it is, then stand back and look at the beauty of it connected in its place. Only then can I admire what I have in Emily and learn from her example. I'm glad that Emily came into my life because, among other reasons, she is gradually showing me who I am.

● ● ●

Beth resides in the southeastern U.S. with her husband and four children. Her oldest daughter, Emily, was diagnosed with Down syndrome shortly after birth. Beth is a teacher, freelance writer, and certified Lactation Consultant, a part-time occupation she initially embarked on in order to help mothers nursing babies with Down syndrome. She also enjoys traveling and photography, especially portrait photography of children.

Craig and Wesley Parker

13.
That's What It's All About!

By Craig W. Parker

"YOU PUT YOUR right hand in, you take your right hand out…"

Our physical therapist started singing the Hokey Pokey with Wes a while back so he'd learn to stand on one foot as he danced. Then we started using the song to work on learning his body parts. Regardless of whether he gets the right part in, Wes always has fun dancing to what is now his all-time favorite song. We've sung it so many times together, we could all sing it in our sleep!

When Wes was born with Down syndrome, I quickly realized that patience and persistence were lessons he would require me to learn. These traits are important for any parent, but especially important for parents of children with special needs. And patience is definitely not one of my strengths. I would describe myself as a very driven person, and, prior to Wes's birth, my main focus, and largely how I defined myself, was based on success in my career. Success depended on me being able to make decisions, implement solutions quickly, and keep to a defined plan and timeline. The transition from a career-focused life to a more balanced one with Wes has not always been easy. But Wes teaches me by example.

My wife and I have high expectations for both of our sons and we haven't changed them for Wes because he has Down syndrome. However, our timelines and paths to meet those expectations have been adjusted, and the amount of effort on his part and ours has increased. On a daily basis, he's challenged by therapists and teachers as well as his parents. Between school and private therapy, he spends more than three hours a week in various types of therapy. This work continues at home as we require him to use his words when requesting things, or when we work together on buttoning his pajamas. I look forward to the day when I can walk down the stairs facing forward, rather than walking backwards to make sure Wes is walking safely down behind me.

Often times, I wonder if it is fair for us to work so hard with Wes and expect so much. But even through his complaining, whining, and squawking, he continues to try; he continues to learn. In all honesty, he learns much more quickly than I do. I was taken off guard the day he pointed to letters inside the cover of one of his favorite books and made the corresponding phonic sounds. And the day he counted aloud the floor numbers in our hotel elevator, I realized I'd be hard pressed to keep up with him!

Wes isn't always successful in his tasks, nor do I always have the patience to help him do things on his own. After all this time singing the Hokey Pokey, he still needs help balancing on one foot while putting his other foot out. There are plenty of times where I give in and pick him up instead of pushing him to walk up the stairs by himself. But the look on his face says, "Give me a chance. Work with me and I can do it. Be creative and I'll show you a different way to do it that makes sense for me." Our morning routine would be quicker if I put his shoes on for him, and our mealtimes would be more peaceful if I loaded the food on his fork. Yet it's in those moments that I realize that I need to offer him the same level of persistence and patience that he offers me. When he wants to give up, that's the exact moment when, for his sake, I can't.

At a recent family wedding the familiar tune began to play: "You put your right hand in, you take your right hand out..." Wes had suffered through some slow songs on the sidelines, growing very impatient for "a big song," even though it was way past his bedtime. On the first notes of his favorite song, he rushed to join the circle that had formed for the dance. My wife helped him use the body parts that the song requested, but he didn't need any help with the clapping and turning! Never missing a chance to be the center of attention, with each verse of the song Wes inched himself closer to the center of the circle. By the end of the Hokey Pokey, he was smack in the middle of the crowd, dancing in all his glory, basking in the smiles and cheers coming from all around the room. I smiled as I watched one of the many "successes" of life with Wes. He was enjoying the rewards of our persistent teamwork and his own unique personality. And that, I realized, is what it's all about.

● ● ●

Craig lives in Victoria, Minnesota, with his wife, Kara, and two sons. He sits on the board of directors for the Down Syndrome Association of Minnesota and chairs their development committee. He enjoys running, traveling, and spending time with his family. His son, Wesley (2004), was diagnosed with Down syndrome at birth and continues to amaze his parents, family, and friends every day.

Joshua and Charity Poleshuk

14.
Independence Found

By Charity Poleshuk

IN OUR RURAL town, going to school is Joshua's social highway. And today is a school day, one of Joshua's favorite days. He is up and dressed at what feels like the crack of dawn. He has told me many times that he is ready to go to school. I have had to encourage him to sit back down to finish his breakfast. He still has time. Joshua is finished with all of his morning routine and he's finally on the porch blowing bubbles, while waiting for the bus. It seems like he has ridden the bus for years; from the early years of going to preschool, to now, at age 13, riding the big yellow school bus independently. No need for me to help him up the step, or buckle him in the car seat; he doesn't even need a hug. When Joshua was first born, weighing no more than a sack of flour, these days seemed hard to imagine.

There is a lesson for Mom here in letting go. For years I have thought of Joshua as being *mine*—Momma's little boy. For I remember all the things that made him my little boy. But the reality is he's growing up, both physically and mentally. He wants a mustache like dad, he whistles at women on commercials, and (scariest of all, for me) he wants to kiss a girl! I can't even call him honey anymore. He told me "Daddy's honey, me Joshua."

Logically I've known these changes would come someday, but still they've taken me by surprise. With his brother, a gradual, natural progression of events led to independence. But with Joshua, everything seems to be happening at once. One day not long ago, the first step onto the bus loomed taller than he was. Now, with a surge of independence and hormones, he is ready to conquer the world. Full of teenage enthusiasm, his favorite words are "I do it, I do it." As much as I have always wanted him to be independent, it's bittersweet to let him try.

This morning, like every other school day, he waits at the side of the street for the bus to stop and then crosses the road to climb aboard. When he reaches the bus, something wonderful happens. Joshua stops and turns to me. Then he raises his arm and signs "I love you" while he yells the words aloud, breaking the silence of the morning. It sounds and looks like a rock star salute, and it would make any mother proud. I realize that now is Joshua's time to become himself. And I am reassured that even as he finds his independence, he isn't losing his love for mom.

It's my favorite part of the morning.

● ● ●

In a quiet town along the Juniata River in Pennsylvania, Charity lives with her husband and two sons, Eli and Joshua. She is a multi-tasking mom who currently balances taking college classes and being an active community member with retaining her creativity. Her boys are the joy and laughter of her life.

Alexander Chervenak with mom, Andrea Chervenak

15.

Brief Encounter

By Andrea Chervenak

IT WAS A bitter cold day in January 2006 when I first entered a sixth grade self-contained special education classroom in a suburban school in western New York. This was my first field experience in a special education setting since deciding to pursue dual certification in general and special education. I was pursuing my master's degree in special education and I needed to complete 150 hours of field experiences.

Thirty minutes before the students would be filing into the classroom, I met with the special education teacher, an energetic woman in her fifties. She explained that there were seventeen students in the class. Pointing to the empty desks one at a time, she named the child who sat there and briefly explained his or her disability. The students faced a wide variety of challenges: learning disabilities in reading and/or math, autism, attention-deficit/hyperactivity disorder, Asperger syndrome, and Down syndrome. I listened intently as the teacher explained in further detail the structure and routines of the classroom. As I took both mental and written notes, I started to feel intimidated.

The halls began to fill with the footsteps and voices of middle school boys and girls, and I eagerly anticipated meeting the students. While the students entered the classroom one at a time and took their seats, I made eye contact with a few of them and smiled, won-

Nicholas Schaertel

dering how they would respond to a new person in the room. By the time all the students had entered, I'd forgotten which child had which disability, and was feeling somewhat overwhelmed. I'd never been in a setting with as many students with special needs in one place at one time.

I decided to introduce myself to one of the students, Stephen, who looked like he needed help finding something in his cluttered, disorganized desk. I bent down to Stephen's level and began to help organize his papers. When I felt a tap on my shoulder, I turned around. Standing with his hand extended to introduce himself was a boy who stood about five feet tall, a few inches shorter than me. He stared at me very intently and without hesitation said, "Hi, I'm Nicky." I shook his hand. He held my hand tightly and reassuringly, as if to say *welcome*. His self-confidence filled me with emotion, and as I looked into his sweet hazel eyes, a feeling of awe overcame me. Nicky has Down syndrome, and although some of his physical features are characteristic of his disability, when I shook his hand I saw not a disabled person but an individual with intensity and conviction of who he is.

Each day I taught and observed in the classroom, Nicky greeted me with the same handshake and smile. He participated in most of the lessons with assistance from a paraprofessional. Nicky had a lot of friends and enjoyed mutual respect with his peers. His energy and enthusiasm were contagious. He was eager to learn; he could write his name legibly, express himself through dramatic play, and make connections with books and movies. More than anything, Nicky had the ability to help others, including myself, see that individuals with Down syndrome are capable learners who should not be defined by their disability.

When my time in Nicky's classroom came to a close, I knew I'd always remember our brief encounter. What I didn't know was that a year and a half later, after graduating with my master's degree in special education, I would give birth to a son with Down syndrome. My husband and I found out about our son's diagnosis when I was about twenty weeks pregnant, after an abnormal ultrasound and AFP screening prompted us to get amniocentesis. Further detailed ultrasounds and a fetal echocardiogram showed that our son had a small hole between his right and left ventricles in his heart called a ventricular septal defect (VSD), which might require repair after birth. This possibility was even more difficult for me to accept than his diagnosis of Down syndrome. Images of my son getting prepped for heart surgery consumed my thoughts. He would be so small and vulnerable, and I would be so helpless.

My husband and I considered our "options." Although it was difficult for me to fathom terminating the pregnancy, I felt our son's diagnosis was unfair. I'd committed my career to working with children with special needs. Yes, I was familiar with Early Intervention Services, Individualized Family Service Plans (IFSPs), Individualized Education Programs (IEPs), and everything I would need to do to advocate for this child, but that knowledge didn't prepare me to be his mother. I felt incapable of providing for a child with special needs, and I grieved the "normal" child I had lost.

But then I remembered my relationship with Nicky. Gradually, the shock of the diagnosis began to dissipate, and the "why us?" comments ceased. I recalled my handshakes with Nicky, and envisioned holding my son's hands. I pictured Nicky's hazel eyes and his intense gaze, and imagined what my son's eye color would be and how he might look at me. I thought about Nicky's many friends and wondered who my son's friends would be. I remembered Nicky's ability to communicate and his love for books and movies, and realized my son would learn to express himself and have his own particular interests. Most importantly, I thought about the positive impact Nicky had on me and others, and I began looking forward to the influence my son would have on me and the rest of the world. My thoughts transcended from utter grief to peace.

Alexander Nicholas was born July 21, 2007. The moment I began to feel contractions, I knew everything was going to be all right. We drove to the hospital at sundown, with the most memorable display of pink, orange, and violet painted across the sky. I said to my husband, "I will never forget this sunset." Nor will I ever forget my brief encounter with Nicky, which in time created an awareness of who I was meant to be: Alex's mom. Thanks to Nicky I knew the ending of that perfect summer day marked the beginning of an amazing life.

● ● ●

Andrea, along with her husband, Nick, live in Rochester, New York, with their two children, Maya (2004) and Alex (2007). The small hole in Alex's heart (VSD) did not require surgery. Alex is a very healthy, active toddler. Andrea is enjoying staying at home with her two children and intends to teach special education when her children enter grade school. This story is dedicated to Nicky and all the other children with Down syndrome who helped her find beauty in unexpected places.

Jamie and Cori Martin

16.
Billboard Boy

By Lisa Muirheid Martin

AT ALMOST EVERY one of my son Jamie's IEP (Individualized Education Program) meetings, I think someone in the room (other than his parents) has described him as unique. At first, I wasn't sure what to think of that word and what it implied. But I've decided I like it, especially in reference to my son. His teachers are correct: Jamie is unique. That's because he's Jamie, not because he has Down syndrome. And just by being himself, he is a walking billboard for acceptance of people who may act or learn a little differently than others.

Jamie is one of the first children with Down syndrome to be included in a regular education classroom in our school district. As a parent I always worry about sending my child off into the unknown, but it has been amazing to see how well the rest of the students in his school treat him and how many friends he has made. We can seldom go anywhere with Jamie without someone saying "Hi" to him. I'll never forget how relieved I felt when his assistant shared that he had a whole group of girls vying for his attention on the playground at recess. "It would really make you smile," she said.

He does make his entire family smile often, although he doesn't always make things easy on us. This is especially true for his younger sister, Cori, whom he loves dearly and terrorizes daily like any other big brother would. She says the worst is when he keeps asking her the same questions over and over, but he is also notorious for chasing her around with whatever she might deem to be "disgusting" or blocking her view of the TV during *Hannah Montana*.

While Jamie may drive Cori crazy sometimes, he is also her best friend and they are usually an inseparable pair, unless he decides it's time to be showing his independence. Some days he does that around every corner—often disappearing around every corner, too, if we aren't careful. And we really try to be careful. But there was the time at the National Down Syndrome Congress's convention when he seemingly vanished in the stairwell of an eighteen-floor hotel! Just when we were getting ready to notify hotel security, my mother, who was waiting in our room, got a call from seven flights up. People in the exact room as ours on a different floor called to tell us our son had knocked on their door, looking for me. We rushed up there to find him entertaining a family with a new baby who was also born with an extra chromosome.

Thank goodness Jamie has a knack for taking care of himself. Last summer we attended a big luncheon at the Illinois State Fair. I know I didn't take my eyes off of him for more than thirty seconds while I gave a friend a hug, and what do you know, he was gone. I started my soon frantic search through the crowd of 500 people, enlisting the help of a few friends. We finally saw him emerge from the other end of the food line with a man who was helping him sit down with his plate. What could I say? He is seven, and he was hungry. Of course, I immediately told him that he'd scared us and reminded him that he needs to stay with me, but I couldn't help but feel a little bit proud of him for getting his own lunch. He changed some perceptions that day of what a little boy with Down syndrome can do all by himself.

There are plenty of other things Jamie can do by himself, some of them hilarious. We laugh regularly at how he can make grown men do things they would never do otherwise. "You stand right here," he'll direct. "Please, pick that up and throw it away." It seems few adults (other than family members, his assistant, and the staff at school) will ever tell the boy no. Ironically enough, he's very good at saying no himself. "No thank you," he'll say ever so politely when we ask if he will give someone a goodbye hug, help clean up a mess, or eat something that isn't in the potato chip family or from a McDonald's sack.

Jamie can be a very sweet boy, as many perceive children with Down syndrome to be, but he also has a defiant and determined streak that shows he is going to think for himself and be his own person, no stereotypes allowed. He likes to help others but also prefers to live on his own terms, always picking out thirty books to read instead of three or asking to do something for "a hundred more minutes please" when the usual request would be "one more minute." While this can sometimes be exasperating, it can also be inspiring. After his class watched the inauguration of Barack Obama, Jamie's assistant shared that he was the only one she saw who kneeled with his hands clasped when he heard the Lord's Prayer being recited. He is never afraid to do his own thing.

Jamie is full of imagination and whether he is forming a rock and roll band or dreaming up his next birthday party, his choice of words is often priceless. How I smiled the first time he told me his Spaghetti O's were "scrumptious," or the time he put his hand to his chin and announced "that's odd" when something didn't work as he expected. And his aunt loves to tell the story of the day she let Jamie look at her datebook, and two minutes later it vanished from the room. "He wanted to help find it so much, getting a flashlight and looking in the oven and behind the couch," she explains. "And then finally, after I'd asked him a dozen times where my book had gone, he replied with a big, silly grin, 'It's in my tummy.'" (It turned up inside the toy box two months later.)

I love how the wheels in Jamie's mind are always turning. Despite the difference in his genetic make-up, he is very much like his second grade classmates who are like little sponges, observing their world around them and opening people's eyes to things they never noticed before. Ordinary things become extraordinary in Jamie's eyes when he notices that the orange and blue cups stacked at a concession stand form an "AB" pattern like he learned in math at school. And the ordinary becomes extraordinary in my *ears* when I hear, "We don't go this way" if we use a different road than normal to get to our driveway. After studying directions, he recently woke up at 3 a.m. and told my sister how to find the McDonald's playland in the next town. "You go left, then right and it is in the Northwest corner," he explained. There are a few miles in between, but he basically got it right. I think I will need to hide the car keys from now on.

Full of surprises, it seems Jamie changes minds and promotes acceptance wherever he goes. He loves music, so we thought he might enjoy dance class. Jamie and his sister, Cori, who is seventeen months younger and almost the same size, did a big "jump" during their jazz routine this year—she ran up to him and turned around, while he pretended to lift her off the ground. Joined by another brother-sister team, they brought down the house with rare spontaneous applause during their recital. After the show Jamie got flowers from people we don't even know. I had to laugh at the grandfather who I overheard saying, "I come every year just to watch him." Of course, there were some granddaughters there for him to watch as well, but I loved the fact that he was smiling and thinking about my dancing son as he left the recital hall.

Another enlightening experience has been community sports. The other families and coaches on his t-ball teams were supportive of Jamie even though he wasn't always the most cooperative player. While he often decided he would rather cheer from the sidelines than stand in the sunny outfield, he would usually take his turn at bat.

One day when the coaches were persuading him to watch the ball, he saw his friend Tyler sitting in the outfield. Jamie got very excited, waved, hit the ball, and ran straight to where Tyler was sitting, batting helmet and all, bypassing the bases. The next time up, he ran the bases like he had hit a homer and everyone cheered for him the whole way. Not quite the traditional way the game is played, but then again, teaching people new traditions is okay too!

Raising a child with Down syndrome isn't always easy, but watching people's perceptions change and their minds open is a blessing I could never have predicted. Just like I could never have predicted my son's vocabulary skills the other night at bedtime. I often call my unpredictable boy "monkey," and when I snuggled up next to him to tuck him in and said "I love you monkey," his reply was "I love you chimpanzee." Always thinking, my billboard boy is, helping those around him accept that being different can be a very good thing, one independent step, one precocious word, and one delightful dance at a time.

● ● ●

Lisa lives in Illinois with her husband, Jim, and children, Jamie and Cori. She works from home and wears many hats, including program coordinator, farmhand, advocate, and volunteer. She loves family, travel, photography, reading, and communicating with others whose children have been blessed with an extra chromosome. Lisa and Jamie dedicate this story to Sam, who earned his angel wings on Jan. 1, 2009, and his amazing mom, MaryAnn.

THE GIFT OF AWARENESS

Ella Kinder

17.
Mulch

By Julia Pewitt Kinder

I'M A DOCTOR so I know about Down syndrome.

If you are a parent of a child with Down syndrome, and you just took a nice long sip of coffee as you settled in to read this essay, then you now have coffee pooled in your mouth as it is impossible to swallow while laughing hysterically. Or perhaps you are drumming your fingers in irritation as you search for my contact information so you can tell me how little I really know.

But that was my first thought four years ago when I was told my baby girl has Down syndrome. I thought, "Well, at least I am a doctor and I know about Down syndrome." Ironically, Ella was born completely healthy. To this day, she hasn't even had a single ear infection. Here I am equipped with my medical knowledge from four years of medical school, three years of residency, and several years in practice, and it doesn't apply. In fact, many of the things I thought I knew about Down syndrome turned out to be false. It was as if "THE UNIVERSE" was determined that I would take a new road in life—and I would start my journey in the dark.

So there I was with a healthy baby who happened to have Down syndrome. I didn't even realize that was possible. I had to refer to my medical books because I thought all babies with Down syndrome had heart issues or gastrointestinal abnormalities or some other problem in the long list of possible complications. In a strange way, I wished I could preoccupy myself with endless doctor's appointments and medication schedules. If Ella had health problems, at least I would have a place to start. I would know what to do.

But all I had, it seemed, were questions: Would Ella crawl? Would she walk? Would we ever understand her speech if she even could talk? Could she learn to use the potty? Would she have friends? Would she go to a regular school? I assumed the answer to all these questions was probably *no*. I always said I would teach my child a second language, but I supposed I'd have to forget that. Violin lessons would have been nice, but I'd have to put that dream away, too. Ditto for my expectations that my child would go to college, drive, work, live independently, and get married. I felt as if I were hopelessly lost on a long and rocky trail. I didn't have the provisions to get started, I dreaded the expedition, and I didn't even know the destination.

Ella was not quite two years old when her Daddy decided to teach her some things about his job. He builds houses. First, he taught her about flooring. Within hours she knew the difference between hardwood, slate, and carpet floors in our house. Then they went outside to discuss brick, stone, and concrete. I was mildly irritated that he was wasting time teaching Ella worthless facts when she needed to learn other, more important things, like the letters of the alphabet and counting to ten. But then, a few days later, we were walking into a restaurant and she stopped and pointed at the ground around the landscaping. "Mulch," she identified, correctly. Mulch isn't the most sophisticated of concepts, but it's not a simple one either. I realized that if Ella at that young age could learn what mulch is, she would go on to learn a lot more than I'd given her credit for. With that one word, the path I was on suddenly became brightly lit with the warm sun.

Encouraged and excited, I returned to school: The School of Ella, seeking a degree in Down syndrome. I wanted to learn as much as I could so that I could give Ella every opportunity possible. In my Down syndrome coursework I've studied physical, occupational, speech, oral-motor, music, and developmental therapies. I've learned about early childhood development. I've learned to teach my child to read. I am practicing yoga. Slowly and painfully, I'm picking up some Spanish. Next week I start violin lessons. The more I learn, the more I realize there is to learn. And everything that I have learned, Ella has learned as well.

Every single night for the first two years of Ella's life, I would go to her room to watch her sleep. I would look down at her and wonder, "Where is this terrible Down syndrome thing?" Ella was a child like any other child; she played, ate, and chased the cat. She had blue eyes and blonde hair and Down syndrome. It was only a small part of who she was; certainly not the most important thing. I had started out on this pilgrimage with the wrong questions. Instead of asking what Ella would *do,* I should have asked who she would *be.* My purpose along the way would be to provide the fertilizer for Ella to become who she wants to be. I could guide our family to our destination; a wonderful life. That was nothing to be afraid of.

I've been in Ella's school for four years now and I am not even close to getting my degree. But I'm listening to what "THE UNI-VERSE" was trying to tell me when I was placed on this new journey in life. It turns out that having a child with Down syndrome was never the problem. The problem was my fear of the unknown and my fear of the future. Through Ella, I've come to truly understand Down syndrome, and I want other doctors and medical students to know more so that they can inspire new parents of babies with Down syndrome. So I travel to medical conferences, schools, and hospitals and present lectures on prenatal testing, delivering the diagnosis, and supporting new families. Most importantly, I try to erase the many myths and misconceptions of Down syndrome and provide current facts and optimism. I like to take Ella along, as my audiences are always more impressed with her than with her mom. She recently read the word "oscillate" to a neurologist. While that is a word to be proud of, I still prefer "mulch." Not only does it stop weeds, it promotes the growth of some of the most beautiful things on earth.

●　　●　　●

Julia is a board-certified family practice physician, writer, and fitness instructor. She speaks nationwide on Down syndrome at medical schools, medical conferences, and hospitals. As a volunteer for the Down Syndrome Association of St. Louis, Julia offers new parent support and educates school children about Down syndrome. Currently, Julia is researching oral-motor therapy and its effects on orofacial posture and speech in children with Down syndrome.

Natalie Bonavita Spencer
and Greg Bonavita

18.

Subtle Wisdom

By Natalie Bonavita Spencer

I HAVE NEVER known life without Down syndrome. From the day I was born, it was everywhere. When I wanted to play with toys, Down syndrome was there. When I wanted the attention of one of my older siblings, Down syndrome was there. When I went to school, to the baby sitter's, to the mall, to Grandma's, Down syndrome was there. But I never saw it.

Gregory Joseph was born in October of 1977; I was born three-and-a-half years later, the sixth and last child to join our family. Throughout my teen and young adult years, each member of the family has told me how they reacted to Greg's birth and diagnosis of Down syndrome. My mother was able to fully accept Greg within the first few weeks following his birth, while my father admits it took him six months to see beyond the Down syndrome and finally "see" Greg. My four older siblings, who were between the ages of eight and twelve, each reported an adjustment period. I, however, can't remember when I first realized Greg had Down syndrome. He was always just Greg.

What I do remember is having a brother who would play Barbies with me and watch the movie *Annie* with me over and over, singing along with all the songs. I was the member of my family best able to understand Greg's "language" and would often interpret what he said for the rest of my family. He may have looked and sounded different to the outside world, but not to me. His tongue sliding out of his mouth when he was concentrating or tired; the "W" position he sat in, with each leg bent at the knees and each foot touching its corresponding hip bone; his full-body laugh, which prevented all sound from escaping and left only a big smile and a shaking body—these were all parts of Greg, not the Down syndrome. I saw him no differently than I saw my other older siblings, or how they, in return, saw me.

As I entered my teen years, Greg and I were the only kids at home, since my older siblings had all married and started their own families. I found myself realizing that I didn't have a typical teen sibling relationship with Greg. I never had to fight for the car, as Greg does not drive. I never had to fight to watch what I wanted on TV, as we both had our own TVs in our bedrooms. I never had to fight for the phone, or the living room when friends were over. There were times I wondered what it would be like to have a "typical" sibling close to my age, but this was my life, and it was okay. Granted, we had our share of times when we bickered as only siblings can—like over who would get the last Oreo cookie. During these times, Greg would get mad and storm out of the room, only to come back a half hour later with the most somber look on his face, sighing deeply, and saying "No happy. Sorry." Greg made it easier to let go of some of the teen angst that we all experience. He taught me that it is possible for someone to give a genuine and heartfelt apology, then move on—a lesson I'm still trying to apply today.

Greg also taught me that it is more than okay to accept someone despite how he or she may look or sound. It's easy to judge a book by its cover, but those who do so may miss out on seeing the person beyond the difference or disability. In our home, we get to enjoy Greg's tradition of calling our father every April 1st, telling him to look at the snow outside, and yelling "April Fool's!" while giggling. We're aware of things we normally wouldn't be interested in, such as WWE wrestling and Power Rangers. We watch Greg get up each morning and independently get himself ready for work, from showering, to dressing, to shaving and packing his own lunch, and finally getting himself on the bus, all the while talking to himself and planning out his entire day for all to hear. We marvel at his ability to find his favorite show on TV at any given moment, despite not being able to tell time. We realize his abilities far outweigh his disabilities.

Now, as an adult early in my career as a speech-language pathologist—a career I wouldn't have known about or considered without Greg—I appreciate the subtle ways Greg has affected my life. He has shown me how to fully accept people for who they are—something he does very easily. He has taught me that there are many different ways to view a situation and to express yourself. Without me realizing it on a conscious level, Greg has influenced how I view my students, many of whom come to me with limited speech and language skills due to a diagnosis of Down syndrome, autism, or overall developmental delay. I know these children each have many abilities that are known to their parents, siblings, grandparents, and extended family members who love them.

Greg has taught me by example that if you can't make yourself understood the first way you try, you try another method. This has helped me to help students like Robbie, who is nonverbal, my height, has the strength of ten of me when he becomes upset, and has autism. Robbie enjoys books and puzzles, and can operate a computer better than most adults I know. He can run faster than I can down the hall and has a great smile. He is an intelligent boy who is learning how to express himself nonverbally. However, he becomes incredibly frustrated and sometimes aggressive when his wants and needs are not met on his timeline. Greg's speech is fairly unintelligible to unfamiliar listeners, and like Robbie, Greg becomes frustrated when he is not understood after a few tries and will occasionally give up. But more often than not, Greg will take a few seconds and will figure out another way to express what he was trying to say. Through Greg's living example, I am aware that although Robbie may not be able to tell me what he wants using clear, precise words, that doesn't mean he can't tell me another way, such as through sign language, pictures, or taking my hand and showing me. When Robbie does this, I see his frustration level decrease, just as I do with Greg when his thoughts are finally understood and he looks at us all as if he is thinking, "what was so hard to understand about that?"

Because Greg can't always tell us what he's thinking or feeling, some may think he does not understand some of the world around him. My understanding that this isn't the case has enabled me to help my student Kiara, who like Robbie is nonverbal. When I first started working with Kiara three years ago, she was very difficult to engage, barely looking at me when I encouraged her to sign "more" or wave "hi." Kiara was very lax in all areas, physically and cognitively. Then, halfway through my second year working with her, something started clicking. Kiara began establishing eye contact more frequently, interacting with adults on her own for brief periods, identifying vocabulary, and initiating requests for objects she wanted by pointing or gazing. She began to imitate some sounds and vocalized more audibly. She would become upset if she couldn't write her own name. She also showed us she was very interested in how things work: she would make sure a zipper was zipped up fully, and tried to take apart toys if possible. She also had a knowing smile when she did something she knew she wasn't supposed to do. Because of Greg, I know that just because Kiara can't verbally express herself doesn't mean she's incapable of understanding when someone's feelings are hurt, or when someone is mad or sad. Kiara, Robbie, and Greg understand much more than you might think at first glance—just give them time to show you in their own way.

The subtle wisdom Greg has shared with me is truly significant. It has affected not only my life, but the lives of others. Because I grew up learning from Greg and realizing he is much more capable than not, I look for what my students and others in my life *can* do. I am willing to give people the benefit of the doubt more readily because of him. I am grateful that my life has always included Greg as my brother, who has taught me so much and influenced my life in so many wonderful and positive ways—some of which I'm just beginning to understand.

●   ●   ●

Natalie lives in Pennsylvania with her husband, Matt. She enjoys her work as a speech-language pathologist. Her brother Greg lives in Pennsylvania with his mother and works five days a week. He is planning to move into a group home as soon as possible, and will expect a phone call before visits.

Donna Hammock and grandson Kevin Miller

19.

Is He Like Me?

By Donna Hammock

"MOM, CAN YOU come to the hospital?" When I answered the telephone, those long-awaited words finally came to let me know that I would be a grandmother again! I had been pacing the floor in nervous anticipation. I jumped when the phone rang and could not answer it fast enough. It had to be my son Larry, and when I realized it was, butterflies went crazy in my stomach.

I scrambled to get ready, thinking what an exciting time this was for my son, having his first baby. But during the drive to the hospital I kept reflecting on Larry's tone of voice on the telephone. I certainly hadn't heard the excitement of a first-time dad. What could be wrong? Fear began to build as I imagined the worst. Could the baby have been born very sick? Or, could the baby have been born like me—a dwarf?

Not that being a dwarf is such a terrible thing. I don't know of any other way to be. But when it came to my grandson, I worried about the difficult parts of being small: the physical pain of bone deformities, the emotional pain of being teased and stared at. I felt terrible sadness that my son, who already had a small mom, might have a permanently small son as well.

These fears seemed to be confirmed when I walked into the hospital lobby and saw Larry standing there with no trace of joy on his face. I approached him, grabbed his hand, and whispered, "Is he like me?" He looked at me lovingly and said he would explain when we got to the maternity ward. Once we stepped out of the elevator, I again asked with a tearful, quivering voice, "Is he like me?"

He gently replied, "No, Mom. He has Down syndrome."

When those words rolled out of his mouth you could have knocked me over with a feather. Time seemed to be moving in slow motion. I knew nothing about Down syndrome, although I'd seen people with Down syndrome on occasion and knew they were mentally challenged. I was relieved my grandson had not been born with dwarfism. However, his diagnosis gave me a whole new set of fears. How in the world was I going to deal with a grandchild who is mentally challenged? Needless to say I was scared to death, due to my lack of knowledge and understanding. But all I cared about right then was seeing my new grandson, Kevin Cole.

The first time I laid eyes on Kevin, I fell hopelessly in love with him. He was born with red hair, beautifully shaped eyebrows, and the most incredible cerulean blue eyes—exactly like his dad's. It was like looking at my own newborn son all over again. I wanted to hold him so badly, but I couldn't because he needed emergency surgery to attach his esophagus to his stomach, a condition sometimes associated with Down syndrome.

Emotions were flying high as I watched Kevin in his little isolette. I thought a mistake had been made in his diagnosis, because he did not look like he had Down syndrome. When I questioned Larry about this, he tenderly pointed out and explained the different features a child with Down syndrome has. I knew from that moment forward my life was going to be very different. As to what extent, I wasn't quite sure, but I made up my mind I was going to learn everything I could on the subject of Down syndrome. I searched, read, studied, and joined a support group. My sense of urgency increased as Kevin's mother showed no signs of being a responsible parent. In short order, Larry filed for a divorce and received full custody of Kevin. His mother never challenged custody rights and went back to her home state. I knew Larry would need my support more than ever.

Four days after Kevin's surgery, Larry lifted our sweet bundle from his isolette and placed him in my arms. His stunning blue eyes were open, and looking at me if to say, "I'm okay, Grandma." As Kevin and I looked at each other I had two weighty questions: Would I be able to play a major part in Kevin's life? Would Larry allow me to help rear Kevin? I'd already become so attached to him and wanted to be his advocate in every phase of his life, but I knew there might be limitations to what I could do. After all, I had a disability of my own. And as Kevin's parent, Larry had the chief responsibility.

Six years later, my two questions have been answered. Yes, Larry has allowed me to help rear Kevin, and I am able to play a major role in Kevin's life. It has become second nature for Larry and me to work as a team where Kevin is involved. I assist with Kevin's daily care, and since Larry has the ability to calm my emotions, I depend on him for comfort and understanding when issues arise regarding Kevin's health or development. Larry and I rely on each other for Kevin's well-being in every aspect of his life, and in the process we've become just about as close as a mother and son can get.

Likewise, Kevin and I have become just about as close as a grandmother and grandson can get. We walk around this beautiful earth, hand in hand, and when he wraps his arms around me, looks at me eye to eye and tells me, "I love you," life cannot get any better than that. Although he's not a dwarf, we are alike in many ways. We experience the same joys life has to offer us, and appreciate the same love and support we get from family and friends. We also face the same trials, and this gives us many growing opportunities.

At a young age, I learned from the example of a beloved uncle and aunt who spent many hours teaching me how to be productive and how to cope with adversity in life. Since Kevin and I are out there in the world together, inevitably exposed to rejection of a sometimes very narrow-minded society, I can teach him the same skills I learned. I can teach him that there will always be stares, name calling, laughing, finger pointing, and general social rejection. I can teach him that people who point and stare just don't understand. In moments of embarrassment and hurt, I can teach him by example to ignore the negative remarks, mind his own business, and dwell on the positives in life.

Recently Kevin and I visited our favorite ice cream parlor. Upon entering, I noticed two mothers with their young children sitting at tables enjoying their treats. As usual, all the kids had their eyes on me. Normally, adults will turn to their children, and with quiet whispers try to keep them from making rude comments. But this time, the moms were focused on my grandson, and could not take their eyes off of him. Kevin and I walked hand in hand over to the counter to order our treats. He told the clerk he wanted, "One coop blue i-ceem, pease." I glanced over at the moms, who were awestruck. I laughed to myself as I imagined what could be going through their heads. You see, Kevin and I are the same height. For a few more months at least, until he grows taller, he's just like me.

● ● ●

Donna lives in Carmel, Indiana, with her husband, Joe, and a Himalayan cat named Suki. Donna has been an artist for many years and has won awards in competitions in California and Indiana. She recently graduated from The Art Institute of Pittsburgh with a degree in web design and graphics. She is devoted to her faith, home, the arts, and especially her family. Her story is dedicated to her husband, Joe, who has been her number one support and advocate throughout the years in all she ventures out to do.

Lisa and Bridget Peele

20.
Bridget's Light

By Lisa Peele

WHEN OUR OLDEST two children were very small, we bought
and renovated a traditional saltbox-style home to accommodate our
growing family. The house sat on a gorgeous, deeply wooded lot
which included a pleasing assortment of redbud, oak, and buckeye
trees. It took us a little while to figure out that while the house itself
was perfect for us, the heavily treed lot, which initially attracted us
to the property, meant that there were no visible sunsets and dark
rooms even on the brightest of days.

When we designed our current home, I wanted windows in every room. "Light is vital," I said to our architect as he drew up plans. "I don't want to have to use lamps during the day any more." He took the challenge seriously, as each and every contractor we met during the building process asked the same bewildered question: "You have *how* many windows?" It might've seemed excessive to some, but not to us. We'd lived in "the dark house" for several years before we fully recognized how much we crave and need natural light. It was several more years still before we realized that light itself would become a central theme in our lives.

As soon as we moved into "the bright house," everything seemed lighter in all senses of the word. Our four children (all under age six) were growing and thriving. We felt a new sense of buoyancy, a light-heartedness, and an unrestricted energy in our household. But as it turns out, the same windows that let light into a home can also let the darkness inside. Shortly after we moved, just as our lives were in full swing, I was diagnosed with a life-threatening brain tumor. Our world seemed to stop spinning, and dusk set in. It was an overwhelming, scary, and sad time, and I secretly wondered whether night was closer than I cared to imagine.

The surgery to remove the tumor took my hearing on one side, but there were no other complications. I not only recovered quickly, but became pregnant with our fifth child just over a year later. We were thrilled and easily slipped back into a happy existence. Yet we were soon once again reminded that while windows provide openings to the outside world, they also let the outside world *in*.

When Bridget was born with Down syndrome, none of us knew what to think, or how to feel. We had no experience with Down syndrome. We only knew the stereotypes, which brought sadness and concern. We grieved the loss of the happy time it should have been, and the loss of the baby we thought we were going to meet. But when we saw Bridget in the NICU for the first time, Chris and I both felt the heaviness and uncertainty begin to fade. We'd come around the corner from the nurses' station to see her lying on a tiny hospital bed, covered in strong, unforgiving light from the warming lamps above. The lighting reminded me of a museum display featuring a rare and valuable piece of jewelry. As Bridget lay beneath it, nearly naked and fully illuminated, our hearts and lives were also laid bare. The light forced us to look at her, at ourselves, and our future. We watched her sleep peacefully, deserving and needing to be loved—just as any other baby. In that moment we realized that Bridget is whole. We began to see her not as a child with a disability, but as a *person* who would grow to express her own interests, talents, hopes, and dreams—just as any other person. We began to understand her potential.

When the warming lights were turned off, there was still a glow that surrounded Bridget. She was radiant. It was unexpected, and we were both moved to tears when we realized that *she* was the light.

***

The little girl with wispy ponytails who plays by my feet today does not yet know that I am writing about her. I've spent many hours these past few years telling our story, trying to show others that Down syndrome is not something to fear.

Down syndrome does not define Bridget. It is a part of her genetic make-up that is distinctly hers, but it is not her—and it doesn't even begin to explain who she is. Bridget is a little masterpiece, with texture and depth and richness to spare. She gives freely of her effort and love. She is spirited and vibrant, content without being complacent. Others may feel that she has much to overcome, but Bridget doesn't seem to see it that way. In her we see honesty, lack of pretense, and uninhibited determination as she goes about her life with vigor and jubilance.

It's interesting how a small amount of extra genetic material in Bridget translates into so much extra in all of our lives. Every day she encourages us to accept our own unique timelines for growth, and reminds us that what matters most isn't what we achieve and when, but how true to ourselves we remain through the process of becoming. We've learned to accept that life is not always neat and tidy (or easy), and that plans can change mid-flight. We've also learned that situations we didn't ask for or want often provide something we need.

A world turned upside-down reveals much about our perspective—it forces us to evaluate ourselves, the assumptions we make about one another, and our beliefs about ideals like success, beauty, and perfection. And while Bridget has taught us significant life lessons, it is the small moments in everyday living with her—the countless little bursts—that fill our lives with meaning and joy. We spend our days together reflecting and accepting, learning, laughing, and loving. As a family, we've realized that we are not uncomfortable with disability; that we are not afraid of the darkness; and that everything seems better with more windows—and with Bridget in our lives. She has restored our sense of buoyancy.

Since our current home has natural light in abundance, it's easy to forget that we once lived in a house with very little light. Likewise, it's difficult to remember life before Bridget. What began with the bright light above her hospital bed and continued as her inner radiance has now developed into a substantial force of its own. Sometimes Bridget's light is a high beam that illuminates clearly and at great range; at other times, it's a gentle glow. But it is constant. With Bridget in our lives, our many-windowed home is luminous and vibrant once again. And even after night falls, sparkles are everywhere, filling every room and glittering with tiny flashes of light.

● ● ●

Lisa and her husband, Chris, have been married for seventeen years. Together, they have five children, Sara (1995), Kyle (1997), Brian (1999), Emmy (2002), and Bridget (2006). Bridget was born prematurely and was diagnosed with Down syndrome at birth. She also required surgery to repair a small omphalocele (an abdominal wall malformation). Today, she is healthy and thriving, and the entire family is involved in Down syndrome advocacy efforts. To learn more, go to www.bridgets-light.blogspot.com.

Joe, Joe, Kevin, Rosemarie, and Colgan Leaming at Kevin's graduation from high school

21.

My Brother Is Not His Disability

By Colgan Leaming

LAST JULY, I took a car trip with Kevin, my fifteen-year-old brother. The music was blasting and the sun was shining through the windows, warming our faces. We were singing loudly to the tune on the radio—Bruce Springsteen, of course. We cruised down the highway enjoying the summer heat and each other's presence. I looked over and couldn't help but feel immensely happy when I saw his face with its beautiful smile that cures all pain and those deep blue eyes that see the world in a perfect light. The song ended, and he hit repeat.

We were going to a summer camp for children and young adults with developmental problems. Kevin has Down syndrome, one of the most common causes of cognitive delays, and he is legally blind. He is also an amazing young man who has many talents to share with the world. Unfortunately, most people miss out on his gifts because they are focused on his disabilities. I wish everyone could see him as I do. He is just Kevin. Simple as that.

A well-meaning friend once told me, "Colgan, it must be so hard having a brother who is mentally retarded." I was so taken aback! Perhaps it was my naiveté, but I prefer to believe it is because I have lived with Kevin for sixteen years now that I see him as he really is. At that moment, my eyes were opened, and I began to realize that many people in the world share my friend's view.

My brother is not his disability. He is a teenager who loves sports and PlayStation, who cares a little bit too much about his hair and is a little bit too confident, who is kind to every person he meets, who makes you laugh so hard your stomach hurts. He's a boy just like anyone else. Kevin does not have "special needs." All he needs is a chance.

Many people believe that my family must experience less of the world because of Kevin. When I think about this, I can't help but laugh. We experience the world just as much as any other family, perhaps more. How, you ask? It's all about expectations. We expect Kevin to do everything the rest of us do. Kevin has hiked the Grand Canyon, played in more basketball games than I can count, seen all that Yellowstone National Park has to offer, played the flute with an Irish band, gone on numerous camping trips with his friends, snorkeled off the coast of the Bahamas, skied in Vermont, seen Bruce Springsteen in concert, joined his high-school crew team, and so much more.

I want to point out that my brother is not an exception; he's a typical child with Down syndrome. The difference is that Kevin is in a community where his peers and teachers know him and treat him as an individual. Not every person with a disability is so lucky.

Having a sibling like Kevin is not a burden. To my eighteen-year-old brother, Joe, and me, it's normal. At a time when people are often overly critical of others, Kevin reminds us that it is truly what is inside us that counts. Everyone in my family agrees that if we had the power to take away Kevin's disability, we wouldn't. It's just not that big of a deal.

So please don't feel sorry for us. Don't feel sorry for my brother, either. There isn't any reason to; he isn't sick. Don't be scared of experiences similar to mine. I can tell you that my life would not be this happy if it weren't for Kevin. More important, have an open mind. Next time you meet a person with a disability, remember that he or she has so much to share with you. Take the time to listen.

That day last summer, as Kevin and I drove along singing to the upbeat music, I glanced at him again and was filled with hope for the world. I wished that everyone could experience that most beautiful sunshine. The road ahead of me suddenly seemed so bright.

● ● ●

Colgan graduated from Millersville University with a bachelor's degree in Special Education and Elementary Education. She has two younger brothers, Joe and Kevin. Colgan has dedicated her story to Kevin, as he has been a huge inspiration in her life.

Juliet and James Leach

22.

Vanishing Beauty

By Mark W. Leach

IT WAS A Monday morning when I first met my daughter, Juliet. Her lips were so rosy, it looked like she was wearing lipstick. When her mother and I spoke, her big, dark eyes locked on our faces, in recognition of her parents' voices. The staff whisked her away to the warming table, taking healthy APGAR scores and weighing her. Then, the neonate nurse, as she ran out of the room, shouted over her shoulder, "Doctor, check the baby. I think she has Down syndrome."

At that point I knew next to nothing about Down syndrome. The literature the hospital sent us home with, which began "BABY

GIRL has Down syndrome. Down syndrome is associated with…"
(a litany of health concerns), was not too helpful. That Thursday,
however, our local Down syndrome support group's executive director and a parent volunteer were on our front porch. We opened
the door, and they showed us that all the doors we thought might
be closed for our daughter really weren't. Within minutes of Juliet's
birth I'd envisioned her wedding—a scene which had been dashed
to pieces by that nurse's words as she ran out of the room. But as we
visited with the executive director, we learned about a couple in our
hometown who would soon be engaged.

After that first week or so, instead of being consumed by worries about what my daughter might not be able to do, I began to
delight and marvel in all the things she could do. Soon, Juliet was
smiling at us when we picked her up in the morning. She would
reach up with her hand to caress our faces with her little fingers as
we gave her a bottle. And, through the help of her early intervention
therapists, Juliet was doing so much more. Now, Miss Juliet certainly
did her bit of fussing—when learning to crawl particularly—but she
always welcomed her therapists with a hug and a smile, and eventually greeted them by name.

There's a common saying that kids with Down syndrome do the
same things as typical kids; it just might take them a little longer. But
with Juliet being our firstborn, I didn't know how long anything was
"supposed" to take. So, when Juliet began feeding herself, whenever that
happened to be, it was a time for celebration. So, too, when she finally
did crawl (after which walking soon followed). And, the moment she
signed "more" for the first time, her mom and I were elated: Juliet had
always been expressive and loving, but now we were communicating!

By watching Juliet grow, work, and learn, I've developed a different view of "disability." For so much of our children's lives we are
told what they will not be able to do or what they may do with a little
extra effort. What I've started to appreciate, though, is how each of
us has our own challenges. Some may be quick to point out that Juliet is a slow learner (at some things), but they happen to be wearing
glasses (like I do). Some may mention Juliet's low muscle tone, never
mind the state of their own.

Furthermore, people often aren't aware of the benefits of some aspects of disability. That same flexibility that causes some to be overly protective of Juliet in gym class is the same softness that gives the most complete hugs as she sinks into my chest. And people tend to get caught up in their assumptions. Juliet the "slow learner" is actually quick to learn, and her areas of focus couldn't be more significant. Juliet picks up names effortlessly. Juliet loves people. In fact, she associates places and events with people she cares about: going to school, Juliet gets to see "Miss Missy" her preschool teacher; heading to church on Sunday, "Pastor Ken." Even whole states have an association. Going to Alabama? No, for Juliet, we're going to see "Nanny and Papoo!"

My increasing awareness of my daughter's gifts and capacity has led to increased concern about what the future might hold for people like her. Despite the positive stereotype of people with Down syndrome being "so loving," they are nevertheless being sought out at a genetic level, with a recommendation that every expectant mother be offered prenatal testing. Because we opted out of the testing, some may say, "Well, then you brought that shock from the neonate nurse on yourselves—you could've been prepared." But a prenatal test would have told us just one thing about our daughter. It couldn't have told us of her rosy lips and dark newborn eyes; it couldn't have told us how she greets me at the end of the day by exclaiming "Daddy!" and leaping into my arms. If current trends continue, as more and more parents elect to have prenatal testing, faces like my daughter's will become more and more rare.

Many people are doing what they can to stem that tide. Some serve as parent volunteers, like the one who visited us shortly after Juliet's birth to share the vast possibilities open to individuals with Down syndrome. Others give presentations to medical practitioners to update their knowledge. And still others fight for legislation to require that parents be provided better information than simply "BABY GIRL has Down syndrome." Yes, my daughter has a disability—but in a sense, each of us do. Likewise, she is a gift to the world, just as each of us can be. She is beautiful in her own way, just as each of us are. My fervent hope is that we will not let this beauty vanish, but rather, that we will cherish it.

● ● ●

Mark is an attorney in Louisville, Kentucky. Juliet has introduced Mark, his wife, and Juliet's little brother to a world of friends and supporters through the local and national Down syndrome organizations. Mark serves on Down Syndrome of Louisville's board and chairs the Informed Decision Making Task Force of Down Syndrome Affiliates in Action. The opinions expressed herein are entirely his and not to be attributed to any of his associated organizations.

Kelly Rose Wesolek, Jeanette Reid

23.

Open Eyes

By Jeanette Reid

My sister shows me every day
To stop and smell the roses
We sing
Dance
Laugh
Doesn't matter who is watching our poses
Doesn't matter if you want to join in,
    because you're going to anyway
Always with the desire

To just have fun and play
We take our time crossing the street
Feeling the breeze on our cheeks
She hears the giggles of the girls in cars
Watching
From afar

My sister shows me every day
To be proud of what you do
To enjoy the here and forget about the crowd
To enjoy all the small things
And to enjoy them NOW!

My sister shows me every day
Not to judge anyone
She walks around saying hello to all
Old, Young
Fat, Skinny
Doesn't matter if you're short or tall
Black, White
Clean, Dirty
She gives a great big smile and wave
Spreading happiness and cheer to all
Wondering
From afar

My sister shows me every day
That everyone deserves a chance
And we should all lend a helping hand
More than just every once in a while

My sister shows me every day
That you're only as happy as you let yourself be
I mean, she's got a busier schedule than me!
She's in Pep Squad, Girl Scouts, Dance Shows, Fashion Shows
Special Olympics, Swimming, Camp,
     and who the heck else knows

But she's never too busy
Never too low
To get the whole family together
To simply tell a joke
She loves to read and go to school
Birthday parties, Tea parties, any party
Family functions rule!
She loves to play and will make you play too
Doesn't matter if you're feeling blue
Reading, Singing, Dancing, Jump rope
Wait there's more, she's no lazy dope
Board Games, Basketball, Baseball, Paint
Puzzles and Movies
She even wants to date!
She teaches me to *never quit*
And that I
Make life
How I want it
She shows me how I truly want to live
She reminds me about family
The support they will *always* give

My sister, her name is
Kelly Rose
She's 12 with Down syndrome
And she will never
Truly know
How blessed I feel to have her in my life
How she makes me want to be my best
And that she inspires me
To inform all the rest:
Having Down syndrome doesn't mean
She can't learn that game
It doesn't mean
That she can't feel pain
It simply means she has some difficulties
Not much unlike you and me

The world would be a better place
If everyone had a hero like Kelly Rose
To teach them about priorities
To teach them to make every action count
Because life is too short
To dwell
On failure
And doubt

The world would be a better place
If we had a hero like Kelly Rose
To teach them to see
That everyone has strengths and weaknesses
And everyone
Everyone
Deserves the chance
To believe

Father, Teacher, Friend, Mother
Sister, Cousin, Aunt, or Brother
You can show others
Just like my sister
Maybe there wouldn't be
So much hate and danger
Show them that differences in people
    doesn't mean we need to fear
Show them to be nice to all, and to break down that wall
Show them that learning from each other is why we're here

Show them right from wrong
And that it's not ok to snicker and stare

Maybe more people would soon realize
Like I did
How to see through open eyes.

● ● ●

Jeanette graduated in 2003 from Elmhurst College with a bachelor's degree in special education and is currently pursuing a master's degree in reading education from Concordia University Chicago. She is an eighth grade special education teacher for students with learning and emotional disabilities who are mainstreamed into the general education classroom.

Amy Aloi and Abigail Vance

24.
Lessons from Abbie

By Amy Aloi

IT'S A TYPICAL morning in preschool and the day is in full swing. We have managed to get to our room, hang up belongings, and complete a messy activity of shaving cream writing. As the last couple of children wash their hands, giggles erupt from the other side of the room. I look over to the housekeeping corner and see Abbie playing dress-up along with two other students. They're wearing floppy hats, high heels, and feather boas. I watch as the three of them balance precariously in the high heels. Almost immediately, one loses her balance, then the next, then the next, until all I can see is a tangle of pink feather boas on the floor. Abbie decides she has had enough dress-up and heads over to play teacher, still wearing her hat and feathers!

My preschool class includes children with a wide range of abilities and disabilities. A few of the students are designated role models, included in the class to help teach others appropriate social skills and model typical behavior. But sometimes, the best teachers are ones we didn't expect. Take Abbie, for example. Her extra chromosome has caused her some challenges, including cognitive and developmental delays. So imagine my surprise when this feisty redhead came along and taught us all a thing or two about what really matters.

Lesson One: Speed is overrated. My first challenge on every school day is getting twelve three- and four-year-olds from the bus to the classroom, which requires making our way through the halls of a bustling elementary school. At first, I was always anxious to reach our destination as soon as possible. But Abbie was never in any hurry. She was on her own schedule and nobody could change that. For weeks I cajoled Abbie, trying to convince her there were many more interesting things down the hall in our classroom that we had to get to as soon as possible. Yet I continued to be met with her firm *no*: feet planted in the middle of the hallway, and hand up signifying a resounding STOP. I finally decided it was me who needed to change, and tried slowing down instead of hurrying up. Like Abbie, I now stop to smell the flowers, notice a ladybug on the sidewalk, and say hi to everyone we pass. Abbie and I are almost always the last to get to the classroom. Everybody else is interested in being first, but Abbie is interested in everything else. Maybe our time in the classroom is cut short by a few minutes, but what we do on the way is just as important.

Lesson Two: Speech is not the only way to communicate. Abbie taught me that just because a person is not saying anything does not mean she has nothing to say. Abbie communicates and gets her point across really well—sometimes we just need to pay better attention. She has an assistive communication device, a small computer with various screens and buttons. However, she uses many modes of communication: signs, pictures, gestures, intonation, and words to make her self understood.

Lesson Three: We teach by example, for better or for worse. I've learned to be on my best behavior around Abbie. She misses nothing and imitates everything! From the way I run circle time to the way I read a story, Abbie has it down pat. She could run the classroom if I wasn't there. Often, as I am reading a story to the class, Abbie will move her carpet tile next to me, take the book out of my hand, and hold it for me. I think she's telling me she can do it better. She sings our weather song with gusto, and never hesitates to remind the other children when it is time to be quiet. She raises her hand when she wants a turn, and will call my name until I acknowledge her. I wonder where she learned that?

Lesson Four: Don't hide your feelings. Abbie has taught me to forgive easily and love unconditionally. She can be mad as heck at you one minute and then giving you hugs and kisses the next. One time, Abbie got upset with me because it was her turn to go to the bathroom. I struggled some to get her into the bathroom and she was yelling "NO" at me the whole way there. After she was finished, I bent down to tie her shoe. She kissed me on the head, said thank you, and happily went back to her game. When Abbie loves you, she loves you with her whole being, body and soul. Her pats are hard, her hugs are tight, and her enthusiasm immense. I cannot count the times she has literally knocked me off my feet with one of her running I'm-so-glad-to-see-you hugs.

Lesson Five: Play is the best work of all. Playing with Abbie is an adventure: you never know if you are going to be a baby, mommy, or beauty parlor customer. I have had my hair brushed, combed, washed, and dried; my nails done and my feet massaged. What luxury for a preschool teacher! I have been dressed up and put to bed; reprimanded for saying ouch (during beauty parlor time) or for talking too much. Her imagination is endless and everybody can play (as long as it's her way). Abbie goes out of her way to include everybody into her play, even strangers. One morning our principal was showing a group of men and women around the school. They came to our classroom during free play when we happened to be playing princess. Wings, sparkly dresses, and magic wands were everywhere. Abbie took notice of the tour group immediately and handed one of the larger men a glittery pink and purple wand. She then tried to lead him over to one of our very small chairs to sit in. He politely declined and the group left to continue their tour. I guess that was his loss!

This will be my last year with Abbie. Next year she will move down the hall to kindergarten and will no doubt influence that class the way she has influenced mine. I will miss everything about her, but feel fortunate to have known her. I only hope I have taught her half of what she has taught me.

●　　●　　●

Amy has a master's degree in special education and has loved teaching preschoolers for twenty years. She lives in Columbia, Maryland, with her husband and three teenaged sons.

Samuel Berendt

25.
Little Brother, Big Impact

By Sarah Berendt

WHEN I WALKED into the room, I could see his tiny head sticking out of the blanket that was spread over the rest of his sleeping body. As I stood there studying his squinty face, my mind raced with different thoughts and questions. *Will he grow up "normal?" Will he have friends? Will he be able to go to school? Will his life consist of bagging groceries?* He started waking up, and his foster mom asked if I wanted to hold him. I took him hesitantly, afraid of dropping his fragile body. Looking in his gorgeous blue eyes, I heard my mom ask if the adoption could be finalized that day so that we could take him home.

When we brought Sammy home on June 1, 2005, I was having mixed feelings about having a brother with Down syndrome. As the summer progressed I read about the possible effects of Down syndrome, and I was scared that Sammy would be diagnosed with life-threatening problems. I didn't want to have to endure a death in the family. Somewhere in my mind I still wanted the doctors to be wrong about Sammy's diagnosis. I thought my life was perfect and I didn't want any changes to occur. I didn't realize it would change for the better.

As time passed, Sammy and I started spending more and more time together. Every night I would sit with him and read him a book. I started trying to teach him how to talk, and I was regularly involved in his physical therapy sessions. As a result, we grew close, and he started showing me the blessings in my life that I had never noticed before. In fact, Sammy taught me that everything is a blessing from God, whether we realize it or not. Before he came home I was self-centered and spoiled; I only cared about me, myself, and I. Sammy helped me understand that I'm not the only person on this earth, and that I need to show everyone the care and love that they show me. I had always hated going to church, but once I realized my need to serve others, I started going willingly and got to know many people.

Since we brought Sammy home I've also had the privilege of meeting many people with different disabilities. I've begun to realize that it doesn't matter how a person looks or acts on the outside; they are still people, and they still have feelings. They have eyes to see what is happening, and ears to hear what people are saying about them. Each of us is unique in our own ways, and in God's eyes we are all the same.

I've also realized the many talents people with Down syndrome can have. For example, although Sammy doesn't speak like a normal three-year-old, he knows at least a hundred signs in sign language. I was surprised that he could easily communicate with us despite his muscle weakness and difficulties controlling his mouth. He has blown people away with some of things he is able to accomplish. We were told that he wouldn't be able to walk until he was about five years old, and he was running by his second birthday.

Even though I love my brother dearly, I still sometimes catch myself wishing that he would just disappear for a while. At times he does things I don't like, such as going into my room and breaking something. Once in a while when he is frustrated, he will hit and bite. But he always knows when I'm upset or mad, and the first thing he does is come up to me and give me a hug and a kiss. Sometimes I wonder if he has a special instinct that tells him when something is wrong.

Sammy just turned three years old. As I look back at our first years together I ask myself what I would have been like if we had never met. Would I still laugh at people who are disabled, or would I stand up for them like I do now? Would I learn to care about more than myself? Would I ever realize all of the blessings that are mine? These are some of the gifts that Sammy has given me. I didn't want anything to do with him at first. But every day when I wake up and see his smiling face, I'm grateful my family was willing to open their hearts for an unwanted child. I often wonder how someone so small could make such a big impact on my life.

● ● ●

Sarah is a fourteen-year-old ninth grader who lives in Adrian, Michigan, with her parents and two younger brothers. She enjoys reading, writing, debating, and taking care of her youngest brother. She often works with her brother and his friends with various disabilities, and is hoping to attend college at Kansas State University to major in occupational therapy.

From right to left: Carin Griffith, Rylee Griffith, Cindy Groom-Harry

26.

Making the Best of Us

By Cindy Groom-Harry

LIKE MOST PEOPLE, I didn't think about "birth defects" when our daughter and her husband happily announced they were expecting a baby. I was ready for my husband and me to be wonderful grand-parents, excited to do all the "right" things with the birth of our first grandchild. I suppose if I'd been asked, I would have said that families of babies born with "something wrong" should either correct what was wrong or learn to deal with a baby that was "defective."

I didn't know what Down syndrome was, really—something to do with a mental deficit—but if asked, I probably would have said that if it couldn't be "fixed," the family should still love the baby and try to pick up the pieces of their disappointment in order to make their family life as "normal" as possible. They would be wise to make the best of it—"it" being a "bad" situation.

Looking back, I'm embarrassed by my ignorant, patronizing (though well-meaning) attitude. I thought of myself as a fairly aware, compassionate person. Actually, I was simply clueless about disabilities. Thank goodness Rylee Jayne joined our family to open a whole new world of awareness. Yes, she had heart surgery to physically "fix" what the surgeon called a heart "defect," but as we got to know Rylee, we knew that there was nothing wrong with Rylee's *true* heart! In fact, *her* heart has magically nurtured and helped *our* hearts grow.

Ironically, this journey began because of an ignorant, patronizing attitude in the heart of a doctor. Early in my daughter Carin's pregnancy, her obstetrician detected that something might be amiss so she recommended that a perinatologist be consulted. Nervously, Carin and Jeremy waited to meet with the specialist. Later, in a tearful telephone call, Carin described how he breezed into the room and abruptly announced that the developing baby's heart was "defective" and gave them one week to decide about "terminating the pregnancy." Then, just as abruptly, he left the room.

After a whirlwind of tears and fears, Carin and Jeremy sought a second opinion from a pediatric cardiologist, who agreed to an appointment—on his day off. His behavior directly contrasted with the first doctor's. With caring demeanor, he performed the ultrasound and patiently showed Carin and Jeremy the images of the heart, confirming the existence of a problem. Then he explained to tearful, breath-holding parents and grandparents that the heart was repairable and that there was no reason the baby couldn't be born…and live well! He did add that this type of heart defect often accompanies other birth abnormalities. But that didn't seem to matter. In the moment, a strong desire to save this little baby's life was born.

The next day, Carin underwent genetic testing. The following week, when she called with the results she gushed, "We'll be having a little girl, and she'll have Down syndrome, but get this! There was one chance in 800 that we'd have a baby with Down syndrome, and *we were picked!"* All of us shared her enthusiasm without reservation. It was amazing—the insensitive, obviously pro-termination specialist not only prompted us to seek and find a more supportive opinion, but also, by contrast, sparked our positive, appreciative attitude for this new little being.

Rylee Jayne Griffith was born on November 6, 2003, a beautiful 6 lb. 2 oz. baby girl with characteristic almond eyes that captivated all of us. Our whole family eagerly waited for Rylee to be old enough and strong enough to undergo heart surgery. When the time was right, we traveled to another state for the surgery, held our breaths, and visualized success during the procedure, and then eagerly waited for the good news that all had gone well. Afterward, we took turns watching over our vulnerable baby covered with wires and tubes. Each day Rylee grew stronger, and so did we as a family. At last, Carin and Jeremy took Rylee home with her healthy heart beating in her little chest. Appropriately, it was Valentine's Day 2004!

Within our family, a good deal of positive momentum had built over the course of Carin's pregnancy, Rylee's birth, and her surgery. This momentum helped us tackle the next hurdle on our path—home care. As a kindergarten teacher, Carin had used up all of her leave time and needed to return to work to keep the family's insurance intact. Because Rylee needed a feeding tube and was fresh from heart surgery, she wasn't eligible for typical daycare or baby sitting providers. Due to our own employment, none of us could stay with her throughout the week, but we did realize that each of us could find a way to baby sit one day a week. Thus the family and friend tag-team babysitting began—and so did the deep, multi-person connections with Rylee. Again, a complicated situation made our family bonding even stronger.

And the magical good will extended beyond family. As Rylee grew, doctors, nurses, therapists, teachers, classmates, other parents, and even bus drivers happily moved one by one into Rylee's world, falling in love with this gregarious little bear-crawling toddler who scooted across the room to give kisses to everyone. (Her exuberant affection is indiscriminate, much to the delight of many store cashiers.)

Rylee is a funny, clever, smart, and incredibly loveable little girl who just happens to have Down syndrome. Yes, she has developed differently than "typical" kids, but she thrives thanks to Carin being such a dedicated teacher, both Carin and Jeremy being committed to getting every medical, educational, and therapeutic opportunity available, and two siblings, Jordyn and Carter, who are such wonderful helpers. As grandparents, we too feel the magic of growth and understanding. Our bright-blue-eyed, chubby-cheeked, tongue-peeking little sweetheart has granted us a completely new awareness, a delightful appreciation for human-ness. We've learned how to love *people* instead of loving accomplishments achieved by people who can do things "perfectly." We've learned that a person's heart matters more than performance. We now have a new definition of "success."

In addition to seeing people with disabilities in a new light, we better understand and appreciate *all* people. Instead of being annoyed with the inconsiderate driver, racing past us, we think of why he may be hurrying home. Instead of being impatient with the grocery clerk who takes longer to scan the items, we take a deep breath and think about her needs and capabilities as possibly being different from ours. Instead of getting angry with people who say "rude" things, we remember back to when we, too, were equally rude and clueless, yet well-meaning people. Then we try to find a kind way to extend awareness.

It's interesting how my original thoughts on "birth defects" like Down syndrome have been turned upside down. I see that what we may initially view as negative can actually provide beautiful results that make people and families closer, stronger, and happier. We don't need to "make the best" of our life with Rylee. She's already giving us the best that life has to offer. And because of her, *we're* making the best of *us*.

● ● ●

Cindy dedicates this story to her daughter, Carin, who has made their family's journey possible with her positive outlook that teaches everyone how to approach the unknown. Carin does her research, relentlessly makes all therapy appointments, completes every IEP, and teaches her children in ways that each learns best. She helps other families with members with disabilities and has an Awareness Alliance that educates the public (for more information, visit www.caringriffith.blogspot. com). The entire family loves and admires Carin so much.

Brenda and Andy Kopp

27.
Do You See What I See?

By Brenda Kopp

VISION:
1. The act or power of sensing with the eyes.
2. The act or power of anticipating that which will or may come to be.
3. Something seen or otherwise perceived during such an experience.
4. Something seen.
5. A scene, person, etc. of extraordinary beauty.

Five years ago while driving back from a family retreat, I was trying to help my husband navigate around a construction zone. As hard as I tried, I just couldn't read the map. He thought I was not concentrating on what I was doing. But I truly couldn't see.

When we got home I decided to go in and have my eyes checked. The doctor told me I had developed an eye condition called macular pucker. This occurs when scar tissue forms on the eye's macula, located in the center of the eye's light-sensitive tissue called the retina. The macula provides the sharp, central vision we need for reading, driving, and seeing fine detail. A macular pucker can cause blurred and distorted central vision. The thought of having problems with my vision was such a scary prospect. Would it progress? Could it improve? The thought of not seeing the faces of my husband and children was very difficult to imagine.

Ten years before being diagnosed with macular pucker, I became aware of a different condition in my vision. It had nothing to do with how well my eyes could focus on things around me. Instead, it had to do with how I perceive and respond to people with disabilities. My diagnosis began on March 15, 1993, the day our second son, Andy, was born. There was no indication ahead of time that he would be born with any disability. But four hours after Andy's birth, our pediatrician told us he was 95 percent sure our son had Down syndrome. Needless to say, we were devastated. So many questions flooded our minds. Would our son be able to walk and talk? Would he live to adulthood? Would he be able to care for himself? Work? Marry? Our vision was clouded by fear, and we couldn't accurately see "that which will or may come to be."

Fifteen years later, our view is much clearer because our focus has changed. In those early days, we were understandably concerned about disability. But now our main focus is capability. Andy does walk (actually, he runs). He talks (nearly constantly!). He loves to work, and he's learning so much in academics and life skills. In so many ways he is like our other sons; it's just taken him a bit longer to learn. We still have some questions and concerns about his future, but now that we can see his potential, we're very optimistic. We believe he'll live a long and healthy life.

Thanks to Andy, my vision has changed in other beneficial ways. For example, the "sensing of my eyes" has greatly developed.

Wherever I go or whatever I do, I notice people with disabilities. They're all around us. Some are distinguished by their physical characteristics, while others have unique mannerisms that might make them stand out. I don't ignore these people like I used to; instead I greet them warmly. My increased capacity to "see" has led to many wonderful relationships. When Andy was born I knew no one with Down syndrome. Now, I have many friends who have children with Down syndrome and other disabilities, and I make a point to invite them to play dates and birthday parties. Grant, Jessica, Scott, and Caleb are the friends in the neighborhood that Andy often asks to have over. They enjoy swimming, watching movies, and bowling. They are thoughtful and kind, play well together and have a lot of fun. I'm also involved in support groups for families affected by disability. Sharon, who runs one of these groups, and her husband, Burt, have been a source of encouragement to us from the time Andy was born. Their son, BJ, is a few years older than Andy and also has Down syndrome. They are positive and encourage us so often when we're in a down time.

As I enjoy these and many other relationships, I notice yet another change to my vision: the increased ability to perceive "extraordinary beauty." This past summer, my husband and I provided temporary employment for several adults with disabilities. We organized ten car washes at several area businesses. We trained each of the adults on the steps to washing a car, and then provided peer tutors to help them get the job done. The joy on the faces of these individuals when they are given the opportunity to work and make a small amount of money is priceless. They are so gifted, reliable, thorough, and willing to do routine tasks, and they love their jobs. Dan S. proudly told us that he had vacuumed 53 cars over the summer. Dan W. was always ready to carry the heavy generators from one car to another to make the task progress smoothly. Gary B. always greeted us warmly with a cheerful smile.

We are always looking for opportunities to provide one-on-one support for other children with special needs at our Vacation Bible School and Sunday School, by adapting Bible verses using song and sign language and reaching out to other families with disabilities.

Jessica's family is a part of our church and she wanted to be involved in Vacation Bible School. Johanna, a high school student, attended as an aide to help Jessica stay focused, provide assistance in crafts, and pull her aside when she needed a break from the routine. Brian is a young boy with hearing and learning difficulties. He was so faithful in attending, but struggled to successfully learn many verses. My husband and I used the modified verses we had used with Andy to help him say his verses. He was so thrilled to be getting the awards like the other kids.

I see many other things of beauty every summer, when our family attends a camp for families touched by disability. At the annual talent show we are reminded of the many gifts of people with disabilities. One year there was a girl with cerebral palsy who signed a song even though her motions were awkward. Another year there was a child who slowly pressed the piano keys as he played his song. Each year we enjoy Paul, a young man with CP, who painstakingly sings "How Great Thou Art" even while on a ventilator. When Andy sings I must readjust my perception of what's "good," since he doesn't carry a tune too well, but he sure worships! I love watching him and others with disabilities learn steps at the square dance, including people who are mobile as well as those in wheelchairs.

In the last five years the effects of my macular pucker haven't gotten any worse, for which I am thankful. Though I don't see things as clearly as I used to, I've learned to adjust to the change and get along quite well. My husband is so supportive in helping me "see" things that aren't clear to me—reading street signs, pointing out my child in the school band, buying me a magnifying glass to see small maps.

More importantly, Andy continues to open my eyes in so many ways. In the process I'm realizing that many of us suffer from undiagnosed vision problems that keep us from really seeing people with disabilities and letting them into our circle. Maybe, when we're in a hurry, we take a handicap parking spot. Or when our child is having a birthday party, we invite all the neighborhood kids except for the one with physical or mental disabilities. I wish I could help others to see more clearly the way Andy has helped me. Yes, it can be scary to realize we need our vision checked, and it can be uncomfortable to make needed adjustments. But the rewards of doing so are more wonderful and fulfilling than we can envision.

●   ●   ●

Brenda is a stay-at-home mom and lives in the west suburb of Chicago with her husband, Bob, and their three sons. Andy, their middle son, was born in 1993 with Down syndrome. Brenda enjoys volunteering at school and church, and loves to travel.

Jennifer Seiger and Charles Seiger

28.
Pass It On

By Jennifer Marie Seiger

"SALLY LIKES JOE, pass it on." When I played games like this in school, it always amazed me how quickly words could spread. Now, as an adult who has a different perspective on the world than I did in my naïve schoolgirl days, I want to stop the spread of some words. Instead, I want to raise awareness and pass it on.

Fifteen months ago my amazing son, Charles, was born. Charles is tiny, funny, and motivated. He's a diligent worker and my driving force. Charles also has Down syndrome. He opened a world for me that I'd always locked myself away from. I never charted this world, and I was afraid of my son being rejected. I was afraid he wouldn't learn. I was afraid that he would never be happy. But Charles saw my fear and smiled it away. At fifteen months he does more than I ever imagined he would, and he has forced me to have the same high expectations I would have for a child with the regulation forty-six chromosomes in every cell. However, this story is not about Charles. He's an important part of it, though, because he was its inspiration.

Four years ago I began fulfilling one of my passions: teaching English. I love bringing literature to life and helping my students see the positive and negative differences that words can make. At the 8th grade level, as many students are trying to find themselves, they seem to lack awareness of others. It upsets me when they call each other names, especially *retard*. I treated that word as profanity in my class long before my son was born, but the kids didn't understand why. Even when I explained connotation and denotation with that word in mind, my students didn't recognize its power and negativity.

That's why I took them to see Karen Gaffney.

Karen is an accomplished swimmer who happens to have Down syndrome. She spreads the powerful messages that you can achieve whatever you put your mind to, and we should accept others in spite of their differences. She offers a new hope to individuals with Down syndrome. In October 2007, the Down Syndrome Network that I am involved in invited Karen to speak at Misericordia College (now University). She addressed teachers and families on two consecutive evenings about her success as an athlete and her academic achievements of full inclusion and attendance at her local college. Karen's talents were inspirational to me as both a teacher and a parent.

Her third session, however, will stay with me forever.

That following morning I brought twelve students from my school to join students from twelve other local schools on a fieldtrip to see Karen speak. The bus ride there was filled with the kids singing and being teenagers. When we entered the auditorium, they became the well-behaved, attentive listeners that I had asked them to be. But something happened when they saw Karen, with her short stature and cute blonde bob, walk slowly on the stage, limping due to loose hip joints. Clearly, they hadn't known what to expect. Karen was different. She walked differently and she talked differently. She also had a zest for life that very few of my 8th graders had yet felt. Karen confidently expressed her motivation to swim competitively, and her determination to conquer new waters both as an athlete and an individual with Down syndrome.

She made it very clear, though, to the auditorium of attentive students that her life was not fully triumphant. Karen did face hardships growing up, particularly with making friends. She mentioned that because she was different, people were sometimes unsure of how to become friends with her. Karen encouraged her audience to make friends with anyone, even people who are different. She described her program called the Friends First Network™, which involves forming a school-wide club where friendships are encouraged and individuals with and without disabilities work together on community service projects. Karen and her program are helping to break down the barriers that separate people.

Following Karen's speech, the students were invited to the Misericordia gymnasium for a program established by the Down Syndrome Network in conjunction with the college faculty and students. The participants were unaware that following the brief, frigid walk to the gymnasium they would have a chance to experience some of the aspects of having a disability.

Upon entering the gymnasium, the students were divided into groups and asked to perform various activities. They started by putting weights on their arms and legs to feel the challenge of walking, jumping, and playing with low muscle tone. Then they wore dark goggles and had to walk in a straight line with distorted vision. Finally, they had to write their name while looking in a mirror to get a sense of what cognitive challenges are like. It took them more time than it would have otherwise, but each of them completed the tasks, just as people with disabilities do with patience and support.

Before leaving, I approached Chad, one of my students from a class in which I heard the "r" word used too often. Chad himself used this word.

I asked Chad, "Now do you understand why I do not want any of you using the 'r' word?"

"Yeah, I get it now," he replied.

I smiled at him and shivered with the knowledge that I had helped make a small difference. Chad realized the power of words, and I realized the power of action. Prior to this event I had always considered myself a dreamer, but with my son motivating me, I have become an advocate.

Later that week, I overheard Drew taunt, "Robyn, you're retarded."

I was about to interject, but I was interrupted by Chad asserting, "Hey, don't use that word!"

Now, I have at least one student who will stop others from making fun of something that they may not understand, and I hope this awareness spreads like a wild fire. Now, my fear that someone may call my son the "r" word someday fades a little. We are raising awareness. We are on the path of acceptance. We are passing it on.

●   ●   ●

Jennifer married her high school sweetheart, Charles, in 2006. Their first son, Charles (2007), was born six weeks prematurely and diagnosed with Down syndrome four days after his birth. Jennifer has been teaching English for five years, and she recently earned her master's degree in education. She enjoys spending time with her family and friends. For more information about Karen Gaffney and the Friends First Network™, please visit: www.karengaffneyfoundation.com.

Danielle (mom) and Zane Perry

29.
The Road Less Traveled

By Danielle C. Perry

WE WERE IN the car for maybe ten minutes when the nausea hit me; I was about to throw up and couldn't possibly continue on to the party.

"Zane, I am so sorry but Mommy has to go back home. I feel sick, Zane. I think I'm going to throw up."

Silence.

"I'm afraid we have to miss the birthday party today, honey. Mommy is sick and has to go back home," I repeated slowly and braced for the protest that was about to ensue.

"Oh, okay," Zane said with a slight hesitation. I waited for the plea to keep on driving to the party but it never came.

"It's okay, Mommy. I'm sorry you're sick."

Shocked and relieved I said, "Thank you, Zane. I'm really so sorry that I can't drive you there right now."

A minute or so passed.

"Is Daddy home?" Zane asked.

"Oh, Zane," I sighed. "Daddy isn't home right now. He's with Jack at gymnastics practice. He can't drive you either."

"Oh. Okay. I'm sorry you're feeling sick, Mom."

And then came the tears. Not his, mine. How many nights I cried, wondering if Zane would ever be invited to a friend's birthday party. Now, because of me, he would miss this one. But that's not what made my eyes well up. That afternoon, Zane understood what was happening, came up with a solution to the problem (Daddy), and tried to make me feel better. A typical six-year-old would have whined and cried or even thrown a fit, thinking only of his own wants and needs—all completely normal reactions to this disappointing situation. But not my Zane. He is full of surprises.

Zane Samuel joined our family two weeks early, two days after Christmas and in less than two hours from first contraction to delivery. Immediately after birth, he let out that hoarse, newborn cry and scored a 9 on his APGAR test. He was chubby and healthy. Perfect.

"Does Zane look like your other son when he was born?" asked our pediatrician. We laughed, "Not at all!" and joked about how even in the womb this child was different from his big brother, Jack. But the doctor wasn't just making conversation; she was trying to tell us they suspected our baby had Down syndrome.

We were shocked, terrified. This isn't possible, we thought, because we had been monitored so closely by high-risk specialists trained to look for complications like those that took our first child from us at just twenty-one weeks into pregnancy. Despite multiple prenatal tests, what seemed like gallons of blood work, and nine ultrasounds, somehow Zane's extra 21st chromosome went undetected.

While Zane and I were still in the hospital, a social worker stopped by to offer us support. She caught my husband and me at a particularly bad moment as we struggled with how having a child with Down syndrome was going to affect our entire family. "We wanted Jack to have a normal brother, someone he could really play with and grow up with...a *best friend*," I explained. Softly and genuinely she replied, "You may have just given him the best friend he'll ever have." Her words were like a parachute that stopped our freefall, glided us past the familiar terrain, and gently lowered us onto our new path.

I'm not a big fan of poetry, but I take great comfort in Robert Frost's perspective on forks in the road. It's been seven years since Zane led our family down this road less traveled. Our path is definitely bumpier, harder to navigate and, at times, intimidating. Sometimes we walk more slowly than others; occasionally we need to stop and rest. We walk hand-in-hand, always.

Sometimes we encounter some roadblocks that are impassible, forcing us to hang a left now and then. But as we turn those corners, Zane will grab a leaf and enjoy the crinkling sound and feel of the pieces as they slip between his fingers. He'll jump right into a puddle, despite my efforts to steer him around it. And he'll point to a puffy cloud in the sky and say, "Hey, there's an elephant!" I'll look up with a smile, grateful that I've been reminded (yet again) to notice the animals flying over my head more often. And I'll appreciate how the sun brightens the way for my little man and those of us walking in his shadow.

Occasionally, our path veers off sharply to a place where thick trees and heavy clouds block the sunlight. A routine blood test that reveals Celiac disease. A hearing loss that now requires hearing aids. A tonsillectomy that ends with a long, painful recovery. But Zane has taught me not to be afraid of the dark. For him, the unknown is just another opportunity to discover. Pain passes. New experiences bring strength and understanding. And the clouds always, ultimately, give way to light.

The darker days also help me treasure the gorgeous ones when the sky is bluer and the sun warmer than I ever imagined it could be. Like the day Zane's first-grade teacher pulled out his reading evaluation. "As you can see, he read 100 out of 100 first-grade words correctly." I couldn't take my eyes off the paper. Then softly, she added quickly, "And he's the only child in the class who did." She knew as well as I did how significant this moment was for all of us.

Most of the milestones deserving of small parties at our house are ones that typical families hardly notice. Opening a snack without spilling it or remembering not to touch the soccer ball with his hands. But this—this was an extraordinary accomplishment. Zane had attained something we couldn't be sure would be attainable (let alone before his typical peers!); and it was awe-inspiring.

But Zane isn't all too impressed by successes or accomplishments, not even his own. He's more apt to appreciate the beauty in the tiniest pebble or most ordinary leaf. And that is, I think, what I love most about my Zane. He takes great pleasure in little things. Stroking my hair when we're sitting together, anywhere. Waking up his little sister, Drew, on weekend mornings. Hugging and kissing his two favorite stuffed animals (Pablo and Dog). Changing into pajamas, reading a favorite story, or eating Chinese food—each of these gets the kind of reaction you'd see when a typical kid opens a birthday present.

I must admit, some of his simple pleasures make me nuts. Like when he flips the pages of magazines or sets up dominoes and knocks them down, over and over again. He insists on blowing out birthday candles, no matter whose birthday it is. And until this Christmas, Zane refused to open more than one or two gifts, ever. He simply didn't see the need for more.

But the little irritations are far outweighed by beautiful moments. I work in a Catholic hospital and our meetings begin with a "reflection." This can be a quote or prayer or story—something that grounds us before tackling the day's work. One time when I led the reflection, I shared a lesson Zane had taught me when he was in kindergarten. I wrote the words: "Over the rainbow I wish to see _____" on the whiteboard, and asked everyone to silently fill in the blank. After a few moments had passed, I suggested that the wishes in that room probably varied widely, from possessions to money, love, or world peace. Then, I told them Zane's wish: To see lots of colors. The faces in the room smiled and nodded in recognition of the truth and simplicity in his wish—to appreciate all that is already right in front of us.

When we tell Zane we love him, occasionally he'll say it back just as my other children do. Usually, though, he grins and knowingly says, "Yeah." It's the happiest, most content "Yeah" you've ever heard. Yeah, he truly feels how much we adore him. It is a beautiful response in its sincerity and simplicity.

Zane exudes tenderness and enthusiasm and somehow brings out these same qualities in almost everyone who interacts with him. People who barely know him seem to have an instinctive affection for him. And those who know Zane well have a special love for him. A recent back injury sent me to see a physical therapist who lives in my town. After a few minutes of small talk at my first appointment, she looked up and gushed, "Oh, you're *Zane's* mom! You are sooo lucky."

Yeah, I said to myself. "Thank you," I said to her.

I needed to walk many miles on this path before I felt lucky. Sitting on my hospital bed that first night, I felt wronged, robbed of the normal child I was expecting. I couldn't fathom how this child would enrich my life. I wish I could take back the unstoppable tears, the worry about his future, and the doubt in my own ability to love and care for him. He deserved better.

Tonight we read a new *Frog and Toad* story at bedtime. Frog was not feeling well and Toad said, "Frog, you are looking quite green." Frog said, "But I always look green. I'm a Frog." Zane giggled. To my surprise, he got the joke instantly. We were still laughing as he climbed into bed. I sang him the same song I have sung to him every night of his entire life, and gave him three big goodnight kisses.

"*Three* kisses?" he asked with another giggle. "How come?"

"Because I love you," I said. It's our little bedtime ritual and we both love it. I closed his door and silently thanked him for leading our family along the road less traveled.

● ● ●

Danielle lives in North Andover, Massachusetts, with her husband, Andy, and their three children, Jack, Zane, and Drew. She's a full-time mom and a marketing/public relations professional who has mastered the art of multitasking. Danielle enjoys writing, reading, playing, and laughing.

Lisa and Robyn Johnson

30.

Change of Heart

By Lisa Rimer Johnson

"BASED ON YOUR age, the risk for Down syndrome is increased."

"Your screening shows an increased risk for Down syndrome."

"I'm sorry, but your amniocentesis confirms the diagnosis of Down syndrome."

As a genetic counselor, I spend a great portion of my time at work talking about Down syndrome. I often say, "I'm sure you've heard of Down syndrome before, but let me explain some of the characteristics: Mental retardation. Congenital heart disease. Slanted eyes. Flattened face. Short stature." I have described the features of Down syndrome countless times. In the past, my list of medical complications would go on and on, spoken almost thoughtlessly to women and couples. How easy it was to describe traits and characteristics and remain oblivious to the fact that I was talking about a *person*. With all of my training and interactions with individuals with a broad range of cognitive impairments, I'd failed to make that vital connection.

And then my daughter was born.

When Robyn came into the world, I was thirty-three years old and had been a genetic counselor for ten years. I had worked in both pediatric and prenatal settings, counseling families after the birth of a child with a genetic condition and counseling couples at increased risk for having a child with a chromosomal anomaly, like Down syndrome. During pregnancy I received prenatal screening, wanting to make sure my child did not have any issues. Despite my normal screening results, I obsessed specifically about Down syndrome, worrying daily that my unborn baby would have that awful condition. I dreamed of her birth and the dreaded words, "Your baby has Down syndrome."

Robyn, my third daughter, was to be born via a planned c-section. My parents came into town to watch my older daughters. Before going to bed the evening before Robyn's birth, my mother and I were looking at the ultrasound photos I had been given earlier that day. I was troubled because I had seen Robyn's tongue protrude several times during the ultrasound exam that had been performed to determine her birth weight. As we were heading up to bed, my mother asked "Who do you think Robyn will look like, Reagan or Riley?"

My response was, "I don't care who she looks like, as long as she doesn't have Down syndrome."

On Robyn's birth day my physician lifted her over the curtain shielding the surgery site. The first thing I saw were my baby's eyes, which featured those upslanting palpebral fissures I so often describe. I knew. I immediately voiced my concerns to my obstetrician, who reassured me that the baby was okay. I saw the joy in my husband's eyes as he held Robyn for the first time, but I could only feel sadness and anger. I actually envied those first few minutes of oblivion my husband had before our world was shattered.

My colleague, Dr. Croom, and another genetic counselor visited me in the recovery area after examining Robyn. "I think baby Robyn has Down syndrome," said Dr. Croom, confirming my suspicions. I could only feel extreme anger. How was this happening to me? I'd had all the screening. This was my worst fear come true. Thankfully, my husband dealt with the news much better than I did. He remained optimistic while I could only go through the laundry list of complications in my head. For every discouraging fact I read about Down syndrome, he countered with a positive point.

Those days in the hospital following my c-section were the hardest of my life. Robyn had to stay in the special care nursery and they would not let me breastfeed until they determined whether she had an intestinal blockage. I had to strain myself both physically and mentally to even go see her. All I could see when I looked at her was Down syndrome. Without being able to feed her and with her not being in my room, I felt no emotional attachment to this baby. Many people tried to provide reassurance during those days following Robyn's birth. They tried to give me information and resources, but I was not ready to hear it. Didn't they know that I already knew everything there was to know about Down syndrome?

I was discharged a day prior to Robyn and spent a night without her at home. When alone, I locked myself in the bathroom and sobbed. I thought about giving her up for adoption. I knew there were hundreds of families waiting to adopt children with Down syndrome. I could always move my family so no one would know what I had done. I wanted to just make it all go away.

But sitting there crying, my thoughts changed. Could I really start over? Robyn couldn't be just erased from my life. And, I truly believed that I could raise my child better than anyone else. I am her mother.

I proceeded to dive headfirst into learning about all the resources and educational materials available to those with Down syndrome. I bought books, joined our local support group, and surfed the web finding success stories about Down syndrome. Still, returning to work after my twelve weeks of maternity leave was extremely difficult. Every time I spoke the words "Down syndrome," I felt like crying. Couldn't they see it all over my face, how my life had changed from those two simple words? Eventually, I was able to detach and not envision Robyn every time I counseled couples.

Since having my daughter with Down syndrome, my view of prenatal testing has dramatically changed. I currently counsel in the prenatal setting and the recent advances in that arena frighten me. Overall, the ultimate, unspoken goal of prenatal screening and diagnosis is to reduce the number of babies born with a disability, and more specifically, Down syndrome. Many in the medical community will be appalled at that statement, as I once would have been. They will argue that prenatal diagnosis only provides parents with information so that they can make their own decisions regarding the fate of their unborn baby. That is true in a sense, but what information is being provided to aid these families in their decision making? Often, outdated numbers regarding the medical complications associated with trisomy 21. And even when current information is offered, rarely, if ever, are stories included of those with Down syndrome participating in their school's sporting activities, graduating from high school, holding a job, living independently, and being an integral and irreplaceable part of their families' lives.

Children with Down syndrome are commonly portrayed as "suffering," but I'm certain that my daughter has not "suffered" from Down syndrome a single day of her life. That is not to say that it is all a bed of roses, but it is certainly not as bad as commonly portrayed. Balanced information, which includes the wonderful advances and accomplishments that have been made and continue to be made regarding Down syndrome, should be shared with all families faced with this prenatal diagnosis. Only then will truly informed decisions be made regarding that unborn life, even if it happens to have Down syndrome.

Genetic counselors are taught to remain nondirective in our sessions. For this reason, I typically do not share with patients the fact that I have a child with Down syndrome. I am often subjected to negative opinions about Down syndrome that I'm sure I would be spared if they knew that I had Robyn. But even though I cannot share my personal experiences with patients, my style of counseling has changed. I no longer feel sorry for them. Instead of only listing medical complications associated with Down syndrome, I try to stress the positive aspects of Down syndrome as well. And, when a prenatal diagnosis is confirmed, my patients are presented with options including continuation, termination, and adoption. In addition, the option of meeting a child with Down syndrome is offered.

As I look into Robyn's beautiful, blue, almond-shaped eyes, I fear that her generation will be the last with Down syndrome. New prenatal techniques will make the diagnosis of Down syndrome easier and earlier in pregnancy. Although I could once easily imagine this world without those with disabilities as a better place, I cannot now. Robyn brings a richness to our lives that was once not there. She lights up the room when she enters and everyone feels compelled to greet her. Having Robyn has shown us the compassion and generosity in others. I still would not choose for Robyn to have Down syndrome. Not because of what it does physically and cognitively to my daughter, but because of how others view her for having that diagnosis. That said, if my choice was to have Robyn with Down syndrome or not have her at all, I would take her and Down syndrome a million times over.

This story is dedicated to Rob, my husband, my rock.

● ● ●

Lisa received her master's degree in genetics from Indiana University in 1995 and has been a practicing genetic counselor since. She resides in Dayton, Ohio, with her husband and three daughters. Since Robyn was diagnosed with Down syndrome after birth in 2005, Lisa's passions include the annual Buddy Walk held by the Miami Valley Down Syndrome Association and National Down Syndrome Congress conferences.

Samantha and Shannon Lee

31.

While No One Was Watching

By Shannon Lee

FIFTH GRADE. IT was a real turning point in my life. While no one was watching I grew taller, came to the realization that boys don't really have cooties, and—most importantly—discovered how much I'd underestimated my older sister Samantha's ability to learn. After all, she does have Down syndrome, and everyone had told me she would be slow. As I sat and watched her struggle with her homework at night, I would wonder how much of it she would remember, and how anything she retained might possibly be relevant to her later in life.

Fifth grade. One of my most difficult academic assignments was learning all the state capitals. Night after night I would sit with my parents at the dining room table with my flash cards: New York—Albany; California—Sacramento; Louisiana—Baton Rouge. Samantha would sit and watch me struggle to memorize the names. I figured it was a good thing she didn't have to learn all fifty state capitals. According to the "educational experts" she would never be capable of that. And even if she could learn a few of them, she would have no real reason to remember them. How would knowing state capitals help her?

That summer my family took a seemingly endless road trip to California. Four hours into our twelve-hour journey, Samantha and I had managed to play all the road games our mom had packed for us. After another hour of "Daddy, how much longer until we can eat?" and "Mommy, I'm bored," my mom, in a desperate effort to maintain her sanity, decided to test my memory by asking me the state capitals. I fumbled through the first four, but then my luck ran out.

"Ohio," said Mom

"I dunno."

"Florida," said Mom.

I answered with the standard fifth-grade shoulder shrug/eye roll.

"Connecticut," said Mom.

I opened my mouth to give some smart-aleck reply, but before I could, Samantha piped up.

"Hartford," she said.

Samantha confidently and correctly named more state capitals—three, then four, then more and more until she had successfully named all fifty! And each time, she answered with matter-of-fact statements, as if Mom had asked her the time or what she had for breakfast. Her calm, cool style was just as impressive as her memory.

I was incredulous as I recalled all the evenings I'd struggled to learn the state capitals with my parents' help. While no one was watching, Samantha had been memorizing them on her own.

For the rest of our trip I pondered how I had allowed stereotypes to cloud my view of what my sister could learn and achieve. I began to wonder how often archaic myths about people with Down syndrome keep them from having a chance at good education, jobs, and acceptance into society. And I realized how learning the state capitals would help Samantha in daily living—and how it would help me. The information itself doesn't matter much. What matters is the process of trying, failing, and trying again. What matters is believing in yourself, not giving up, and finally achieving success. With success comes self-confidence, and with self-confidence comes eagerness to try other things. Even without success, you know you gave it your best effort—and that's the most important thing.

It's been ten years since my family's road trip to California. To this day, Samantha can name all fifty state capitals. My best record is twenty (on a good day).

Today Samantha has a very active life, vocationally and socially. She works two jobs, one for Oregon State University cleaning and maintaining the main student lobby. Many of the students stop and chat with her. She really enjoys having the college athletes stop and say hi. She also works for a trucking company as a clerical office assistant, handling the mail, ordering supplies, and doing other basic clerical jobs. She has a large circle of friends. She bowls, swims, loves to dance, and has a very cute boyfriend. My sister's abilities remind me of a certain saying: *Don't tell me the sky's the limit when I know there are footprints on the moon.* Samantha continues to walk in amazing, unexpected places—and this time, people are watching.

● ● ●

Shannon graduated from Oregon State University in June 2009 with a degree in Human Development and Family Sciences. She is currently working as a counselor in the juvenile justice system. The joys in her life are her faith, family, and friends. If God hadn't chosen Samantha to be her sister, Shannon would have chosen her to be her best friend.

THE GIFT OF FRIENDSHIP

Carrie Bergeron Desai and Rosemary Reimer

32.

Better Caught Than Taught

By Rosemary Reimer

"JERK!" JOEL SHOUTED at Ben, his face twisting with anger. "You missed the ball. What a retard." And these two boys were friends.

Stationed halfway between first base and the swings, I was enjoying the sun on my face and the chickadees chattering in the spruce trees at the border of the school playground. My class was a good bunch; basically responsible, cooperative, and friendly. They had persevered on today's tests and deserved some free time. Now our twenty free minutes on the playground at the end of a busy sixth-grade day had turned from a reward to be celebrated into demeaning putdowns fueled by frustration and ignorance.

It was just a brief time until dismissal, insufficient to deal with Joel and Ben's exchange. For the rest of the afternoon, I thought about ways I could try to change my students' attitude. From my experience as a teacher, I knew young people understand fairness and are sensitive to others if taught. But from my experience as a godmother, I also knew that such lessons make a deeper impression if they're *caught*.

In 1976, my goddaughter Carrie was born with Down syndrome. Exactly two months after her birth, her life was celebrated at her baptism, and my husband and I became her godparents—in fact, our children claimed that we were Carrie's "Godfamily." The years that followed were full of prayers, hopes, worries, firsts, and celebrations. Early on, our Carrie's life included infant stimulation, speech lessons, ear infections, and heart surgery. Then came elementary school, a blend of mainstreaming and self-contained classes, reading, and a "super swimmer" award. In junior high and high school, Carrie was a chorus member and a budding poet.

Knowing she was already an asset in our school community, I invited Carrie to come and talk with my sixth graders. On the Monday morning following the playground incident, I announced that I was concerned about attitudes and that I had invited a guest speaker for that afternoon. What body language! Eyeballs rolled and a few "oh greats" were mumbled. What a reversal when I mentioned Carrie's name.

"Oh, she rides my bus," echoed two students.

"She volunteers in my brother's kindergarten class," stated another.

That's when I knew all would be well.

Shortly before Carrie's arrival that afternoon, we stashed our electrical circuit projects on the counter and straightened the rows of desks. I gave my final "guest in our room" speech just before Carrie knocked on the door and peered through the window. I knew Carrie would reach my students' hearts. Her honest, totally loving demeanor touched everyone who got to know her. I beckoned for Carrie to enter.

"Hi guys. Thanks for inviting me and thank you to my god-mother for arranging our meeting. You know this was my science class when I was a sixth grader. I'm a junior now."

Carrie's blonde hair framed her face, which held a broad smile. "I came to talk about people with disabilities. What's a disability?" she asked the class.

"My dog's deaf, so that's like he has a disability," Joel volunteered. "He's still a smart old dog."

The class good naturedly giggled but Carrie jumped in and affirmed Joel. "Your dog has a disability and is a bit different than other dogs. Is it hard for him sometimes?"

"He gets around the yard just fine and we just have to use hand signals," Joel replied.

"You know," he chuckled, "my Dad and I still talk to him and call his name, out of habit I guess."

Carrie straightened up and said, "I have a disability. I have Down syndrome. I was born with Down syndrome. You can't catch it like a cold. Down syndrome never goes away. It means that I have an extra twenty-first chromosome in every cell and that it just takes me longer to learn some stuff like reading and especially math."

No boys drummed pencils, no papers rustled, no desks squeaked, no girls twirled their hair. Forty-four eyes focused on her alone.

"Sometimes I'm sad when people make fun of me or of anyone with a disability. I get really angry when someone says *retard*."

Joel and Ben glanced down and guiltily tipped their heads toward each other. A few other students took an extra breath or adjusted themselves in their chairs. A couple of girls snuck a peek back to the boys in the middle of the room. Then the attention reverted back to Carrie.

"When I was born the doctors discovered I had a hole in my heart. I had heart surgery when I was two years old. When I was little I was sick a lot; bronchitis, scarlet fever twice, and ear infections. My family is the best and is always there for me. My brother Jamie let me play his drums and kept bullies away. I have my own drum set now. I have two sisters, Wendy who sang and read with me, and Katie who is my fashion advisor and I can always talk with her. I'm the youngest. My dad taught me to ski, and my mom played game after game of Scattergories with me...."

I stopped hearing Carrie's words and focused on my students. Their faces said, *We understand your pain and your joys, your loneliness and your laughter.*

Carrie was concluding and her comments brought my attention back to her. Her voice was strong. "Remember guys, we all have abilities and we all have things we do real well and we all have stuff we need help with. It's okay to be different but it's not okay to hurt someone's feelings just because they are different or have a disability."

When Carrie finished talking, the room was quiet. "Any questions?" Carrie asked.

The students bombarded her.

"Who's your favorite movie star?"

"What's your favorite song?"

"What's your favorite color?"

"Do you fish?"

"Do you ride snowmobiles?"

"Do you dance?"

I smiled; these were questions they asked each other when making friends.

After Carrie answered all the questions, a few students gathered around her. "I had a hole in my heart too and the same surgery," announced Eric.

"My uncle had a fever real bad when he was little and he was always in a special class. You should hear him sing. He's great and can imitate Elvis Presley," boasted Ryan.

"My sister has Down syndrome," Nicole revealed.

Every head turned in her direction. "Nicole, I didn't know that!" chorused her group of friends.

Nicole nodded. "She's going to Pre-K next year. I watch out for her all the time. She loves to be tickled."

My eyes moistened and I collected myself. As a teacher, the past period had been one of those magical moments when a class connected with a concept and their lives could be richer. How very simple. Talk to each other. Listen! Truly listen, not just to words but to hearts.

The bell rang; it was time for Carrie to say goodbye. Nicole and some girls hugged her. Eric and Ryan hovered close. *Yes,* I thought as I watched the new friends together. *The importance of valuing each other is best when caught.*

●   ●   ●

Rosemary is a retired elementary school teacher and a watercolorist who was born in England and educated in New York City. She has a deep love of history and relishes travel, in reality or virtually through a great book. However her greatest adventures have been as wife, mother, and grandmother. Her godchild Carrie Bergeron Desai graduated from community college, is an advocate for others with disabilities, and is married to musician Sujeet Desai, who also has Down syndrome.

Brad Hennefer and Drew Berlinsky

33.

My Stereotypical Perfect Life

By Drew Berlinsky

College Essay Question: If you could name one experience in your life that has changed you for the better, what would it be?

I'VE HAD THE stereotypical "perfect life." I have two loving parents that give me everything, two brothers that are like friends and many friends that are like brothers, and four grandparents that are all still alive and self-sufficient. With a childhood as flawless as mine, I didn't think that any one person could change my life for the better.

But at the age of fourteen, that one person entered my life, and his name is "B-rad."

Brad Hennefer, or "B-rad" as I like to call him, has a genetic condition known as trisomy 21, or Down syndrome. We met on the first day of basketball tryouts during my freshman year of high school. Halfway through the try-out, the coach had all of the players find a partner to complete the next drill. The coach asked me to partner with Brad. My first thought was this was going to be awkward for me. However, after five minutes of being paired together, and a deliberate disobedience of the coach's orders not to talk during practice, Brad and I had developed a friendship that was no different than the relationships I made with the other kids at try-outs.

One week later, the team was boarding the bus to head to our first away game. I knew who I wanted to sit next to. I had asked Brad to sit with me not because he had enough chips and sodas to feed a family of twelve, and not because I was trying to do the right thing, but because I was fascinated with him. From that point on our friendship grew and strengthened. By the time summer rolled around, we shared a passion not only for basketball, but also for golf. But while I had only just begun to play golf, Brad had been playing his entire life. At this point, I realized that there were few things I could do that Brad could not.

I cannot relate a cute or amusing anecdote about Brad because he was all about quick-witted snippets that were purely about the time, place, and moment. What I can say is that all teens, whether or not they have Down Syndrome, can appreciate sophomoric humor. We can all tease each other about girlfriends. We can make fun of the stereotypes that threaten to separate us in society, and make sure they never separate us as teammates or friends. With Brad around, every practice, every game, and every chance meeting in the school hallway produced a laugh—and when we meet up again in five, ten, or twenty years we'll still be sharing those laughs.

Now that Brad and I are beginning our senior year of high school, we are closer than ever. We have spent three years together playing for the high school basketball team and have enjoyed each other's company on the golf course many times. Spending time with

Brad is not charity, or a gift of pity. It is a friendship that I hope will last beyond high school. My experiences of friendship, team-work, and laughter with Brad during our high school years have been incredible. My appreciation for what Brad has given me can-not be described in words, but only in my efforts to help him and the organizations his family is involved in. With B-rad by my side, my "perfect life" may not be stereotypical, but it has become more perfect than ever before.

●　●　●

Drew is from Cherry Hill, New Jersey. He is currently a freshman at the George Washington University majoring in finance. He enjoys play-ing sports and is a member of the Sigma Phi Epsilon fraternity.

LeAnn Brilz

34.

Adventures with LeAnn

By Kimberley Williams

I LOVE MY work as a developmental therapist, teaching life skills to children with disabilities in the community. One afternoon in the beginning of autumn I was asked to meet with an eight-year-old girl with Down syndrome and her mother, who was seeking the services of a developmental therapist through our agency. When I opened the door to the office, there in the reception area sat a little blonde girl with her head down, staring deep into the eyes of her Barbie. Kneeling down beside her and peeking into her eyes, I said "Hello LeAnn, my name is Kimberley. What's your Barbie's name?" She took a quick look at me and then turned her attention back to her Barbie, swishing and turning the doll as part of some make-believe adventure.

LeAnn's mother was carefully watching us interact to see if the two of us would make a good match. I wanted to work with LeAnn and wondered how I could make a connection with her. Should I ask her more questions? Try to play along? But LeAnn soon provided the perfect solution. She sat up, looked at me with her big blue eyes, and said, "We go swing now?" Then quickly she jumped up and ran to where her mother sat. "Mommy, we go swing now?" As Mom agreed, we all walked into the resource room, an awesome sight to any child's eyes: lots of games, toys, books, and yes—there in the middle of the room was a giant square swing. Quickly she ran toward the swing, thrust herself onto it, belly down, then pushed off the ground with her feet like a rocket taking off! That was the beginning of our adventures together.

I'd never before worked with a child with Down syndrome, and I was excited to have the opportunity. According to the agreement with Leann's mother and my agency, I would be picking LeAnn up after school and working with her on safety, writing, hygiene, and social skills. This would take place at the agency's resource center as well as out in the community, doing activities such as swimming, dancing, shopping, and playing at the park. I was a little nervous, but very motivated. I could sense LeAnn's tremendous potential and wanted to give her every opportunity to meet her goals.

To my delight, LeAnn seemed excited by our partnership as well. When I picked her up from school for the first time, she greeted me with great enthusiasm. "Kimbury!" she exclaimed, hugging me tight, then introduced me to her teacher and classmates. We headed out the door with LeAnn holding a Barbie in one hand and my hand in the other. My learning to speak LeAnn's language was our first shared adventure. Walking across the grassy field, she said hi to the other kids or simply shouted "happy birthday pizza!" Right away I understood the "happy birthday" part, but not the "pizza"—I thought she was saying "peace out!" Once we reached my Jeep, LeAnn struggled to pull herself up onto the seat. When she was in position and I started to buckle her up, she looked right into my eyes. "I do it," she said firmly. I understood *those* words loud and clear. But as we pulled away in my Jeep, she kept saying "Kimbury, singer, singer." I couldn't figure out what she meant until she started to sing!

LeAnn and I had many adventures at the park. The first thing she always wanted to do was swing. Keep in mind, not all swings are equal in size—but with all her might LeAnn would fight to get herself onto whichever swing struck her fancy. After a time she would sweetly say "Kimbury, you help." I would guide her to hold the chains, position herself on the seat just right, and then with a couple pushes she was pumping her legs and singing the Sesame Street theme song at the top of her lungs. One day after finishing the theme song, she went on to sing all the other songs on the tape—in order! I thought, *that's a smart little girl.*

LeAnn's perceptiveness never ceased to amaze me, even when some concepts went a little over her head. One afternoon when it was time for me to leave, I told her that I was going home to Michael.

"Michael?" she asked.

"Yes, Michael," I replied. "He's my husband. We're married."

She just smiled. But as I walked out she said, "Kimberley you go home now to Michael?" When I said yes she smiled again and said, "Married, Husband?" I said yes, and she gave me a big hug. I was driving home thinking how great it was that she listened and then repeated back to me what I had said. But that was just the beginning. That weekend LeAnn drew a picture for me featuring four people. On Monday as I took the picture in hand, I asked, "Who are these people, LeAnn?" and she pointed to them and named them in order from bigger to smaller: *Michael, Kimberley, Married,* and *Husband.* We had quite the giggle at this very sweet picture—she'd thought *married* and *husband* were my children!

But there were other times LeAnn had to set *me* straight. One day as we were crossing a bridge on our way home from school, I glanced downward at the creek and saw a deer. I quickly pulled over to a parking area. "LeAnn, there's a deer down there!" I exclaimed.

She hesitated and shook her head. "No," she said emphatically. But I insisted that we hop out of the Jeep and go look at the deer, knowing that this would be such a great learning opportunity. Once out of the Jeep, a trail led us along the side of the creek, which was lined with birch trees. As we gently walked, tiptoeing and looking for the deer, LeAnn grumbled and dragged her feet.

"Come on," I whispered. "Let's find the deer!" We crept along for a couple of minutes until we reached the spot where I'd seen the deer, but to my disappointment there was no deer in sight. There was, however, a cute family of ducks.

"Look, LeAnn!" I said, pointing at the ducks and thinking she'd be excited.

She looked at me with mild disdain. "Uh-uh, Kimbury. That's not a deer. Those are *ducks*." I laughed all the way home, and I still laugh whenever I remember that day.

Each day was its own new adventure with LeAnn, and brought many wonderful teaching moments and satisfying progress. Over the course of our relationship, LeAnn's art work went from large scribbles to focused, thoughtful coloring. Daunting tasks such as writing out her letters and safely crossing the street became exciting accomplishments. The first time she fastened a button by herself, we were both so proud that we couldn't wait to show her Mom. Seeing LeAnn's face with each new success brought me a thrilling feeling I cannot describe.

When I first met LeAnn, I had looked forward to watching her reach new goals, but I had no idea she would become a true friend in my life. On weekends she called me to say hi. She invited me to her birthday party. We giggled and played when we went swimming together, and I even got to play in the snow with her and her grandma during Christmas break. Once when LeAnn had pneumonia, I helped take care of her at her home. We watched a movie together, with her head on my lap. At one point she looked into my eyes, smiled so sweetly, and said,

"Kimbury, you're my best friend!"

Swinging and singing with LeAnn has filled me with laughter and joy. But our quiet adventures touch my heart the most.

●   ●   ●

After living in Idaho for two years, which is where Kimberley had the privilege of working with and getting to know Leann, she and her husband relocated back to California. Even though Kimberley and Leann have not seen each other for over a year, their bond is still strong and they talk on the phone every week. Kimberley continues to work with children who have special needs.

Denise and Ana Sawyer

35.

Friendship Ball

By Denise Sawyer

"PASS IT TO ME!" I can't tell you how many times those words exploded out of my daughter's mouth during the recreational basketball season in our hometown. And I never thought that anyone on her team would ever pass it to her during a game, especially during the final game of the season.

Ever since infancy, Ana has been throwing anything that she could get her hands on—bottles, toys, food, books. Amazingly enough, she had fairly good aim, even as a very young child who struggled with learning any new physical skill. Her accuracy improved each year in spite of the loose joints and ligaments that she has due to the Down syndrome. By the age of three, she could dribble a basketball better than her older brother. Maybe this was because she is very stubborn and was bound and determined to do whatever her big brother did, or maybe it was because of the encouragement of a family friend who loves all sports but particularly basketball. Whatever the reason, Ana would go out on the driveway and shoot basket after basket—never getting discouraged when she missed the basket more times than she made it.

When she was old enough to join the Mulvane Recreational Basketball Team in third grade, we signed her up. She was so excited about playing— although she wasn't thrilled about running back and forth across the court. Running was hard work for her, but throwing the ball toward the basket was her forte. In fact, there were numerous times during the first season that she preferred to sit on the bench and cheer on her teammates. In return, her teammates encouraged her to go back out on the court and play when it was her turn. Ana didn't have an alliance to the team that she was a member of; she rooted for both the team that she was playing on and the opposing team because she had classmates on both teams. Ana didn't see it as a problem to encourage members of both teams. She just understood that they were her friends and that is what one did for friends—clap and cheer them on.

When fourth grade rolled around, Ana still wanted to play on the recreational basketball team, so we signed her up again. Now she knew more of the rules of the game, and knew that if she were open she should shout, "Pass it to me." During practices, her teammates passed her the ball, but unfortunately they never did during the games. It was heartbreaking to watch her play so hard at each game and never get a chance with the ball. Her father and I understood that the team wanted to win the game but it would have meant so much to Ana to actually get a chance to shoot the ball. Ana never gave up, though. All season she ran back and forth on the court, never having the opportunity to dribble, pass, or even attempt to make a basket—until the very last game of the season.

The clock was ticking down the final minutes of the game. Ana was standing a few feet from half court and yelled once again, "Pass it to me." I was just thinking that she was wasting her breath when I noticed her teammate with the brown ponytail stop a foot away from Ana. She looked around at the members of both teams on the court as if to say, "Okay—let's do it." Turning toward Ana, she calmly called her name, "Ana."

Ana turned toward the young girl and before I realized what had happened, she efficiently passed the ball to her. Surprise crossed Ana's face as the ball actually came in contact with her hands. Ana cautiously dribbled down the right side of the court and with great concentration, raised her arms and let the ball fly toward the net. During this entire period, members of both her team and the opposing team stood as still as statues in a park, allowing her to take her time and not even attempting to take the ball away from her. And as team members and people along the side of the court watched, Ana's basketball headed toward the backboard and swished down through the net!

I was up on my feet, jumping up and down saying, "I can't believe it—she did it!" Ana spun around, raced towards the other side of the court, arms raised in victory with a glorious smile on her face yelling, "I did it!" But she wasn't the only person in that gym smiling—so were all the members of both basketball teams. Meanwhile, the audience clapped and hollered along the sidelines.

A short time later, Ana's team once again had possession of the ball. When Ana yelled, "Pass it to me!" her teammate complied. And like a replay on tape, Ana dribbled toward the basketball net while members of the two teams remained stuck like glue to their places on the court. This time, her shot fell short of the net. But it didn't matter to Ana. Her face had a huge smile across it and she had a bounce in her step as she chased after the ball. A curly haired, brunette member of her team came up to Ana and gave her a "high five" in recognition of her attempt.

After the game ended, I approached the referee, an older woman with short, gray-streaked dark hair wearing comfortable blue sweats. All season she'd watched Ana call for the ball, but never get it. Her eyebrows rose as I walked up to her. "Ana was thrilled when she made that basket. What an awesome moment," she said.

I stepped closer and asked in a quiet voice, "Did you arrange for that to happen? Did you talk to both teams?"

She shook her head in response. "I had nothing to do with it." My face registered my shock. "They've been wanting to do it for weeks now," she explained. "It just took them awhile to coordinate it with all of the team members."

I felt the tears start to roll down my face when I realized it was not a "set-up." The opportunity had been planned by team members and coaches who truly cared about Ana. Some may assume that Ana's teammates finally passed her the ball out of pity. But anyone who saw the faces of her team members that day knew that there wasn't any pity involved. Ana's friends took it upon themselves to make sure that she had the opportunity to truly be a member of the team and shoot a basket—not only once, but twice. I'm not sure who was more elated, Ana or her teammates.

Ana is a person who only sees others in a positive light, gives people hugs during the sad times, laughs with them during the good times, and cheers for them no matter what team they are on. She was a true friend to her teammates. And when they passed her the ball during those last precious moments of the game, they returned that friendship in full.

● ● ●

Denise, a special education teacher at the secondary level, lives in Mulvane, Kansas, with her husband, Scott, and two children, Arron (1995) and Ana (1997). She is actively involved in her church and is secretary for the Down Syndrome Society of Wichita (www.dsswichita. org). Ana now plays basketball (along with many other sports) on a Special Olympics team and continues to receive most of her education in an inclusive setting.

Rylee Hageman, Nichole Stumbo, Constance Glandon, and Jennifer McLeland

36.
Treasure Hunt

By Constance J. Glandon

I REALLY LOVE treasure hunts. It's so much fun digging for clues and searching to find the hidden prize. In order to win, though, you have to keep your eyes wide open. This is also true when you're looking for treasures in daily life. I found a special gift in three little girls with Down syndrome who belong to my church congregation, but it took me a long time to discover it.

I grew up in a town of 1,200 people in rural Iowa, so you could say that diversity was a new concept to me. We had no people of color in our town, and a disability was defined as having no sporting or musical talent. Sure, we had a few kids in school who were considered "slow" and today might be labeled "developmentally delayed" but I don't ever remember being around anyone who had Down syndrome.

So to be honest, when I heard that a family in my congregation had just welcomed a new daughter with Down syndrome, I did not consider the diagnosis a potential gift. The baby, Rylee, had some pretty serious health issues with her esophagus and stomach, and I spent quite some time praying for the family to just be able to get through the situation. In my ignorance, I somehow expected that the family would accept the circumstances and "move on," although looking back I have no idea what I meant by that.

Because Rylee had many complications related to Down syndrome, I didn't get much opportunity to be around her as an infant. Most of the time it seemed like she was either having a surgical procedure or was recovering from one. I was intimidated by her health status and it wasn't until she was older and stronger that I really got to know her.

When Rylee was about two years old, she intrigued me when I saw her at social gatherings and church. I came to see her as the little blonde princess with a sweet yet precocious personality. Whenever I saw her, she was dressed beautifully, smiling, with a twinkle in her eye that said, "I'm ready to take on the world." I'd expected her to be listless and uninterested in other people, but nothing could be further from the truth. Wearing little white knee-high boots, she would climb the steps in the sanctuary, determined to reach the drum set before her mother could get to her. The mischievous grin on her face made me laugh aloud. And when her daddy held her in church, she would lay her head on his shoulder and give me a smile that dared me to not love her. Getting to know Rylee was my first clue that children with Down syndrome can be a hidden treasure, an unexpected delight.

About five years after Rylee came into my world, I got my second clue to the treasure map. A young couple at our church announced they were having their first child. We were excited and happy for them, and as is my practice, I asked God to give them "good gifts." Little did I know that many months later they would bring home a beautiful baby girl named Jennifer who also has Down syndrome.

After seeing how sweet, loving, and funny Rylee turned out to be, I was anxiously waiting to see just what Jennifer would be like, and she hasn't disappointed me at all. From the moment I first saw her, so tiny in her stroller, I could tell that she was going to set the world and our congregation on their ears.

Jennifer is a little firecracker, and just thinking about her makes me smile and laugh aloud. Her impish grin and huge, expressive eyes are beyond charming, but what makes me giggle the most is how fast that little girl can move. She's turbo-charged! I love to watch her run. As is true of many children with Down syndrome, Jennifer has shorter than average stature. The first time I saw her walk, she went right under the table and didn't even mess up her hair. The next time I saw her, and pretty much every time since, she has been running. Running in circles with other children, running so Mommy and Daddy have to catch her, or running after our dog while squealing with delight. Jennifer helped me see the bigger picture of the beauty and diversity of children with Down syndrome, But I still had much to learn about the vastness and richness of the treasure.

Fast-forward two more years to when our Youth Pastor, Andy, and his wife, Ellen, had their second child, a little girl named Nichole. My family had come to know Andy and Ellen pretty well—my teenage girls were involved in the youth group that Andy leads, and as a family we had babysat for their first little darling, Ellie. This wonderful couple lived far from their respective families, and while there were plenty of people in our congregation willing to help out, we were one of the first families to offer our child-sitting services when Nichole came along. Thankfully for us, they took us up on our offer. I wish I had noted the exact date of her first visit, because it very well could be a Glandon family holiday. Nichole was about three months old. It took her roughly five minutes to steal our hearts, including my husband's and our ten-year-old son's. After years of not wanting to admit he was old enough to be a grandparent, my husband said he was finally looking forward to being a grandpa, especially if the babies would be "like Nichole." And I wholeheartedly agreed.

One of the first times I held Nichole, she placed her chubby little hands on my face, looked me in the eyes, and held my gaze as if to say, "Hi, I'm Nichole, and I am going to be a wonderful part of your life." She loved to be rocked and cuddled, and I was more than happy to do as she desired. Seven months and many babysitting visits later, our family continues to be completely enraptured with Nichole. Her beauty captivates us, her personality thrills us, and her smile melts our hearts. Every time she reaches a new milestone like sitting up, crawling, or pulling herself up to the couch, I break out in spontaneous applause. She is my third clue on the treasure map, and I could not love this little girl any more if she was my own child. When I look at her I do not see a "Down's syndrome child," I see a child with Down syndrome, a child with a soft, expressive, loving, heart. I see a beautiful flower—not a dainty fragile rose, but a happy sturdy daisy.

A princess, a firecracker, and a flower: these are symbols of the three little girls I love, and marks on a treasure map leading to an understanding of Down syndrome, a brighter enjoyment of life, and a deeper appreciation for all people. These days, when I mention to people that we have three little girls with Down syndrome in our congregation of 275, they often look at me with a quizzical expression and ask me if there is something in the water. And with a bemused look I answer, "Yes. Blessings."

● ● ●

Connie lives in Charles City, Iowa, with her husband and three children. Writing is one of her passions, along with church and softball. Connie is an avid reader and writes a monthly column for a regional newspaper. While she has a job at a local college, her dream is to become a full-time writer.

Kristine Johnson (birthday girl); Kristi's mom, Sharon, far left, Amy, Jake, with Nick Kearin, Mary, Nikayla, and Ray

37.

Birthday Blessing

By Amy Kearin

LATE WINTER, NINE years ago, we found something unexpected hidden under our kitchen towel: a birthday announcement and list. It was titled "Kristine Johnson's 31st Birthday, June 29" and it listed a handful of items she would enjoy for her next birthday. Over the next six months, similar lists showed up throughout the house every time our friend Kristi came to visit. We came to realize that Kristi plans her birthday party—princess cake and all—every day of the year. She absolutely loves not only her birthday, but everyone else's. She enjoys making cakes with her mom for her friends and family, and wrapping up gifts for everyone she knows. This exemplifies her joy, her daily celebration of life, and her love for all her friends and family, which have greatly blessed our home for nearly a decade.

Our family of six met Kristi and her loving mom, Sharon, in a Special Olympics gymnastics program. The first day we met Kristi, we were in awe of her beautiful gymnastics and graceful dancing. She had a loving smile that lit up the whole room, and eyes which smiled as well through her thick glasses. Without them, she is legally blind. When Sharon introduced us to her, Kristi hugged each one of us with sincere warmth, as if she had known us her whole life and we were her best friends in the world. Our children were surprised and touched by her sweetness and wonderful laugh. We noticed a gentle strength about Kristi that was very endearing. As she walked around the room thanking and hugging people, it didn't take us long to realize that she has open arms for everyone.

Kristi inspires our family with her many gifts and talents. We grew to love her at Special Olympics practices and competitions, because we could see the joy that gymnastics and dance gave her and the happiness she found in sharing her talent with others. We're so proud of Kristi for serving as a Global Messenger for the Special Olympics (which includes giving speeches in front of large crowds) and winning gold medals in gymnastics, but even more proud of her hopeful, always positive attitude, even when she's dealing with muscle aches and nerve pain. Her other talents include acting, singing, playing tennis, golfing, power lifting, swimming, karate, horseback riding, and playing bocce ball. She doesn't let her eyesight or heart problems get in the way of reaching her goals. She perseveres through every obstacle and shows outstanding determination. Her mother, Sharon, deserves a great deal of credit for being Kristi's coach, teacher, guide, motivator, supporter, and biggest fan.

Early in our friendship, Kristi started coming over to our home every week to do gymnastics, dance, play, and eat. She always walks in the door with big hugs and gifts wrapped up for the whole family. Nothing makes her happier than giving to others. When she plays ball with our son, Ray, her contagious laugh melts away any problems of the day. When we sit down to eat, Kristi enjoys every kind of food she's given, from hard-boiled egg yolks to chocolate milk. And when she's on a diet she says, "I can't have cookies, only cake and ice cream!"

During our visits we love to dance with Kristi and listen to her sing, especially songs from church and "Annie." She encourages our girls, Nicki and Mary, to sing their hearts out like she does. The kids love to draw and write with her, and Kristi has taught them how to draw rainbows, angels, flowers, butterflies, and hearts. Along with her birthday lists, she usually leaves sweet cards and prayers for each one of us. One of the last notes we found read, "I love butterflies. They are beautiful. I love God and I love you very much." We have a special book filled with Kristi's drawings, writings, cards, and photographs. It sits on a shelf next to the books we keep for our four children, Ray, Nicki, Mary, and Jake.

It's been our privilege to share Kristi's friendship with our extended family, friends, and our children's classmates. She is embraced by everyone she meets, because she embraces them first. Anyone can see that she is a remarkable individual. Kristi loves going to "Grandma Cookie's" house to put the chocolates on the cookies, fresh out of the oven. (She loves to eat them too!) Grandma Cookie adores Kristi and always welcomes her help. Throughout the years our older kids have enjoyed having Kristi help out with gymnastics during P.E. class at their school. Nicki is always so proud to have Kristi come. She loves watching her friends' amazement at Kristi's flipping and leaping abilities, as well as her ability to reach out to everyone she meets. Nicki currently enjoys doing gymnastics with Kristi at the same gym. Sharon and I enjoy watching our daughters love the sport together and build a unique friendship that will last a lifetime.

A few years ago, Kristi did something that was truly courageous and inspiring. We asked Sharon if she thought Kristi would be willing to speak at our church during "Respect Life" month, calling attention to her own life being valuable and every human life being precious. Sharon said "yes" without hesitation and wrote a beautiful talk that Kristi delivered to the church community of thousands, at five different church services. She began her talk with her own words: "Before I was born, my parents prayed for a baby. They asked God to send them a special child. And he did. I was born thirty-six years ago and by the way, I also happen to have Down syndrome. The doctors told my parents that I might not live through childhood because I have a hole in my heart. I think, because of this, my parents loved me more than ever. They have worked very hard so that I could have as many opportunities as every other child. I have a brother and a sister-in-law that I love very much."

Kristi went on to share some of her goals and accomplishments, hobbies, and enjoyment in helping others and loving her family and friends. She closed her talk with the most poignant words about God's place in her life and His love for all of us, then spontaneously added, "and I mean it!" Our family and every person in the church sat motionless, with open ears and hearts as Kristi spoke with such conviction and love. She then sang and gracefully danced with her arms to the song "Every Life Is Precious."

It's difficult to put into words just how important Kristi has become to our family. One evening out of the blue, our son Ray said, "Mom and Dad, we really should adopt a girl with Down syndrome." We listened very carefully to him and began praying for guidance. Was this to be for our family? A short time later, Ray answered the question himself. He simply said, "No, we have Kristi, and she is part of our family." She truly is, and we couldn't be more grateful. We're excited for our youngest son, Jake, to grow up to know and love Kristi. And of course, we're honored and delighted to celebrate Kristi's birthday every year. Our children love blowing up colorful balloons, frosting the cake, wrapping presents, and giving Kristi a birthday party to remember. We're so grateful to Kristi for continuing to enrich our lives, bless our home, and touch our hearts.

● ● ●

Amy lives in Southern California and is a wife and mother of two sons and two daughters. Individuals with special needs have been touching her life for the past twenty years, in her positions as a volunteer, live-in camp counselor, special education teacher, and Special Olympics coach. Amy and her family loved writing this story together, and they thank God for Kristi.

LeAnn K. Brilz, Lori J. Charlier, Emma A. Charlier

38.
Delighting in Each Other

By Lori Charlier

EMMA RAN ACROSS the school yard and hopped into the van, slamming the sliding door behind her.

"Mom, guess what?" Without waiting for my response, she excitedly proclaimed, "LeAnn did so good today! She got to stay in our class because she sat in her chair real quiet."

I smiled at her exuberance and asked, "Who is LeAnn?"

"She's my new friend who sometimes comes to our class with a helper," Emma replied.

I was touched by my daughter's obvious affection for LeAnn. Ever since I was in 5th grade, I've been involved with helping kids and adults with intellectual disabilities. As a former special education teacher, I wrote the educational goals for my students and worked to help them fit in as much as possible; I tried to arrange friendships for my students by recruiting recess buddies, seating them next to children who showed kindness, and enforcing my expectations for respect. But even though I've spent decades as a caretaker or teacher for people with intellectual disabilities, I've never been simply a friend.

Emma and LeAnn's friendship quickly blossomed after that first day, and watching their relationship grow has been an enormous source of joy for me. They love coloring with markers in coloring books, reading books, playing hide and seek, swinging on the swing set, and solving jigsaw puzzles. No matter what they're doing, they help each other along the way. LeAnn always gathers the coloring books and markers and sets up their spots to color together. Emma reads books aloud to LeAnn and LeAnn turns the pages. LeAnn and Emma take turns pulling each other in our wagon if we have to walk a far distance.

Sometimes they even get into a bit of trouble together. One day while swimming at the community pool, LeAnn and Emma were wrestling in the water and laughing uncontrollably. They caused such a ruckus that a lifeguard asked them to stop!

But their teamwork never fails to warm my heart. One afternoon I watched them tackle the challenge of climbing up the wall of a huge inflatable bouncing structure: Emma was at the top of the wall reaching down for LeAnn's hand. She was cheering for LeAnn, saying "Good job! You can do it! You're almost there!" LeAnn was trying so hard and calling back to Emma, "Nemma, Help me! Help Me!" When LeAnn finally reached the top out of breath, they both laughed as they slid down the slide together into the play area.

Despite the obvious sincerity of Emma and LeAnn's interest in each other, sometimes I still fall into old assumptions. One day I was visiting school during recess and saw them playing on the playground with a group of girls. LeAnn was swinging one end of the long jump rope while another girl held the other end. After they practiced turning the rope together a few times, they were ready for the line of girls (including Emma) waiting to take their turn jumping into the middle of the turning rope. Each girl would jump and count to ten or try to say a jump roping rhyming song as they took their turn. LeAnn was smiling and obviously loved playing with the other kids.

When the bell rang I commented, "Emma I like seeing your friends let LeAnn play jump rope."

Emma responded with surprise in her voice, "Mom, LeAnn always is the turner because she is good at it!" She didn't see any reason *not* to include her. It was merely a natural outcome of their friendship.

Emma and LeAnn are now in 4th grade. They're not in the same class, but they never miss a chance to greet each other with a hug, and can't wait until days off from school when they can play at each other's homes—they even use calendars to count down the days. The last two years, they had a great time together at the local Down Syndrome Buddy Walk, and will be participating again this year. Emma has learned some facts about Down syndrome through books and discussions, and is eager to learn more. She tells us that when she grows up she wants to adopt a baby girl with Down syndrome. That's a long way off, to be sure! But in the meantime she is loving LeAnn and learning a lot from her friend, and I'm learning a lot by watching them.

They're not friends because of goals, strategies, or rules, as I would have planned as a teacher or even as a mother. They're not friends because they have to be, or even because they should be. They're friends because they delight in each other.

● ● ●

Lori lives in Boise, Idaho, with her husband, Henry, and their three children. Lori currently provides care for two children with special needs. She loves including these children in her family's daily routine. Also, she occasionally supervises a group home for adults with minor disabilities. Lori enjoys tandem bike riding, African dancing, helping at her church, and scrapbooking.

Brent Oberhelman, athlete, and Ron Wasoba, coach

39.
Thanks, Brent

By Ron Wasoba

WHEN WRESTLING SEASON came around and Brent heard that some of his homeroom buddies had signed up for wrestling, he asked me, the wrestling coach, where to sign up. I had known Brent for a few years, and during my thirty-two years of teaching and coaching experience I was pretty set in the ways I did things. But from the moment Brent came on board, many of my coaching philosophies were changed for the better. I knew that this once quiet and reserved student was going to change his and our lives forever. He was going to compete on a wrestling team. He was going to be a part of a team.

The moment he came into the wrestling room with a reserved expression on his face, his teammates encouraged Brent that he could be a part of the team. But I was concerned, because like many children with Down syndrome, Brent had had heart surgery at a young age. I wasn't sure he could handle the exertion. His mother assured me that when he got tired he would let me know. Sure enough, when he got tired he just sat down and said, "No more, Mr. Wasoba!" His teammates and I got a big kick out of it, and many of them were saying the same thing when they thought we were working too hard during some of our practices! In fact, we took a hint from Brent and instituted nightly "Brent breaks," during which we talked about competition and improving each week.

In our workouts, we get pretty worn down by the hard effort. I've found that adding music to the practice helps take the wrestlers' mind off their fatigue. We soon found out about Brent's love for music and his ability to play air guitar. Soon all his teammates were joining him. Practice was never boring with our new teammate around. And neither were other events like team pictures. Before our first meet Brent had to put on a wrestling singlet for the first time for team pictures. "No way," he said; "It will hurt me." The photographer was about finished with all the other wrestlers' individual shots, and my plan was soon to be tested. Knowing that Brent loved Mountain Dew, I had purchased a liter bottle in case he needed some coaxing. Sure enough, he put the singlet on and was in our team picture. And of course the other kids needed some pop as well!

Our first wrestling meet with Brent was unbelievable. Several of his 8th grade teammates literally held his hand going to the locker room. I was warmed with emotion when his teammates helped him get dressed for the meet, even before getting themselves ready. When we went out on the mat to warm up, I was proud to see Brent staying focused and doing what all the others were doing. A couple of the boys walked him to the scorer's table, where he needed to check in. This was all done without any prearrangement on my part, much to my surprise!

When it was Brent's turn to compete, the whole gym seemed to stop and focus on his performance. He was absolutely jumping with excitement as his teammates and the crowed cheered him on! His teammates and our fans were all so proud as he put his leg band on and stepped to the mat. His opponent could tell Brent didn't have many skills, but when he took Brent to the mat, Brent avoided the pin with a stand-up move that we had practiced night after night to perfection! Tears of pride came streaming down my face, and I could see some of his teammates felt the same way. Even though Brent lost the match, the team and crowd understood how great it was for him to compete. I stressed to my athletes that just like Brent, even if we don't win all of our matches, each time we step on the mat we are winners.

Our second meet, four weeks later, was also an away meet. What warmed my heart was that this once reserved young man showed great gains in confidence. For the first meet, Brent had ridden on the bus by my side, very quiet and scared. But for the second meet, Brent asked me if it was ok if for him to sit with the wrestlers at the back of the bus. Then the kids yelled for Brent to sit with them. Several tried to get him to sit by them, but he ended up sitting by his practice partner: Alex Zinnel, the smallest team member and Brent's favorite teammate. As the bus took off, many kids asked Brent to move to their seat. Even though we have strict rules about staying seated while the bus is moving, the bus driver and I didn't say a word as each of them got to "share" Brent on the ride. The student who I thought would take some extra work was actually no bother at all as each team member made sure he got dressed and to the gym, as well as to each match on time!

As the season went on, the other athletes showed Brent different moves and helped him practice, which greatly improved his performance and increased their own skills as well. Their camaraderie expanded and increased. Brent participated in traditions such as showing the team his favorite move. We all marveled at how he had become one of us. I was amazed at how much Brent had changed my perspective on life and on sports.

Two years later, after Brent moved on to high school, I was asked to be an official at the high-school level wrestling meet. Many of the athletes from my eighth-grade team were still competing together, and best of all, Brent was among them! As I officiated over the match, I was excited to see how much Brent was still enjoying the sport. More tears of joy came down my face as I noted how Brent stayed true to form and performed to the best of his ability.

After the match was over, Brent's response was his typical, "Thanks, Mr. Wasoba." As I regarded this neat young man that had touched so many so deeply, my only response was, "Thanks so much, Brent."

● ● ●

Ron lives in the Midwest with his wife, Pat. They have three grown children: Jennifer, Kelly, and Keith. Ron has been a science teacher and guidance counselor at Humboldt Middle School in Iowa for thirty-two years.

Andy and Stephanie Meredith

40.

Part of the Pack

By Stephanie Meredith

TWO WEEKS BEFORE Andy turned eight years old, he was invited to his first Cub Scout activity by the Scoutmaster at church. In Sunday school, Andy often fidgeted and kicked on the pews until the closing prayer released him to run in the gym with his posse of eleven-year-old boys who were in a different class. At his first official Scout event, where all the boys were combined together, Andy beamed as he scrambled with his older pals, Davey, Kenny, and Sean, to pick up a block of pine and wheels for the upcoming Pinewood Derby.

When he proudly dropped the rattling box in my lap, I was disappointed to find that the block of wood was raw and plain—not like the painted and polished cars I had seen boys race on slick plastic tracks at other Pinewood Derbies. It would require work and strategy at the Pinewood Derby workshop to build the car, and insider tips and tricks from my husband, who was raised in a family with seven Eagle Scout brothers. I dreaded the tedious process of carving the piece of wood into a car that was fast enough and cool enough to fit in at the race, and, even more, I worried that Andy would get run over by the jostling competition or bored by how long a Pinewood Derby could drag on.

Andy only had one requirement though: the car must look like "Red"—Dad's Mini Cooper. Father and son eventually compromised on making an Audi A6 Avant wagon, since it would be the best fit for the shape of the wood, but it would indeed be red. Since Dad would be out of town during the Scout workshop, we printed a photo of the Audi to try to figure out how Andy and I could transform a block of wood into a sports car.

Driving up the dirt path to the Scout Master's home on a wet Saturday in January, I looked forward to Andy's first Pinewood Derby workshop building a car with the other boys. As we pulled in I saw outdoor heaters scattered across the porch, which was covered with tools and sawdust. I had no clue how to make the car or use the tools, but I trusted that the Scout Master would guide us. So, I pulled the orange fleece sweatshirt over Andy's head and took my first tentative step onto the Georgia clay path leading to the house.

As we clambered up the broad wooden steps, I wondered if we had come on the right day or if I was late, as usual, since no other boys were bustling around the machines. Apparently, everyone else knew what they were doing and stayed at home, so the Scout Master patiently devoted all of his attention to us while I continued to nervously glance up at the driveway to see if anyone else would come. The Scout Master (aka Akela) instructed us to look at the picture of the Audi and draw an outline of the car with a Sharpie on the block of wood. He nodded with a half-grin as I clumsily drew the outline of a sports wagon over the rough surface, and Andy didn't wander away as usual but stood at attention over my shoulder while I worked until the "car" seemed close enough and ready to cut.

Akela made the first cuts into the pine while Andy watched. Then, the Scout Master wrapped his husky, calloused hands over my boy's soft hands, and Andy pulled back the saw on his own. I nervously looked on as he learned to use a guide to cut the large chunks of wood with a handsaw and to refine the lines using a hacksaw.

After Andy grew tired and went to eat cinnamon toast with Akela's teenaged children, I finished the project by sanding the car to give it the curves that made it look more like the real thing. I worked in frosty silence, as no other cars pulled into the driveway on the isolated country road. I wondered if we were making a Derby car that would actually be able to compete with the others if no one else even needed to show up at the workshop. I remembered the painful twinges I'd felt after Andy turned one and all my friend's children began to walk without any extra help. Then they started to run before I could even coax Andy to cruise along the wall. Would this be the same?

Once my husband returned home from his business trip, he assured me that we could refine the car with finishing touches. Dad wanted to help by using some secrets from his own father, a veteran of countless Pinewood Derby races. Granddaddy had showed him how to strategically drill holes in the bottom and fill them with lead and how to sand the seams of the wheels to make the car go even faster. Then, Andy worked with Dad to meet the most important requirement of all—painting it red. They added several coats of red spray paint to make it shiny, and Andy put pin-striping stickers across the top. The day of the race, Dad kept fussing with the graphite paste accidentally wiped on the side, but Andy held the car tight and insisted on taking his "Red" to the Pinewood Derby by riding in the Mini Cooper.

When we arrived at the Pinewood Derby in the church gym, we saw other boys lined up in front of "The Pit"—a room where the Cub Scouts weighed their cars, repaired wheels, and added graphite paint if their cars did not weigh exactly 5 ounces. Younger siblings flitted in and out of the room as excitement mounted. The cars reflected the imaginations of the boys—Andy's red Audi; Conner's rounded silver Porsche; Jared's orange race car with white numbers; and even Kenny's car that looked like a block of cheese with a clay mouse.

After the boys added the finishing touches to their cars, the leaders whooped and hollered to congratulate Andy as he placed his car alongside the bright display of cars. We all gathered in the gym decorated with checkered flags while Andy disappeared into the cluster of scouts, sidling up next to Kenny, the hands-down favorite from his posse. Bright and funny, Kenny walked with Andy to pick up a proper meal at the races—a hotdog, popcorn, soda, and a cookie. It was no surprise when Andy insisted on two hot dogs and even less surprising when the woman serving the food easily gave in, but I let it slide that night.

The program started with a flag ceremony. Andy placed his hand over his heart as he had learned to do at school, but as a more experienced Scout, Kenny looked over and subtlety lifted Andy's hand from his heart to his head, making the Cub Scout salute. Andy proudly stood among his pack wearing the navy Cub Scout shirt with the number of his new troop stitched on the sleeve. The Scout Master, wearing pit crew overalls with a blue cardboard car strapped around his waist, introduced himself as his professional racing alter ego, Billy-Bob Joe. He explained that the heats would consist of races between three cars, and that all of the boys would have the opportunity to race each other at some point. He emphasized the Cub Scout motto, "Do Your Best."

And so the races began. When their names were called, the boys moved toward the track to place their cars in position and waited for the lever to send the cars zooming down the rickety wooden track, which had flags that popped up when the first car hit the finish line. After several heats, Andy was called forward for his turn. Because Andy was unsure of exactly what to do on his first round, volunteers helped him place his car on the top of the track, and his smile erupted when the lever was released to send the cars rocketing down the path. When he was called for another heat, he knew just what to do and sprinted toward the track. Andy pumped his fists in the air as he approached each race and the audience grew more and more enthusiastic each time he placed the car in position. Chants of "Andy, Andy,

Andy" echoed through the gym for the boy who was so genuinely enjoying the race. He won some and lost some, but each time he celebrated at the start of the race just as much as he cheered at the end.

The crowd's enthusiasm was infectious as teenage siblings of the scouts wandered into the room after a youth group activity in the building, and they joined in the cheers for all the children. Shouts of "Go Jared!" and "Yeah Davey!" filled the room. That night, no one argued about who won the race or what numbers meant the best time. Parents clapped Connor on the back for making the shiniest Porsche, and children cheered together for Justin, the small boy who had just moved to town and decisively won the race. All the boys won prizes as unique as the cars they made. Andy claimed his prize for "Best Showmanship." The Cub Scouts lined up to display their cars for the final photo with their arms boyishly slung over the other members of pack—and my Andy right in the middle of them.

● ● ●

Stephanie is the mother of a son who was born with Down syndrome (2000) and two younger daughters. Her son, Andy, attends a Cub Scout troop where they live in Canton, GA. When she is not mothering a rowdy Cub Scout, a witty princess, or a fearless toddler, Stephanie also works as an editor, a part-time college English instructor, and a technical writer, including writing the Canister Down syndrome guides (www.canisterbooks.com).

Front row: Andrew Warren, Kelly Roper; 2nd row: Robin Warren Siegel, Donna Roper;
3rd row: Kevin Ewing, Christine Young, Dana Young;
Back row: Kathy Ewing, Gail Williamson, Blair Williamson, Susie Schallert

41.

Friends Indeed

By Dana Young

IT'S A BEAUTIFUL, warm spring day and I am fortunate to be spending it with great friends. Five of us are enjoying a leisurely lunch at a local restaurant on a lazy Saturday afternoon. As we eat, we share our concerns, our joys, and lots of laughter. On the surface, it might appear that we don't have much in common. Donna works from home helping to run the family business. Gail is the executive director of a nonprofit organization. Robin works part time in retail and donates time in volunteer service to her community. Kathy is retired from her job in the medical field. And I am an administrative assistant at a local university. Some of us are liberal, some conservative. Some of us are religious, some are not. We have different backgrounds, different economic levels, and different points of view.

In the booth next to ours is a group of six young adults, three men and three women. Like us, they are obviously enjoying each other's company, laughing and joking with one another. They talk about what to order, the dance some of them attended the night before, and what their futures will be like. Sometimes they whisper among themselves, making one wonder what secrets they are sharing; at other times they are downright boisterous. It is obvious that they have a comfortable familiarity and know each other well. Just another group of friends out for lunch, with one minor exception—all six of the people in the next booth have Down syndrome. They are our children.

Blair, Susie, Andrew, Kelly, Kevin, and Christine are remarkable individuals. Blair is rarely seen without his camera in hand. In fact, he was the official videographer at Christine's thirtieth birthday party. But mostly he takes still photos with his digital camera. He then loads them onto his computer and makes amazing slide shows set to music.

Susie is Blair's girlfriend. Blair's mother brings her along to our gatherings. At age forty, Susie is the "senior citizen" of the group. Susie plays hand bells and the piano. She swims every day to keep her girlish figure.

Andrew is madly and hopelessly in love with Kelly. He proposes regularly and presents gifts and cards every time he sees her. Attending Disney ice shows is his favorite activity. Andrew is incredibly artistic and is able to do amazing things on the computer. He can also crack his mom's passwords to order things from Ebay!

Kelly's beautiful auburn hair is the first thing you notice about her. That, and her infectious smile—it is impossible to be around her and not smile yourself. Kelly loves to dance. Just put the music on and she will move gracefully and fluidly. She is a joy to watch.

Kevin is a ladies' man. He loves all women and flirts unashamedly. It's hard to watch sometimes when his love is not reciprocated, but he always makes a full recovery–so many women, so little time!

Kevin is a writer. His seemingly continuous flow of imaginative and creative stories—all starring him, of course—is amazing.

My daughter Christine is my first-born child, my pride and joy. She and Kevin used to be a couple. Although no longer romantically entwined, they remain very good friends; their break-up was handled maturely and with respect for each other. Christine is very proud of her job in the shipping department of a local manufacturing company—and the paycheck that comes with it.

Two groups of friends, linked by one common thread: Down syndrome.

We became acquainted because our children are members of the Born to Act Players, a performing arts group for people with disabilities. As our children rehearsed, we got to know each other, discovering that we faced many of the same issues, had similar outlooks on how to deal with them, and—perhaps most importantly—we could find humor in our situations. We started going to lunch together occasionally, and the friendships grew.

When Christine was younger, I searched for support and guidance in raising her. I attended parent groups and contacted organizations looking for help. While those contacts were not in vain, they were quite limited. This was in the days before the Internet. I couldn't just Google "Down syndrome" and find information or support. The information I could find was usually out of date (the books in my local library still referred to Christine as a "Mongoloid idiot"). Many children with Down syndrome were still institutionalized in the 1970s, so there weren't mentors in the community. There was a lack of other parents who were successfully raising their children And most of those with whom I did have contact had lower expectations than I had for my child. What I needed, I realize now, was friends who understood. Around the table at lunch this day, I have those friends—friends who have been there, friends who "get it."

While it's wonderful that we can all understand the issues involved with having an adult child with special needs, our friendships transcend the chromosomal link. We celebrate with one another and we grieve with one another. We call each other to share good or bad news. Mainly, we support and laugh with each other. When I had some minor surgery, these friends took my daughter for three days. The Born to Act Players were putting on a show that weekend, and my friends worked together to make sure that she was well taken care of and where she needed to be. She ate at their tables and slept in their homes. They made sure that she was at the theater when she needed to be, helped her with costume changes, and applied her make-up. Sometimes one of us will take another's offspring for a day, just to give the other parents a break. One mom has sewn costumes for the children of those of us who find sewing to be a challenge. We have all enjoyed working together on projects that enrich our children's lives. We are on the same journey, and there could not be a better support system when a detour is encountered.

As our lunch winds down, we are reluctant to part ways. All of us—moms and our adult children—must return to our busy lives. But it will be a little easier because of the time we have spent together. I never dreamed that my child's diagnosis would lead us to lasting, close friendships with people we so thoroughly respect and admire. Yet sometimes the most wonderful gifts are hidden deep within challenging circumstances. Down syndrome is the link that has given two generations the gift of friendship, and all of our lives are much richer because of it.

● ● ●

Dana stays very busy keeping up with the hectic social schedule of her daughter Christine, who is the oldest of her three adult children. She also has three amazing grandchildren. Dana lives in southern California and is involved with the Down Syndrome Association of Los Angeles. She believes that life is better if you try to find humor in any situation.

Tess Fuller with friends Beth Smith and Savannah Redden

42.

True Success

By Nina Fuller

WHEN MY DAUGHTER Tess was a baby, she had dozens of adoring friends. In our home and at our boys' school and sports events, teenage girls hovered over Tess on a regular basis, goo-gooing over her extreme cuteness. But these weren't baby friends from the neighborhood, or preschool playmates—they were pretty, teenage girls with designer jeans, shiny lip gloss, and a glimmer in their eyes as they approached Tess. Each of my sons caught on fairly quickly that when they held their little sister, they would draw swarms of teenage admirers. They used their baby sister as a chick magnet and it worked!

Tess outgrew her brothers' arms and toddled her way into the hearts of thousands of adults who were surprised to see such a high-functioning child with Down syndrome. As a professional speaker, I would share our personal story about Down syndrome with audiences all over the country. In conclusion, I would introduce Tess and watch with motherly pride as she received standing ovations from audiences as she confidently toddled on stage. After my speeches, people would gather around to talk to Tess and get their picture taken with her. With her engaging presence and bright smile, Tess changed their thinking about Down syndrome, and they readily embraced her.

When Tess entered school, we were directed to a developmental kindergarten and then a Life Skills class. There were many positive elements about this elementary school setting: smaller class size with more concentrated teacher-student-aide time, practice of skills that would help Tess function in the outside world, and effective reinforcement of basic academics. With the combined efforts of home and school, Tess started to read on her own! She was able to engage in conversations with her teachers and aides about places she had been traveling and events and people she had met, and to use the typical banter that should take place among peers. Teachers often commented to me that Tess spent her free time talking with the adults. They loved her sense of humor and her honesty.

But in a way, Tess's comfort with adults highlighted a drawback to that particular classroom situation. Tess had been relating well to teens and adults her whole life, but she had no *real* friends, no peers with whom she could relate. I take that back—she and Nick were best buddies until second grade, when the gender conflicts began. Boy would tease girl. Girl would sulk all day and wait to retaliate. (But they're still talking marriage—at least Tess is—and one day, we shall see.) Since Tess was the only girl in her class, we knew the situation wasn't likely to improve. And as Tess got older, the self-contained Life Skills class wasn't challenging her enough academically. My husband and I realized that we needed to take a good, in-depth look at our other options.

Option one: Public school, with time split between Life Skills and General Education with typically developing peers. We'd tried this for two years previously, but the teachers were unable to learn how to accommodate Tess in their classes and failed to meet her needs academically and socially.

Option two: Public school, full-time General Education. Not appealing, given our prior experience. We'd learned from our split class experience that even the personal aides were not properly trained in assisting students—if Tess even received one. Plus, we worried she would fall through the cracks in a classroom of twenty-six or more students.

Option three: Home School. Some distinct advantages, but some significant disadvantages as well. Tess needed friends, and she needed accountability to other adults.

Option four: Private School. This seemed to be the best setting for Tess to reach the social, academic, and even spiritual goals we'd set for her. Tuition was expensive, but the academic and social price we were paying in public school was even more expensive.

Before the start of the new school year, we checked out a small Christian school in our community, and were excited to learn they were interested in having Tess as a student. We were not promised the moon, but we were received with open arms by the faculty. We also had high hopes that Tess would be warmly received by her class-mates, especially the girls. Finally, she'd have some real friends! They would invite her over to play, and she would have girl friends come play at our house.

But it wasn't as easy as I'd hoped. I'd forgotten about the pecking order that exists in many typical classrooms, especially among girls. Tess was used to being the center of attention at school and else-where. Now she was the new girl at school and had to learn to adapt to the social setting. There were times during the first few weeks that Tess was frustrated and got a bit aggressive with a couple of girls. I realized our goal of making new and healthy friendships would soon be lost if we did not intervene.

First, I explained to Tess that in order to have friends, *she* must *be* friendly. She needed to show kindness and gentleness. We talked in detail about some of the ways she could do that, and she agreed to try her very best.

Next, I got permission from the teacher to address the students one afternoon when Tess was absent. I explained a little bit about how Down syndrome makes it hard for Tess to speak clearly, and acknowledged that sometimes she gets frustrated because of this challenge. I thanked each of them for being patient with Tess. I pointed out that this was her first experience being in a regular classroom and that she was working hard in areas they find easy. I also reminded them that it's hard to be the new kid in school no matter what the situation. And, since this was a private Christian school, I was able to lead the class in a prayer. I asked God to bless them as they showed friendship to Tess and modeled appropriate behavior so she could learn how good friends act.

After I left, I thought about how I could show my appreciation to these girls and boys for their willingness to be friends with Tess. An idea began to take shape, and the following day I sat down and created invitations for a friendship party at the local bowling lanes. This wouldn't be a birthday party or a class fieldtrip, simply an opportunity for classmates to have fun together.

What I didn't know was at the very same time I was making the invitations, Tess's classmates were making friendship cards of their own! As Tess climbed in the car the following afternoon, she excitedly showed them to me one by one. One card read, "Tess, you are my best friend." Another, covered with multi-colored hearts and too big for basic postage, stated, "Tess I love you. I wish I WAS you." Tess giggled over each card, read each word to me, and even blushed when she read a card from one of the boys!

As the day of the party approached, I wondered how many of Tess's classmates would be interested in attending. Would they even take the invitations home to their parents and plan to come? Tess was excited at the opportunity to have a party with friends, and I hoped she wouldn't be disappointed. Then, one by one, parents called to confirm they would be with us. I felt so uplifted and encouraged by their willingness to participate.

As it turned out, nearly all of Tess's classmates attended the party, which was a great success. The students cheered for one another, and especially for Tess when she bowled a spare or a strike! High fives and lots of laughs were shared as classmates learned Tess was just like them in many ways. Friendships began to grow, and Tess had the time of her life doing the three things she loves most in the world: going bowling, eating pizza, and laughing with other kids.

Tess continues to thrive in private school. We are so thankful that the principal and teachers have been willing to learn how to modify the curriculum to help Tess, and we enjoy working with them to ensure that Tess reaches her full academic potential. But when I think of how well Tess is succeeding in life, the first thing that comes to mind isn't her progress in math and reading. It's the sight of her typically developing classmates encouraging her in the classroom, engaging her on the playground, and enjoying friendships outside of school. My daughter, at age thirteen, finally has a group of peers who include her in their lives. True friends, I believe, are true success.

●   ●   ●

Nina is the founder of two nonprofit organizations, S.M.I.L.E. on Down Syndrome and Living Proof Testimonies, and cofounder of a brand new online outreach at www.specialmoms.us. Nina is in demand as a keynote speaker, and has been able to share her personal story and message of hope as a guest on several television and radio talk shows throughout the country, as well as in print media. Her most recent book is Special Strength for Special Parents. Foremost, Nina is a committed wife of thirty years to Andy, and mother of five, ranging in ages from twenty-seven to five. The youngest two have Down syndrome: Tess, their biological daughter, and Hope, their daughter adopted at one day old.

43.

A Crash Course in Friendship

By Shannon Cooley

TWELVE-YEAR-OLD ZOË WAS excited to attend her first year of girls' camp, an annual event sponsored by her church, but her parents had mixed feelings. Although Zoë was a very smart and active girl with Down syndrome, she had never before spent a week away from home. Her parents finally agreed that she could go, as long as there would be someone there whom Zoë knew well and trusted. I had been a nanny for their family since Zoë was six years old, and Zoë and her siblings saw me as an older sister. Even though I had moved away earlier that year, Zoë's mother called and asked if I would travel the seven hours and go to camp as Zoë's companion.

I eagerly agreed to the arrangement. But during my drive to the camp, I had a lot of time to think about the coming week, and worry began to dampen my enthusiasm. What would I do if Zoë decided she didn't like sleeping in a tent? How would she react to so many people that she didn't know? Would we even have cell phone reception if I needed to reach her parents? I didn't know what to expect. As it turned out, what I received that week was a crash course in acceptance, patience, and love for which I will be eternally grateful.

Zoë reminded me to look beyond the labels. The first day of camp, the leaders anticipated the need to alter activities for her, but I convinced them to let her try on her own. We found her a seat next to a girl she already knew, and she was handed two pieces of rope, a stick, and a paper with instructions for knot-tying. All the other girls were curious about Zoë, and wanted her to succeed. Carefully the girls on either side of her demonstrated each knot, and Zoë copied their movements. Before long, she had successfully completed the knot-tying certification, just like the other girls her age. I was reminded of many other times Zoë had shown me that she was capable of far more than most realized. From beating the entire fifth-grade at a "hoops" contest to getting 100% on her spelling tests in a normal classroom at school, Zoë has always pushed the limits of her disability, confounding those who would see her only as "special needs." Having known her for so long, I was very aware of how capable she is, but it was rewarding to see others recognizing her abilities as well.

Zoë also reminded me about the value of patience. During our previous arrangement I'd had a lot of practice managing her need for structure and her sometimes-stubborn moods, but this new situation required more ingenuity than ever. She needed constant reassurance of where she was and what she would be doing next, which was often difficult to offer due to changes in the weather, menu, or other circumstances. At times Zoë would decide she was not interested in the current activity, and once she spent an hour sitting under a picnic table petting a dog while the other girls were working on First Aid.

As I struggled to find ways to keep Zoë comfortable and involved, I often turned to music. Having played the piano for years, I knew the influence music can have on emotions and attitudes. I discovered that if the other girls joined me in a rousing chorus of "Rudolph, the Red Nosed Reindeer" it was enough to lift Zoë's dragging feet and send her running ahead on our four-mile hike; conversely, gentle children's songs from church helped calm her as we tried to sleep in a tent with water seeping through the walls and ceiling, while peals of thunder shook the ground beneath us. As Zoë drifted off to sleep in that tent each night, I was inwardly praising every musician who'd ever written a children's song. A leaky tent in a thunderstorm is an uncomfortable place for anyone, and had I not discovered a way to calm Zoë's fears, I doubt we would have been able to finish out the week of camp.

Most of all, Zoë reminded me about the power of love. Again and again she would notice and remember small things people did, such as leading a camp song or helping her cook a marshmallow, and then she would bring it up the next time she saw them. I would see tired girls' faces light up as Zoë would announce "Kaylee my friend, help me roast marshmallows!" or "Alligator, your song, want it at my birthday!" The cheered-up girl would then tell anyone who would listen how much Zoë had appreciated her contribution. As I watched Zoë in action, I felt like a proud new grandmother flaunting a photo of her grandchild. But although I smiled knowingly at these girls' reactions, I myself was not immune to her charm. At seemingly random times, but often when I most needed it, Zoë would come close and whisper conspiratorially, "I love you Shani." Those four simple words would make up for hours spent coaxing and trying to be patient despite my own weariness or frustration.

Zoë gave her love freely, never questioning whether it would be returned, and I watched as her unconditional love helped those around her to find charity. As girls reached out to befriend and help her, they became more willing to reach out to one another. The result was a harmony that could never have occurred had each girl been focused on her own struggles or worries, such as the bugs, thunderstorms every night, or the teenage drama that can so easily occur when you gather that many girls in one place.

At the end of the week, Zoë and I were both exhausted but happy. She returned safely to her family, loudly singing camp songs everywhere she went. She had made many new friends, and influenced so many lives. One of them was my own. As I gave Zoë a hug and said goodbye, I knew she didn't understand it could be another year before she saw me again, but her hug couldn't have been any more enthusiastic had she known. As I traveled home, I smiled, thinking back on the week. I went to camp to help Zoë, but in the end, she helped me more than I could repay.

● ● ●

Shannon is a junior studying English at Brigham Young University-Idaho. She and her husband recently returned from China, where they taught English for one semester. The year after writing this story, she returned to camp with Zoë, and had another great week. Zoë continues to expand her own horizons, learning to ski and teaching everyone around her to love.

Joaquin Andres Sanchez and Andres Calvo Sanchez

44.
Joaquin and Andres

By Jennifer Varanini Sanchez

WHEN MY HUSBAND, Hector, and I learned we'd be adding a third son to our family, we were thrilled—although nervous about how we would handle all the testosterone! Immediately the search was on for the perfect name. For the first name we agreed on Joaquin, which means "founded by God." But what about a middle name? Our first two sons, Diego and Mateo, had been given middle names in honor of their grandfathers, and we wanted something special and familial for the new baby as well. I was a big fan of Tomas, my dad's favorite name and confirmation name. But

Hector favored Andres, the name of his favorite nephew who lives in Mexico City.

Hector has always had a special place in his heart for Andres, his sister Silvia's first son. He was with Silvia when she received Andres's diagnosis of Down syndrome, and as Andres grew up Hector formed a strong bond with him. I kept pushing for Tomas, thinking it sounded great with Joaquin, but Hector felt very strongly that he wanted to name this baby Joaquin Andres, to honor his nephew. So the decision was made. Little did we know that Joaquin and Andres would share more than a name.

The pregnancy was uneventful and healthy. We declined the blood screening for alpha-fetal protein, and opted instead for genetic counseling (since I was thirty-seven years old) and an ultrasound exam, which revealed no markers or flags for Down syndrome other than my age. I delivered Joaquin at thirty-eight weeks, and nobody suspected anything was amiss. But in the weeks that followed, Hector and I had the feeling that something was different about Joaquin. For me, it was what I'd call mother's instinct—I sensed in the pit of my stomach that there was an unresolved issue. Hector remembered the way Andres had looked as a baby, and thought Joaquin had that same look. By the time Joaquin was two and a half months old, we couldn't let it go any longer, and we requested a karyotype.

Thoughts of Andres were the first things that ran through my head when we got the results. "What are the chances?" I thought. We had named our son Joaquin Andres after our beloved nephew who has Down syndrome, and now we were learning that Joaquin had Down syndrome as well. It was surreal.

Silvia was the very first person we called when we got the news of Joaquin's diagnosis. We spent a few hours on the phone with her, comforted to remember what a good life she and Andres share. At eighteen years old, Andres loves to swim, see movies with his friends, hang out with his brothers, and, most of all, read books (his favorites are those in the Narnia series). He loves school, will soon graduate from high school, and plans to go to college. Thanks to Andres and Silvia, we had a shining example of how life can be with a child with

Down syndrome and that gave us immediate peace and hope in a time of great need.

Shortly after Joaquin was diagnosed, we took him to Mexico to meet the extended family. We gathered at the home of Victor (Hector's brother) and his wife, Ana Paula. The occasion was the fiftieth wedding anniversary of Hector's parents, and it was the first time in many years that the entire Sanchez family was reunited. Hector's parents renewed their wedding vows at their home and there was a big reception in Victor and Ana Paula's backyard with all six of Hector's siblings and the fifteen grandchildren.

We told Hector's parents about Joaquin when they picked us up from the airport the day before the party, but we waited to tell the extended family until everyone was together on the evening of the party, and the special occasion had nearly concluded. Silvia had decided not to tell Andres until the rest of the family was informed, as he might have a hard time keeping the secret. Therefore, when we introduced Joaquin at first, the family greeted him just like they had our other two boys. Despite the likeness in appearance Hector had noticed between Andres and Joaquin, no one suspected they had the same diagnosis. It was the hardest thing to wait and not tell everyone right away, but we didn't want to detract from the beautiful event of the vow renewal and the celebration afterward. After dinner, with much nervousness, we asked everyone to gather around us and then we shared the news.

"Joaquin has Down syndrome," we explained.

Hector's siblings were immediately supportive and received the news graciously. But we noticed that Victor, Hector's brother, had a peculiar look in his face. "I knew you were going to say that," he said.

Hector and I were surprised. "How did you know?"

"Because of Andres," he said, explaining that just half an hour earlier Andres had come upon Ana Paula carrying Joaquin up the stairs.

Ana Paula nodded. "When Andres saw me carrying Joaquin, he stopped and put his hand on Joaquin's head. From what he said, I got the feeling Joaquin might have Down syndrome. But it didn't seem to make any sense, so I didn't tell anyone except Victor," she explained.

"What did he say?" I asked.

"You're like me. You're just like me."

We were amazed. Did Andres see a part of himself in Joaquin? Was he referring to the fact that they share the same name? Was it something deeper than that?

We'll never fully understand what Andres meant, but we do know it was a powerful moment for the whole family. And Andres and Joaquin seemed to form an unusual bond during our stay. Andres never left Joaquin's side, and spent hours playing with and talking to his baby cousin. Both boys were so peaceful and content together. It was really wonderful to witness their interaction. Although Joaquin was too young to respond to Andres other than by smiling and gazing at him, it was clear that a special relationship was forming, a relationship we believe is "founded by God."

● ● ●

Jennifer is a stay-at-home mom of three busy boys and is co-owner of an online children's boutique. She lives with her husband, Hector, and their children in Sacramento, California. To follow the family's journey with Joaquin (2008), visit www.trisacharm.blogspot.com.

Mason Ponte (grandson) with Michael Pearce

45.

My Best Friend

By Michael B. Pearce

EACH OF US has events in our life that we recall with minute detail, even years after they've happened. Among mine is the birth of my five-year-old grandson, Mason. While I remember the births of my other three grandchildren, my memories are a bit hazy, and I sometimes need my wife to remind me about the dates and details. This isn't the case with Mason. Every minute of his birth day is a vivid picture in my mind.

I clearly recall meeting him for the first time; he was as cute as any baby I'd ever seen. My daughter had had a troubled pregnancy and I'd had my share of worry about this growing baby, but there he was, radiant in his mother's arms. Then, unexpectedly, the doctors came in and asked us to leave. My wife and I sat in the waiting room for what seemed like eight hours, although it was really only about forty-five minutes. Finally, the doctors came out of the room. They walked past us without acknowledging us, nor giving us permission to go back in. But we took their exit as our signal, and headed back in to see our newest grandchild, only to find the room far more somber than it was when we'd left.

It was then that, with some difficulty, my daughter told us that Mason had Down syndrome. The doctors could tell by the lines in his hands and feet. At first I thought they must have been mistaken. I can still feel the emotions that came over me when reality hit—they were complex and all over the place. I was never sad, but I was confused about what this diagnosis might mean for my grandson and for all of us, and worried for my daughter and her fine husband, Mark. They wouldn't experience, in exactly the same way we had been anticipating, the son we had been talking about for months. I began to realize that all the dreams I had for my grandson just wouldn't be, and I didn't know what would take their place. That next Sunday at church, one of our members put his arm around me and told me, "You've just received a very special gift." That was a much-needed positive thought I could hold onto.

Shortly before my daughter was discharged from the hospital, we had a conversation, just the two of us. She lay in her hospital bed, and I sat in the armchair close by. With concerned eyes, she looked at me and asked, "Dad, how are you doing?"

I knew what she meant. Could I accept this fate and deal with it? Was I disappointed? Could I be a grandfather, proud of my grandson, looking forward to celebrating all of his successes? I might be tempted to feel sorry for myself, but I noticed she wasn't feeling sorry for herself—she was moving on.

At first I wasn't sure how to respond. But as I sat there, some words suddenly came to me. They weren't anything I had thought of; they just came out—a person of faith might say God gave them to me. "You know, sweetheart, I'm realizing that it won't be long before my other grandchildren see me as just an old man who tells dumb jokes. But Mason will need me for the rest of my life. As far as I'm concerned, I've just met my best friend."

And that's the way it has turned out. Mason runs with outstretched arms to greet "Papa" every time he sees me. He's never too busy or preoccupied when I come to visit. We play baseball together in the backyard, we take outings to the park and the ice cream store, we watch together as demolition crews tear down great big buildings in our city. Mason has a wonderful personality, he likes to tease and joke. His classmates ("typical" children) invite him to their birthday parties and run to greet him when we show up at the door. He's not the same as they are, and they know it, but he's a special friend and they embrace him and his differences. His parents are role models for us all: patient, yet firm; keeping realistic expectations, yet assuring Mason in every way that he will have a good and productive life.

I still worry about my grandson. He has any number of health issues. His mother is a world-class nurse, but when Mason gets sick, he gets really sick, and it scares me. He doesn't really understand boundaries yet, and that scares me. He's not without his challenges. At the same time, he's come so much farther than I could've hoped in those first few days, when suddenly I saw people with Down syndrome everywhere I looked.

Mason is a bright, fun kid. He's gentle and kind, yet he has his own strong will which I enjoy seeing, even if it frustrates his mom and dad occasionally. He takes me as I am, and makes me feel good about being with him. He is my loyal supporter, my pride and joy. Yes, Mason is my best friend.

●   ●   ●

Michael lives in Bellevue, Washington, with Susan, his wife of forty years. They have two daughters, both married, and four grandchildren. Mason is the second of the four grandchildren, and the only boy. Michael is a partner in OneAccord, a frequent speaker, and has published numerous business articles and one book on professional sales titled Don't Shoot the Piano Player. *He enjoys golfing, traveling, scuba diving, reading, and spending time with his grandchildren.*

THE GIFT OF COURAGE

Sterling Grooms and Tommy Kremer

46.

Brave in the Attempt

By Tommy Kremer

Let me win; but if I cannot win, let me be brave in the attempt.
—Special Olympics motto

FOUR YEARS AGO I got a call from my sister-in-law, saying her volunteer organization was looking for a weightlifting coach for some Special Olympics Athletes. After pausing for a second I said I would do it. I'd been coaching weightlifters for twenty-eight years, and I have a degree in Nutrition and Exercise Science from Virginia Tech. I felt this opportunity was a way to give back. My sister-in-law said I'd be coaching a man with Down syndrome, which didn't seem like too big of a deal. Little did I know what effect it would have on me.

I met the guy at Winchester Fitness, a facility which generously donated time and space for us to train. His name was Sterling Grooms. He was thirty-two years old, somewhat shy and unassuming, but boy, was he strong. As the meeting progressed, we joked and laughed a lot, so he liked me. But the organizers and myself were a bit apprehensive about how Sterling would do. I had never worked with an athlete with special needs and the area leader said he was unmotivated to work hard. But I was able to change that.

Sterling and I motored right along and developed a close bond quickly. We trained two days on, one day off. I was his training partner, doing the same lifts and exercises he needed to do to prepare for competition, and he would try to out-do me. We motivated each other. If I saw he was getting bored I would change the routine. We were like peas and carrots—always together.

Our first meet was the VMI Games, hosted by the wonderful cadets from the Virginia Military Institute in Lexington, Virginia. Sterling was excited, but I was nervous because I didn't know what to expect at such an event. When we entered the venue I was a bit overwhelmed by all the athletes, volunteers, and spectators in attendance. The sight was truly impressive as well as intimidating. But Sterling was an old pro, so he helped me figure out where to go and what we needed to do.

After an opening ceremony, the athletes gathered in their prospective competition areas. Sterling and I headed to the gym. When we got there, I started introducing myself to the other coaches, but Sterling knew everyone already. Checking out the competition, I quickly realized Sterling was the man to beat. That didn't help my nerves, though. As our start time drew closer I started to get excited, but figured I needed to concentrate on keeping Sterling focused. I soon found out that he doesn't need to keep focused—he just goes out there and does it.

Let the games begin! A powerlifting competition is comprised of three lifts: the bench press, squat, and deadlift. The VMI football players were on hand as volunteers, spotting the lifters and changing the weights for the competitors. As the meet progressed, the football players were incredibly impressed with the athletes' strength. I was nothing less than blown away by the ability of these athletes, including Sterling and all his friends. This was true competition the way it was intended: no stare downs, no *I'm going to beat you*, just admiration and applause for the efforts of all. Sterling won the competition by benching 245 lbs., squatting 275 lbs., and deadlifting 345 lbs. I was elated that he won, but even more impressed by the spirit shown by all the athletes. When I congratulated Sterling, he just smiled and said, "Wait until Richmond."

Richmond. He meant the state-level games, a very big event. I mean *big*. I wondered, what did I get myself into? I soon found out. After three months of intense training, we arrived at the games. The campus at The University of Richmond was full of athletes, coaches, chaperones, volunteers, and spectators. A mind-bending spectacle. It was no big deal to Sterling, but I was a nervous wreck. As a Global Messenger for Special Olympics, Sterling gave a speech at the opening ceremony, in front of a packed arena. He blew everyone away with his encouraging words about what Special Olympics means to him. I was sobbing like a baby. Afterward, Sterling patted my shoulder and said, "It's okay." That made me chuckle.

The weightlifting competition was held the next day. Sterling and I got up early for the weigh-in. Sterling was 180.5 lbs., which was perfect for his 181-pound weight class. But when I saw the other competitors I got nervous again. There were some *big* boys in Sterling's class. He told me not to worry. He said, "Tommy, I will win." At the time I didn't know that he had never lost once in the eleven years he'd been competing.

That day Sterling continued his streak of victories with lifts of 275 lbs. in the bench, 365 lbs. squat, and 405 lbs. on the deadlift. The win landed him many admirers and status as a local celebrity.

We set our sights on the Special Olympics World Summer Games in Shanghai, China. Sterling and I were hopeful he'd be chosen, but it wasn't a sure bet. After many suspenseful weeks I got the call from Sterling: "Guess what Tommy, I'm going to China." He had trained so hard his whole life, waiting for an opportunity like this. Boy, was I happy for him! I called everyone in my family to let them know, and they were really excited too. But after I calmed down, I thought, Oh my gosh, what have I done? Sterling had won every competition he had ever entered, but now he must do it on the world stage, the biggest stage of all. I tried to help Sterling understand how big of a deal this was, and that he needed to dig deep. I knew he wanted to win so badly, yet I wasn't sure he could. But then Sterling's words resonated in my mind: *Tommy, I will win.*

The next time we were together I asked him if he really wanted to do this, and he said yes. I asked if he was sure, and he said yes. I asked if he really thought he would win. He said yes. So that was that. We moved forward with the training, and it went very well. Sterling began fundraising for the trip, and since he was the local celebrity, he got a lot of press. Every bit was well deserved. Many people donated money to support his shot at gold, and Sterling was on his way.

Now that Sterling was an athlete for Team USA, the coaches from Olympic Headquarters in Colorado Springs were his new trainers, which meant I didn't get to go to China with him. I wished so badly that I could go with him, and Sterling wished I could come too. But I got to attend the send-off party in Richmond for all the Virginia athletes and their families—that's right, I was now family. As Sterling traveled, he called me during every layover—New York, San Francisco, Alaska—and told me about all the new friends he was meeting along the way. When he landed in China and began training with his new coach, I was jealous. Sterling had been all mine, my pride and joy.

The day of the competition, I was a wreck. Sterling's meet took place late at night in my time zone, but I told him to call afterward no matter what the time. His brother called around 11:00 p.m. and said Sterling had won gold in the squat event and the bench event. I was elated, and so wound up I paced the floor while I waited for the news about the deadlift event, which was Sterling's best lift. At 1:00 a.m., the call came: Sterling had won the deadlift, and therefore the whole event for his weight class! He benched 267 lbs., squatted 385 lbs., and deadlifted 447.5 lbs for the victory. I was so ecstatic I ran through the house screaming, waking everyone up. I couldn't sleep at all. Then

Sterling came on the phone. We talked for about forty-five minutes. I told him how proud I was of him, and he was so happy. "I told you I would win, Tommy," he said. "I wish you were here too." We talked for such a long time, he used up almost all of his calling card minutes. When he called his Dad, he only had time to say, "I won! But sorry Dad, I can't talk long. I talked too much to Tommy."

The champ came home as a bona fide celebrity. He was asked to participate in the Shenandoah Valley Apple Blossom Festival, and I got to ride with him in the parade. Sterling was beaming the whole time, and I was touched by the appreciation shown by the spectators who gave him standing ovations along the way. Together we attended the sports breakfast where we heard motivational speeches from Jerry Rice, Gale Sayers, Kelly Washington, and Nadia Comaneci. Then it was Sterling's turn to address the packed crowd. Like usual, I was nervous. And like usual, Sterling did a fantastic job. He is truly an amazing speaker. After his speech he hugged me, and the whole place erupted in cheers and clapping. Another standing ovation. Sterling was on top of the world, sharing hope and courage and inspiring all of us to follow our dreams.

Sterling and I continue to lift weights together, although we don't train hard like we used to. But we enjoy each other's company, and we laugh at each other in our daily routines—sometimes we laugh too much! I just want to thank Sterling for being my friend and taking me on this amazing journey. What a ride. Thanks, buddy. I'm extremely proud of your accomplishments and of the person you are. You won your competitions again and again, but even more importantly, you were brave in the attempt.

● ● ●

Tommy lives on the east coast. He is a Virginia Tech Alumnus. He has a beautiful mother, father, brother, and sister-in-law, and has three awesome nephews who are the best. He enjoys sports, fitness, and coaching kids.

Diane and Michelle Chrisman

47.
Defining Moments

By Diane Chrisman

YOU KNOW THOSE defining moments in life when something happens that changes everything you planned on and expected your life to be?

The first defining moment in my life came in September 1989, when my husband, Dan, came home from work with disappointing news: the company he had worked for for thirteen years had been sold. I had news of my own that he wasn't happy about—I was pregnant with our fourth child. We lived with stress and uncertainty through the winter, and in the early spring the company was sold again, this time to four crooks who drained the company dry, pocketing all the employees' health insurance premiums, income tax withholdings, and 401K contributions, which left us penniless. A nightmare come true, and it only got worse: a month after our daughter was born, we found out that she had Down syndrome. Overwhelmed with paying for all the medical bills from her birth, we now could not obtain health insurance because she had a "preexisting condition."

My husband, along with three partners, started an industrial insulation company to provide for our family. While he was busy building the business, all of Michelle's therapy, love, and care were my responsibility, along with keeping the rest of our family intact. This was an extreme challenge. Even in 1990 there was little up-to-date information on Down syndrome—our pediatrician even mentioned that there were "places to put her"! I spent a lot of time researching treatments, therapies, anything that would improve the quality of my daughter's life. I found myself consumed with her daily care, which included IEP meetings and monthly changes of speech, occupational, and physical therapists. The stress took its toll both emotionally and physically. When I could no longer pick up my toddler without pain, I was diagnosed with fibromyalgia, and began a search for relief from medical doctors as well as alternative therapies.

Thankfully, things began to get better for all of us. After three disappointing years of putting up with the public school's idea of "educating" my daughter, I decided to home school Michelle and take the credit for teaching her colors, numbers, letters, and how to say and write her name. Home schooling was always fun because everything we did could become a lesson. For one of her very first lessons, we gathered up everyone's stuffed bears and counted them, sorted them by size and color, then by owner. Michelle loved to make lists of all the characters in her favorite movies and TV shows, which became the catalyst for her learning to read. I would take pictures of her doing different activities, such as painting, cup stacking, completing workbooks, and horseback riding, and we would then make story books to read at bedtime. To practice counting, Michelle had 100 plastic bears that we would take turns hiding under cups to determine how many were missing. Our days were relaxed and entertaining and I was able to teach to her strengths of learning visually and kinesthetically.

When Michelle was nine, she began to participate in Special Olympics. Her Dad would try to get home from work in time to take us to her practices, and eventually became Michelle's unified partner in bowling and bocce ball, which enabled her to share learning experiences with her father as well. Michelle doted on her Daddy, always glad for him to come home so she could "help" him around the house and yard, and occasionally he would even take her to work with him, where she would make copies on the copy machine. Although there was always stress of some kind sneaking its way in, our family life had greatly improved since the early years.

And then, the next defining moment came.

February 25, 2003. Our three older children were young adults; Michelle was twelve. Dan came home from work at the usual time. We ate homemade tacos for dinner, then I cleaned the kitchen while Dan rode the exercise bike. I settled in the living room to read a book and Dan went downstairs to watch the KSU Wildcats basketball game. At 7:30 p.m., he came upstairs for a glass of water, then went back downstairs. At 8:30 p.m., Michelle went downstairs to say her special goodnight to Dad. A minute later, she called to me, "Mom, I can't wake up Daddy."

I went downstairs and saw that our lives had been turned upside down. Dan had apparently suffered a heart attack and passed away. After I called 911 and performed CPR, our house quickly filled with police, firemen, and EMTs. But their efforts to revive Dan were to no avail. I was not only devastated but bewildered; Dan had never been sick a day of our twenty-six years of marriage. I'm ashamed to admit it, but I'd assumed that having a special child was extra insurance against tragedies like this.

Grief does one of two things to families—brings them closer together or tears them apart. In many ways, ours was torn apart. The three oldest children were preoccupied with attending college, searching for jobs, and pursuing their own dreams. The burden of our family's grief fell upon my shoulders and Michelle's. There were days that we just simply existed rather than go through the motions of school and living. Shared mealtimes ended: gathering as a family was already uncomfortable, and sitting at the table was worse because Dan's seat was empty. Michelle had to hold me in my tears as often or more than I held her in hers. But as a result, our mother/daughter relationship became a deeper friendship, and, slowly and painfully, our new life moved forward. We returned to the routine of schoolwork, got more involved with Special Olympic sports, and relied on God to get us through this difficult time.

Michelle was at the age to begin religious instruction at our church, which would culminate with her sharing her faith story with the congregation and then being confirmed. Because of her learning challenges, which by this time also included some hearing loss, I included her religious instruction as part of her home schooling, using lots of arts, crafts, and sign language to reinforce the written words.

During this period, I read about a member of a popular Christian band who had lost his father and had written a song about wondering what his Dad was seeing in heaven. I arranged for Michelle to use this song as part of her confirmation, and set the date for Father's Day, in honor of her Dad. As the sun shone down upon her through the skylights, she presented her faith story, signing the words to the song, "I Can Only Imagine" by Mercy Me. Needless to say, there wasn't a dry eye in the congregation as Michelle expressed her faith, courage, and love for her Dad. It was a powerful defining moment to watch my daughter stand up in front of the congregation and minister to them. I was awed by the strength God had given me and my family to carry on.

Our next defining moment came in 2005, when we were forced by financial and familial reasons to leave our home with all its memories and move to a smaller house. Michelle and I became an even stronger team, depending on one another for love and companionship. With her brothers and sister living in their own places, I had to teach Michelle to share in some of the responsibility of taking care of our house, and we found a rhythm that works for us. We were able to continue home schooling, and we played a lot of games and did a lot of artwork together. Because of her activity in Special Olympics, we spent more time in the car, going to a practice nearly every day of the week and competitions once a month. After a long week of school and sports practices, we would reward ourselves by taking in a Friday afternoon movie.

To this day, I work very hard to help Michelle become her best self and she helps me do the same, simply by being who she is. Sometimes people tell me I need a break from Michelle, a job that doesn't include her. It's true that our lives are sometimes hard, often lonely, and always expensive. I continue to spend a lot of time worrying and second guessing my decisions about her life. But I wouldn't have it any other way.

Michelle has self-confidence that many people envy. She is a good consumer: she makes people do their jobs, whether finding a store clerk to locate an item on her list, a waitress to refill her drink, or a lifeguard at the pool to keep a closer watch on everyone. If she has money in her billfold, she will pick up the check in a restaurant, or put it in the offering plate at church or the Salvation Army bucket. I can count on her to help in any situation, even when she really doesn't want to. She's always striking up conversations with strangers and is willing to try new things, which is how we discovered her gift for photography. Her quirky sense of humor fills our days with laughter and her joy at the little things helps me not to take stress and worry so seriously. The person I have become because of Michelle is someone I admire.

Our most recent defining moment came on June 9, 2008, when Michelle and I appeared before a judge to establish my legal guardianship of her. Michelle had turned 18, which meant that she was considered a legal adult; entitled to vote, get married, and make her own financial and medical decisions. Was she capable of these decisions? As much as we had worked on money skills, she still thought that she could buy a forty-four dollar DVD set with whatever dollar bills she had in her billfold. With her hearing loss, she might not be able to comprehend the questions nurses and doctors would ask of her. Reluctantly, I determined she could not make her own decisions. In the eyes of the law she became my total responsibility, and after all I'd invested in teaching her over the years and all she'd accomplished, I felt as if I'd stripped it all away from her. I could only hope that she would trust that my decisions for her life would be in her best interest.

I did not realize how hard it would affect me emotionally to take this step alone, as a single mom. Having no one to lean on and share in this decision was heart wrenching. But my heart was touched when the lawyer asked her who she would want as her guardian, and she answered "My mom." Once again, her love sustained me through a difficult time, and we survived this moment as we'd survived the others. I'm sure we'll have more defining moments come along as the years go by, but I'm willing to bet that we'll get through each one with the love, courage, and faith that we have *together*.

● ● ●

Diane spends much of her time in her car, driving Michelle to her activities and sports practices. She also enjoys being artistic with painting and mosaics, and using her musical talents by singing, playing piano and guitar, and composing music for church, weddings, and funerals. She loves coaching Special Olympics sports and is the coordinator for a club for young adults with disabilities that meets once a month. In her spare time, she tends to her home, her daughter, and two dogs in Blue Springs, MO.

Tanner, Teagan, and Tyler Klingenberg

48.

Rearview Mirror

By Juergen A. Klingenberg

SHE RUNS INTO the family room, eyes darting side-to-side, somehow knowing that the boys are close on her heels chasing their favorite playmate. Our tiny two-and-a-half-year-old, bald-headed munchkin is again seeking a hiding spot during a game of "Where's Baldo?" Playfully, the boys stumble over toys and furniture, opening squeaky cupboards and avoiding the obvious hiding place behind the couch pillow. They ignore her increasing giggles to prolong the game just a few more seconds before starting the chase all over. As we watch, thankful that the hair loss seems to be the only lasting ill effect from her chemo treatments, we reflect on that fateful day nine months ago, when with sad eyes we looked into the rearview mirror while heading to the hospital to begin our battle against the deadly disease of Acute Myeloid Leukemia. There sat our daughter, oblivious to the trauma ravaging her body and the further trauma of treatment that was to come.

It's hard to remember the first time we looked in the rearview mirror with such sadness, back when our daughter was only two weeks old. Minutes earlier my wife, Holly, and I had left the pediatrician's office with the much unexpected news that our newborn tested positive for trisomy 21. Our initial reaction was, *Trisomy what?* The doctor looked at us with apprehension, repeating slowly and cautiously the words "Down syndrome," while handing us some informative papers to help us understand. Our oldest son, Tyler, witnessing as the shock and devastation slowly drained the blood from our faces, bravely came over, and stated, "It's not the end of the world, she just may need a little extra help sometimes." But it certainly felt like the end of the world in those dark, early hours of the unknown, when our minds filled with unwarranted fear, our hearts seemingly broken beyond repair. When I looked in the rearview mirror and saw our tiny daughter, my horrible thought was *What is that thing in the back seat?*

But in our minds, that devastating "diagnosis day," or "D" day as we called it, is overshadowed by a day that made Down syndrome pale in comparison: the day we met Cancer. The exact moment is etched in my mind forever. Having received the results of our daughter's blood tests, my wife walked into the room pale and shaken. "It's Leukemia," she uttered. I couldn't breathe, but somehow managed to whisper "Her hair...." How could this happen to my sweet, tiny, innocent baby girl? How could she possibly fight this insurmountable challenge? How could we? How could we tell the boys? What if she dies? She can't. *She can't!*

During my endless trips between home and the hospital, as I looked in the rearview mirror and saw the empty car seat, I had plenty of time to reflect on how we'd taken for granted the beauty of life, with its ordinary days and simple achievements. How the stress of a long workday would be washed away as she would greet me at the back door, smiling, with her arms stretched out, signing a double handed "I Love You" and accentuating that with a loud and proud, deep toned "I uv u...."

Even now, my heart still aches as I remember the look of terror on my daughter's face, lying in the PICU connected to that horrible bundle of tubes, wires, and lifesaving machines. Only my love for her gave me the strength to carry on. At her bedside, I'd sit for hours and silently ask her to fight, fight, fight.... And fight she did! Her positive attitude and amazing resilience worked miracles, as did her trisomy 21 diagnosis, which helped her survive and beat the deadly cancer. *Fight! Fight! Fight!* she'd chant while pumping her tiny fists high in the air. It became our battle cry for nine months as we rallied to bring her back to full strength and reunite our family at home. And when she did return, I looked into the rearview mirror with the broadest smiles and tears of joy.

These days, as we travel for monthly oncology check-ups, I look into that same mirror and see an amazing three-and-a-half-year-old girl with wild, curly hair and beautiful brown eyes. With an infectious smile, she asks for the "edphoone" (headphones) so she can listen to Elmo's laughter during the drive. In her short years she has already faced many more challenges than most of us will ever have to endure. Those experiences led me to fear, to doubt, and to question my faith, but in the midst of that darkness my daughter taught our family laughter, courage, joy, and a true understanding of unconditional love. The boys have become impervious to her irrelevant diagnosis of Down syndrome. In fact, our younger son asked if she still had it. He doesn't see her as different. She's just his little sister, a perfect person to torment and love in classic big-brother style. Like right now. The game of "Where's Baldo?" has just ended, and the living room is full of the joyful noise of two laughing boys—and one giggling girl. Her name is Teagan, which means "Beautiful Princess." *And she is!*

● ● ●

Juergen lives in Saratoga Springs, New York, and shares his life with his wife, Holly, and their three children, Tyler, Tanner, and Teagan.

Their daughter Teagan was diagnosed with Down syndrome two weeks after birth and AML Leukemia at nineteen months. A graphic designer by trade, Juergen enjoys being involved with the local Down Syndrome Resource Center, creating many of their marketing materials and publications. To read more about Juergen and his loved ones, visit their family website at www.teamteagan.com. He dedicates his story to Teagan, his beautiful princess.

Brent, Colleen, and Ryan Bailey

49.
Heroes

By Colleen J. Bailey

HERO: "A PERSON of distinguished courage or ability, admired for his brave deeds and noble qualities." Heroes save us. Heroes overcome adversity. Heroes inspire us. Heroes change us forever. When our firstborn child arrived in our twenty-first year of marriage, my husband and I were elated. When we received the diagnosis of Down syndrome, we were devastated.

Four weeks after Ryan's birth, I sat alone and cold on a remote country road staring at all the prescription bottles I had grabbed before leaving the house. Sleep deprivation had set in after weeks of worrying about my newborn's health and future. He didn't have the strength to breastfeed. I felt like a failure. I thought that someone else would be a better mom. My husband rushed home from work to join the search for me. While family and friends were praying, flashes of my newborn's innocent face and gentle disposition gave me the courage to return home. Ryan needed a hero. And while I was pretty sure it wouldn't be me, I was determined to find him one.

A year later we met Rachel, a young adult with Down syndrome who cheerfully took pictures at a luncheon our local Down syndrome group hosted for champion swimmer Karen Gaffney. At first, I was just impressed that Rachel could use a digital camera. My admiration grew as we formed a friendship. Rachel has worked in a local CPA office locating and managing documents with ease because of her extraordinary memory, and also, more recently in an upscale delicatessen. While visiting Rachel at her office for her television interview about the Buddy Walk, I noticed how friendly she was to all her coworkers. Her volunteer association with the national AMBUCS group resulted in our son receiving a specially designed Amtryke bicycle for people with mobility challenges.

During Ryan's second year, we met Lisa. Ryan's speech pathologist had told us about an amazing young woman with Down syndrome who was on tour with the national Women of Faith organization. After some inquiries, Lisa's mom and I began communicating. I was treated to a private performance of Lisa's beautiful sign language accompanied by Sandi Patty's music. A year later, after attending a taping of her performance for a televised TBN concert with Sandi Patty, I overheard ladies talking in the restroom. "That Lisa gave me chills," expressed one concert patron. "Did you see how passionate that young girl was in her performance?" another one asked. I just listened from behind the closed stall door and smiled. Did I mention Lisa performed on the Dr. Phil show too and now has her own website and talent agent?

As Ryan continues to grow, I'm grateful for heroes like Josh who are exceptional role models. He was raised to respect ladies and was named 2007 Goodwill Ambassador for our local Buddy Walk. Every time I see Josh, he kisses my hand like a true gentleman. His character is invaluable in this world and a real gift that stands out in a crowd. The first time we met, he offered me not just a serving of pretzels, but the entire unopened family-size bag! Josh's parents emphasized appropriate behavior as he grew into adulthood, which makes him a true delight and joy to be around. Thanks to him, my husband and I have a clearer understanding of how we want to raise our son.

My other heroes include the individuals and families in the Down syndrome community we've been privileged to meet since Ryan's birth five years ago. I used to fear their company, thinking I would break down and cry. The sight of another family reminded me of the uncertainties and challenges we were facing, which somehow made it harder to cope at first. Tears of joy are more often the case now, and the quiet goodness, determination, and courage of these friends brings me peace. When Alex was introduced to us she was prompted to count in Spanish—and she was only four years old! Dylan came through his open heart surgery as a newborn and is thriving in school now. Alexis is the little princess and pride of her family. Kirsten reminds us that life is fragile and moves her parents on to greater purpose. Allison recovered from leukemia treatments at a very young age and now plays actively with her sister and friends. Natalee has such a gentle spirit and shares her toys readily. Sweet Kate wasn't phased about her recent heart surgery. Blessed stillness in my heart has replaced so many fears I once clung to desperately.

Other heroes of mine include people and families I have not had the privilege to meet in person, yet have had a powerful impact on my life. The writers of the first volume of *Gifts* propelled me onward and upward to greater heights in my wonderful journey with Ryan. Each author offers something similar and something different that we're sharing as moms. On the last page of the book, Jennifer Groneberg writes, "He is the child that I wanted, *that I did not know I wanted*. He is my son." I echo those words.

Thanks to my heroes, I no longer doubt my ability to love and care for Ryan. I watch him listen and learn on a daily basis, and he inspires me to do the same. At the church where my dad is pastor, I once listened to Ryan recite all of Psalm 23, holding a big microphone in hand and bringing the audience to tears. Recently I listened to his insightful thoughts regarding the world economy: "All these people. It's a big mess. Eat oatmeal." Of all the heroes I've met since his arrival, Ryan is my greatest. I can still see those dark newborn eyes that sweetly gazed into mine when I told him goodbye on that terrible day shortly after his birth. Somehow I sensed he was communicating to me that I'd be back.

It hurts to look back on that awful afternoon when I considered taking my own life, but at the same time I'm amazingly grateful and humbled to have experienced a pain and heartache so great that I can understand when another mom says, "I don't know how to do this." When I meet such parents in my local area, I offer them a complimentary copy of *Gifts* from our East Texas Down Syndrome Group and hope they will meet some of their own heroes within its pages. Then I think of Ryan, and I thank God for this boy, this challenge, and this joy that surpasses any experience I've ever known.

● ● ●

Colleen lives in East Texas with Brent, her husband of twenty-six years. Her son Ryan (2003) was diagnosed with Down syndrome at birth. Colleen's recently published writings include "Signing with Sandi" in Windows Into Heaven *(2008) and marketing materials for Amazing Grants, Inc. She is active with the East Texas Down Syndrome Group, having previously served on their board. Other heroes of hers include her husband and parents.*

Heidi and Jacob Moore

50.

The Power of One Phone Call

By Heidi J. Moore

WHEN MY SON Jacob, who has Down syndrome, was three years old he found it hard to interact with the outside world because sign language was his only viable means of communication. His speech wasn't developing as fast as his desire to speak to the world. He had so much to say to people, but they did not always understand him, and that brought him great frustration.

We did our research and discovered that there was amazing augmentative technology that allowed children and adults to touch pictures on a computer screen and hear the words pronounced aloud.

This touch screen computer would allow my son to express his basic needs and wants with his family and the world around him. We went to our local children's hospital, and they determined that he had the ability to use a fairly sophisticated device, but it cost six thousand dollars. After discussions with the school, it became clear that they were not going to purchase the computer that was recommended by the hospital specialists.

I refused to take no for an answer. I had never had any formal training in advocating for Jacob, but, like all mothers, I had the love, desire, and compassion to make sure he received all the supports he needed to maximize his potential in life. I found out we could pay for the computer through Medicaid, but it was a very difficult system to navigate. After talking to a few parents about my concern, I decided to call my state senator. I thought his career background in medicine might grant him compassion and understanding of my son's need for this equipment. I was a little intimidated to call him at first but then I realized that his job was to represent me. So I thought, "What have I got to lose?"

When I called Senator Tom Price (who is now U.S. Representative Price), I asked him, "How would you feel if someone took away your voice box? How would you feel if you could not express your basic needs and wants with your family? How can the state put a price tag on being able to communicate with the world?" This got his attention, and I was able to make my case for Jacob's need for the communication device.

Within three hours of my conversation with Senator Price, I received a phone call from Medicaid wanting to know how they could help me. I stated that I had requested authorization to purchase the computer and had not heard back from them in over two months. Much to my surprise, Medicaid approved the purchase practically on the spot. A few days later I got a phone call from the computer manufacturer, DynaVox Technologies, stating that not only had they received an approved purchase order for Jacob's computer, they had also received approvals for over fifty families who had been waiting for over a year and a half!

At that moment, I started to understand the power of advocacy. I raised my voice with the initial idea of simply helping my son. However, my phone call exposed a greater problem, and suddenly children all over the state of Georgia would soon be able to tell their parents that they were hungry, or cold, or that they loved them. I wasn't in a position of power to actually make any changes myself, but I was able to help those in power see the problem, and they responded. Because of my phone call and a state official who was willing to listen, we were literally able to give the children of Georgia a "voice."

Fast forward to today. Since my first brush with advocacy a few years ago, I have gotten involved in many areas of need in the disability arena. I have organized two healthcare rallies at our state's capitol. I have been involved with various state committees regarding Medicaid waivers, home and community based programs, and special education reform. I started out with an advocacy distribution list of 100 members after my first healthcare rally. Today, I have a distribution list of over 2,500 members. More than ever, I understand the power of networking, educating, and developing alliances in all areas of my children's lives. This willingness can bless the lives of many families beyond my own.

I share these experiences not to boast, but to hopefully inspire others to look around and see how they might act as advocates for their children. Fortunately, we don't always have to have the answers or even the direct power to make the change ourselves. We can literally speak for our children when they cannot. Sometimes, just being willing to pick up the phone and talk to the right person can open doors that once seemed impenetrable. There is a definite need to educate administrators, legislators, and others in positions of influence about the needs of children with disabilities, but how can they "fix" the problem if they don't know it exists? This informative role is one that parents can excel in, because they are motivated to the greatest extent possible, and therefore they have the power to motivate others.

I'm pleased to say that for four years the augmentative computer did help my son to develop his vocabulary and language skills, as well as to communicate with his world. Today, he is speaking simple sentences and continues to use sign language as a backup form of communication. I'm just so glad I made that one phone call.

● ● ●

Heidi lives in Alpharetta, Georgia, with her husband, Steven, and two children, Jacob and Jared. Heidi is very involved in many organizations and committees throughout Georgia. Currently, she has a distribution list of more than 2,500 members to promote awareness of the advocacy issues that affect children and adults with disabilities, and empower parents with information to help make necessary changes for individuals with disabilities. Heidi can be reached at heidijmoore@ comcast.net or www.heidijmoore.com.

Beverly Beckham and Lucy Rose Falcone

51.

Loved and Cherished, She Thrives

By Beverly Beckham

I STRAP HER into her car seat and tell her that we are going to the doctor. And she smiles at me and says, "Mimi's house."

"First we're going to the doctor, Lucy, then you can come to my house, OK?" And then we sing, in big, booming voices, "Police officers, firefighters, a doctor, or a nurse. They help me if I'm hurt. They help me if I'm hurt!" over and over until we arrive at Norwood Hospital.

Lucy, my granddaughter, is almost five, but she was only three days old when we came here for the first time—the entire family, her mother and father, aunts and uncles, her grandfather and I. "She has three holes in her heart," Dr. Geggel told us. It's not unusual for children with Down syndrome to have holes in their heart, he explained. Sometimes the holes close on their own. Sometimes we have to operate. It sounds worse than it is. Don't worry. We do these operations all the time, he told us. Calm and kind and quietly caring, he was then and continues to be.

We came here regularly, to this satellite of Children's Hospital, to have Lucy tested. She was so tiny then, the smallest of babies, poked and made to lie still, constantly being assessed and evaluated.

No one could get her blood pressure, the littlest cuff too big for her arm. But even if a cuff had fit, the pressure wouldn't have registered because it was that weak, because her heart was that compromised.

I took her to a healing priest when she was four weeks old and he held her up like a trophy and announced that he had cured her and a church full of people clapped. But he was wrong. Lucy had surgery at Boston's Children's Hospital a month later and there were complications. And when we got her back, she still wasn't cured.

When she was four months old she had to have more surgery to fix what went wrong. Now, every June, just before her birthday, we come to Norwood to have her tested.

A wisp of a girl, 32 pounds and 3 feet 2 inches tall, she walks into the examination room, her hand in mine, and her lower lip quivers.

They want to give her an echocardiogram, which requires that she be naked from the waist up and lie still on a flat table in a dark room for about twenty minutes while a technician spreads gel on her chest and uses what looks like a microphone to take pictures of her heart.

I lift her up and show her the monitor and explain to her that this is just a different way of taking pictures. "So the doctor can see what's inside of you, LuLu." As if they could ever see all that is inside this child.

I unbutton her shirt and then I sing to her, a song from "Signing Time": "Lay down on your bed, pull the blanket high. Turn out the light. Welcome the night. Dream, dream." And she relaxes and lies down and I stand behind her and sing the song again and again, and it is like a prayer and a spell.

When I was five years old, I was in a hospital for a few days and woke up one night screaming for my parents. A nurse held me down. I remember being small and terrified and overpowered.

After Lucy's echocardiogram we go into another room where we play "My turn." The physician's assistant listens to my heart, then she listens to Lucy's heart. She checks my blood pressure, then she checks Lucy's blood pressure. Then it is Dr. Geggel's turn to check everything. And then it is time for an EKG. More sticky stuff on Lucy's chest. More lying down. More keeping still.

I think she'll lose it here. But she doesn't. She is all guts and grace, this little girl who, if she'd been born a couple decades ago, most doctors and books would have dismissed as a child unable to understand anything, not worth the bother of loving and teaching and raising.

It kills me to think of children like Lucy whom our society wrote off for years, who were warehoused on the advice of experts, who were abandoned and then ignored. It kills me to think of experts today advising women to abort children like Lucy.

She runs down the hall when the tests are finished, laughing as I chase her. It is one hour and eight minutes later, a long, long time for a little kid to be quiet and patient and good. Dr. Geggel is pleased with Lucy's test results. But like the rest of us who love Lucy, he is equally pleased with Lucy herself.

●　　●　　●

Beverly writes a weekly column for the Boston Globe and a biweekly column for Grandparents.com. She's a contributor to the Chicken Soup for the Soul *book series and author of* A Gift of Time, *a collection of personal essays, and* Back Then, *a memoir of childhood. She lives in Canton, Massachusetts, with her husband, Bruce, and just across the street from her oldest grandchild, Lucy Rose, who brings her joy and makes her proud every day.*

Brett and Guler Banford

Truly Rich

By Guler Banford

I GREW UP with eight siblings in a one-room, twelve-by-twelve-foot house with no indoor plumbing, no electricity, no water, and very little food. Other people would give us used clothes, vegetables and fruits they grew, or a lamb they'd butchered. We'd gather watermelons that fell off trucks heading to the market. Many times our main meal was bread dipped in olive oil. We each had one outfit to wear, and when it got dirty we'd wash and wear it again. We played with rocks and dirt instead of toys. But we didn't care about any of these hardships. Yes, we were poor, but at the same time we were *truly* rich—because we were so loved. Walking home from school with my mother or father I'd hear people jokingly say, "Mr. or Mrs. Kazancioglu, since you have so many other children, why don't you give me this one? You'll never miss her." My parents always said, "*No way!* She's our little girl. We can't live without her."

This is what I remember when I meet or hear of parents wondering if they could welcome a baby with Down syndrome into their family. It hurts to think about aborting, it hurts to think about giving the baby up for adoption, and it hurts to think about giving birth to a disabled child. But for me there was never a question of what I should do when Brett came into my life. I did what I would have done with any other child: help him, teach him, protect him—and most importantly, love him. True, there were hardships. Brett required more teaching, more patience, and more visits to the doctors, and I got less sleep. When he was younger, some people would stare at us and might've considered us poor. But we felt rich.

These days, people around the world are enjoying Brett's many treasures. When Brett was eleven years old and really active, we needed to gear that energy in the right direction and use it in a positive way. I ran into a woman in my childcare classes who had just gotten back from a trip to Europe. She told me about the Special Olympics competitions her child had participated in, and immediately I knew I wanted to get Brett involved. Since there wasn't a young children's Special Olympics team in town, we were up to the challenge of starting a new team of our own, and in September 1993 that's what we did. The team was named "Dyno-Stars," and the team members were Brett and his classmates. Our family, friends, and coworkers came to our aid by coaching and volunteering many hours.

Now, sixteen years later, we have about two dozen athletes on the "Dyno-Stars" team. They compete in many different sports, are state champs in basketball and volleyball, and are some of the best swimmers in Utah Special Olympics. Through our involvement in Special Olympics, Brett gained not only physical fitness, but spiritual and social growth. He's also learned patience, endurance, compassion, and acceptance.

For the last several years, Brett has been a global messenger for Special Olympics, and was recently inducted into the Special Olympics Hall of Fame. While fulfilling his Global Messenger duties, he has met many celebrities, gotten positive media exposure, and developed his public speaking and interpersonal skills. In 2004 he was an Olympic torchbearer for the Greece Summer Games, inspiring greatness in all people.

Brett has many athletic interests. He loves snowboarding, alpine skiing, basketball, and golf, and he has a second degree black belt in Taekwondo. But by far his biggest passion is hip-hop dancing. Music is in his soul, and rhythm flows through his veins. When the Back Street Boys were really popular, Brett would watch their music videos and teach himself the dance steps. Sometimes when he was in crowds or in the hallways at school, he'd start dancing, and immediately people would form a circle around him to cheer him on.

The *So You Think You Can Dance?* TV reality show auditions came to Salt Lake City in February 2008, when Brett was twenty-five years old, and he really wanted to participate. Even though I had never seen the show and didn't know what we were getting ourselves into, we went, without any prepared music or choreography. Brett's magnetic personality immediately caught the producers' eyes, and he wowed them with his dancing skills!

Soon afterward Brett got the callback for the solo dance, which was supposed to be choreographed. Not knowing much about hip-hop music myself, I called a friend at 10:20 pm the night before to ask for song suggestions. The next morning Brett went on stage never having heard the song before. He winged the choreography and did a fantastic job. The judges said he was a lot of fun to watch and he had musicality and great moves, but wasn't good enough to continue on in the show. Brett spontaneously replied, "I'm here to prove people with disabilities can have normal lives and live it and that it isn't about winning or losing but to have fun." On May 28, 2008, Brett's audition and spontaneous comments aired on national TV. He touched and inspired many people, with and without disabilities, across the nation and all over the world. It's been chaos at our house ever since: making appearances at nonprofit fund-raisers, galas, balls, and television and radio stations to advocate for people with disabilities and to educate the public through Brett's example of ability and skill.

Most recently, Brett became one of the USA ambassadors for Best Buddies International, an organization started by Anthony Kennedy Shriver. He encourages people to form lifelong friendships with an intellectually disabled buddy.

Brett has brought so many blessings into our lives and has inspired so many people in his twenty-six years. As a family, we are truly rich. Not because Brett is famous, but because Brett is Brett: cute, compassionate, outspoken, creative, talented, and fun. Who knows what will come next in our amazing journey? Whatever it is, we're ready for the challenge. Brett probably won't be able to have two of the things he wants most: a supermodel wife and a driver's license (in our big city, driving is treacherous). But I'm beginning to learn to expect the unexpected. After all, eating bread dipped in olive oil is now gourmet!

●　　●　　●

Guler and her husband, Marlo, have been married for thirty-two years. Marlo works for Qwest Communications. Guler recently retired from AT&T and is currently mom-managing Brett's endeavors. They have two sons, a new daughter-in-law, JenneVee; a gorgeous granddaughter, Sailor Rae; and a service dog named Mister. Adam (1979) is the owner of a Taekwondo school in Sandy, Utah. Brett (1982) is a spokesperson for the "R-WORD" campaign, works as a bagger at Harmons Grocery store, serves on the Law Enforcement Torch Run Council, and is a USA Ambassador for Best Buddies International.

Jacob Borkin and Kimberly Bedford

53.

My Journey with Jacob

By Kimberly Bedford

THE MORNING JACOB Borkin began school was a typical morning in my infant-toddler class at St. Francis Children's Center. As the eight students arrived, there was classical music playing in the background to provide a peaceful ambience for their free play/exploring time. Like I do for every new student, I had prepared Jacob's cubby and cut out his "First Day" crown that he would decorate and take home at the end of the day. I had talked to the other children about a "new friend" starting today named Jacob, and when he arrived with his mother, the children were very excited. In keeping with tradition, they greeted the newcomer with an enthusiastic, "Hi Jacob!" Mrs. Borkin smiled wide, and I gave her a welcome hug. I looked at Jacob, and his adorable eyes said a thousand things to me: *Are you going to play with me? Care for me? Love me?* And if he read my eyes in return, he knew at that moment we would begin a wonderful journey together.

I was thrilled to have Jacob assigned to my classroom. However, I wondered if he could sense my uncertainty. Until that point, my background did not include any experiences working with children with special needs. I was worried about making mistakes. I was concerned about how I was going to foster his development in all areas and help him achieve his full potential. To learn more, I decided to search the literature and ask colleagues to share their experiences in working with children with Down syndrome. My colleagues in the Birth to Three team taught me not to be afraid of challenging Jacob in the same ways I challenge other children in my classroom. As a result, over the past few years that Jacob has been my student, he has developed in numerous ways, such as demonstrating the use of expressive and receptive language and overcoming many physical challenges.

This learning journey began as the special education teacher and therapists started their interventions with Jacob in my classroom, and I learned activities to build into his daily routine. For example, under the direction of the occupational therapist, Jacob had so much fun when I bounced him on the therapy ball. At first I was nervous thinking he might fall off, or might sense that I was doing this activity differently than his therapist. While I did sense a mild hesitation on his part, once he was bouncing on the ball, he laughed and the reluctance vanished. When we finished, I said and signed "all done," and he giggled with delight!

Jacob is a very quick learner and as time went on, talking and signing helped him make connections with everybody around him. Music helped accelerate the process. From our earliest days I recognized that Jacob enjoyed singing and movement; this was most noticeable during group music time when he became excited and very animated. In the beginning, Jacob would clap, wave his hands, and raise his feet up and down to the beat of the music. He now can follow along with the finger play movements and sings aloud with the words of the songs.

Jacob reached a huge milestone in his motor skill development when he was able to get himself from sitting to a standing position. Once he mastered this, I would place objects he wanted in front of him to encourage his cruising along furniture. I tried to create opportunities throughout the day that encouraged his upright mobility, knowing that this would open new avenues of exploration for him. Jacob now is able to hold onto objects, pull himself up to a standing position, and cruise from place to place. I am eager to see him take his first steps and will continue to encourage him until he reaches his goals.

In addition to Jacob's gains in speech and mobility, I am most proud of what I taught him in respect to feelings. As Jacob got older and wanted my attention, he would grab my face. I would say to Jacob: "That hurts," and then I would take his hand and demonstrate a "gentle touch" on my cheek. Eventually, he caught on and seemed proud when he understood what "gentle" means. It did not take long for Jacob to sense that he could express his wants and needs and that I would understand him.

Being with Jacob for almost two and a half years has taught me that when we are really interested in learning about something we mustn't be afraid; we must trust and believe in our abilities and we'll be fine. Any anxiety or nervousness I might have had about teaching a child with special needs has vanished. Our journey has come full circle. Now when Jacob and I look into each other's eyes, his tell me he is sure of my love and caring for him; and in my eyes, he sees gratitude for an amazing little boy who has given me confidence as a teacher. He has taught me the truth of the motto etched on a stone outside of St. Francis Children's Center: "All children can learn, if we can learn how to teach them."

● ● ●

Kimberly currently teaches at St. Francis Children's Center, a school specializing in the integration of children from diverse backgrounds and abilities. This fall Kimberly will continue working on her bachelor's degree in education.

Left to Right: Emma, Meredith, Brianna, Michael, Kristopher, and Micah Cornish

54.

Journey to Hope

By Meredith Cornish

WHEN MY HUSBAND, Mike, and I found out that our eight-week-old baby girl had Down syndrome, we had some adjusting to do. We had a two-year-old son, Kristopher, and now a daughter, Brianna. The most difficult part of her diagnosis wasn't Down syndrome, though—it was the news that her heart had formed with a large hole in its center. Brianna had a Complete Atrioventricular Canal Defect (CAVC) as well as an Atrial Septal Defect (ASD) and a Ventricular Septal Defect (VSD). She would need open heart surgery before she was six months old.

After Brianna's successful surgery, we began to believe that her diagnosis of Down syndrome was an answer to many heartfelt prayers. In the past, Mike and I had discussed special needs adoption, but we weren't sure we were ready for a lifetime commitment. After all, we were in our early twenties and had our whole lives ahead of us. But we continued to pray about the possibility of adopting a child with special needs, and once we'd recovered from the initial shock, we believed Brianna's diagnosis was our *yes*.

When Brianna was eighteen months old and we felt more settled, we contacted Reece's Rainbow, a Down syndrome adoption ministry, and looked through pages and pages of little faces of children who needed a home. Many of the children were sick, malnourished, had heart conditions that were not repaired, or because of age would soon be transferred from infant homes to mental institutions. There, the life expectancy is ten years—for children who survive the first year. Choosing just one child from so many needs was a difficult process and we had a hard time narrowing it down by gender, age, and location.

We finally did make a decision and began the process of adopting a four-year-old little girl with sandy-colored hair, green eyes, and a cautious smile. She lived in Eastern Europe (for privacy reasons, I'll refrain from naming the country), and was walking, talking some, feeding herself, and generally doing well. In the end, we chose her because we wanted another little girl who would grow up with Brianna. She was going to age out of the "baby house" soon and her future would be bleak without a family. We expected to travel in March or April to bring home "Aleksa."

By October we had completed our homestudy, finished the majority of our paperwork, and were waiting on just one final form. Everything was going faster than anticipated! But we were in for a few surprises along the way. First was Aleksa's transfer to a mental institution during the paperwork phase of our adoption. The fear and sorrow knowing that "our child" could be in a place where she'd be restrained to her bed, fed once a day, and live in deplorable conditions was more than we expected to face. After her transfer, we were able to have some of the processes of the adoption expedited and traveled to meet Aleksa in early January, leaving Brianna and Kristopher at home in their grandparents' care.

The second big surprise was the intense resistance put up by the director of Aleksa's institution. He blatantly refused to allow us to adopt her, based on his view of Americans and his idea of what our motives might be in wanting a disabled child. Although terribly un-fair, his authority overruled the paperwork granting us visitation. We immediately took steps to intervene, but unfortunately, his political involvement in the small town made it impossible to proceed. Dur-ing our two visits with Aleksa we tried to convince the director of our sincere love for this child. But in the end, although we were able to see that she was being dressed, fed, and not left in a crib alone, we had to say goodbye. Our adoption was denied.

We went back to our small hotel room in this city where not a single person spoke English, or even smiled. It was about ten degrees below zero, there were no restaurants, and the only food we could find was water and some bread and cheese. Over the weekend, as we grieved the loss of our hopes for Aleksa, we felt battered down and defeated. But we regrouped, and quickly realized what the next step would be for us:

There was another little girl living in a baby house, a girl from a different region of the country whose adoption had fallen through. She would be five in just a few weeks, and would be transferred to the mental institution. Because of her heart problems and poor physical condition, we knew the transfer would be deadly for her. After much thought and discussion, we decided we wanted to offer a home not only to this child, but to a second child with special needs as well—any child the Department of Adoptions would allow us to have. We signed paperwork to request permission to meet and adopt the girl who was aging out of the baby house, and any other child with spe-cial needs at her orphanage who was available for adoption.

A week later, we'd heard nothing but difficult news and stalling. "There are no other kids." "They can't fit you in yet." "Maybe tomor-row...." But tomorrow turned into "Another day, perhaps." It was a lonely way to spend time in a foreign country, and the anticipation was difficult. Thankfully, during this waiting time we stayed with a

Christian couple who spoke English, and were also able to meet up with several other families adopting through Reece's Rainbow. Both of those things helped to lift our spirits tremendously.

Finally, at the end of that week's wait, our facilitator called and said, "Be there at one o'clock." We quickly dressed in our winter coats, hats, mittens, and boots and walked the two miles to the Department of Adoptions. Outside, our facilitator told us, "There's a baby available. I don't know anything else, but they'll tell you upstairs." Our hopes soared as entered a small room with two chairs, a small table, and a long desk. They put out two sets of referral paperwork—one for our requested five-year-old little girl and the other for a sixteen-month-old "baby" boy. He had only been released for adoption that week.

Two days later we took a thirteen hour trip on an old rickety train with toilets that didn't flush and beds that folded like bunks out of a wall. Each time the train stopped I fell from the top bunk, but we were on our way to meet our children! After this sleepless night on the train, we went to the orphanage where our children lived and we fell in love instantly. The "baby" was exactly that. At eleven pounds, he was the size of a three-month-old. He had blonde hair that stood straight up and he kept pinching his mouth to make "fish faces." His body had been wracked with sickness, though, and he frequently spit up entire feedings. Even when he kept the food down, it went through him too quickly for any nutrition to be absorbed. With his ribs sticking out and his bloated belly, he looked like one of those emaciated children pictured in *National Geographic*.

Our little girl was tiny too: seventeen pounds at almost five years old. And she wasn't in much better physical health. She had a contagious smile and was able to roll over, but wasn't able to hold her head up well, sit up, or put any weight on her feet. We learned which heart condition she had, and it was one that should have been repaired before she was a year old: an AV Canal defect (the same heart defect our daughter had repaired). She had pulmonary hypertension as a result of it not being fixed. Despite the children's poor health, we were told by the orphanage doctors and later by our daughter's cardiologist that they would survive the trip home. That was all we needed to know.

Still, so many questions about their futures flooded our minds. One day, would they learn to walk and talk? Would they like being part of our family? Would they enjoy our holiday celebrations, our cozy evenings at home, our Saturday outings to the beach?

Over the next weeks, we visited the children twice a day to get to know them better. Our little boy was half asleep during most of our visits, but smiled occasionally for brief moments and tried to hold his head up a little. Our girl loved to have the freedom to explore her surroundings and especially liked being pushed on a swing.

Micah Daniel and Emma Hope became a part of our family the day before Emma's fifth birthday. We had "court" in the judge's chambers and this hour-long finalization was the end of two weeks of work. We went out for pizza with our facilitator and had a quick celebration, but the waiting time was beginning again. It was another two weeks before the court paperwork was complete and we could have custody of our children. Then almost a week another week passed before we could get their new birth certificates, passports, visas, and come home.

Five weeks after we met them, those two tiny children entered our home for the first time, slept in warm clean clothes, and woke the next morning to meet their new brother and sister. Since we'd arrived at around two o'clock in the morning, the only members of the welcoming party were grandparents patiently waiting at home. Thankfully my sister and the grandparents had made preparations, and there were two cribs set up and the right-sized pajamas ready for the children to wear. After a few minutes of visiting, both kids went to sleep   Micah in the "boys' room" and Emma in the "girls' room." Kristopher and Brianna didn't stir.

The next morning, Kristopher and Brianna were surprised and happy to see everyone was home. Emma was awake soon after they were and Brianna was quick to go rub her head, pat her back, and sign "baby" to her. Micah soon awoke, which meant Brianna was in heaven with not just one but two babies to cuddle with! Kristopher was most happy to have his parents home at last, but talked constantly about his new brother and sister. The kids all took to each other quickly. Because Emma had been used to having all of her time to herself, she got over stimulated by all the attention at first, and Brianna was sad when her sister didn't want to play. But by the end of the day, Brianna figured out that it's okay not to cuddle all the time and Emma found out that cuddles from a sister are okay after all.

Over the following weeks, we visited cardiologists, pediatricians, and a host of other specialists. We are blessed to have family nearby and some close friends who pitched in to help with Kristopher and Brianna so they didn't have to attend every appointment. The transition was very easy for us all, though, and we were quickly in a good routine as a family of six.

Micah's health greatly improved as soon as we decided to try changing his diet from milk- to soy-based. He immediately started to gain weight and became more alert and responsive. Gross motor skills came quickly for him once his strength increased, and he was soon holding his head up, then sitting, then crawling.

Emma's condition didn't improve quite so dramatically, as she still had many unresolved medical issues. After being home for a month she had a heart catheterization procedure, which showed progressed pulmonary hypertension and possibly irreversible damage to her lungs. Later that day, the cardiologist told us that Emma would not be able to have heart surgery, and would die within the next few months. Our hearts fell to our feet. We'd already scheduled her surgery for later that week, and it was canceled. We were sent home with a terminal diagnosis.

But neither Mike nor I were willing to accept this as the final answer. The very next day I brought Emma to our local cardiologist and told her the prognosis we'd received. *"No,"* the cardiologist said adamantly. "That's not an option. Emma is a different child than when I met her one month ago, and she deserves a chance. If she's going to die either way, then we'll do the surgery and find out." The cardiologist called the surgeon's office and convinced him to see us.

In the meantime, Emma was seen by an ear, nose, and throat specialist, who told us her tonsils and adenoids needed to be removed. Her tonsils were almost touching, which would make it difficult to remove the ventilation tube after Emma's heart surgery. In addition, her adenoids were causing chronic illness, which weakened her significantly, making heart surgery more risky. We moved forward with the procedure to remove them. It was rough on Emma and required a week-long hospital stay, but finally she was able to swallow liquids again. We scheduled the heart surgery for eight weeks out, and then took her home to heal. But healing didn't come. Instead, Emma's health deteriorated. She was tired and weak, and her oxygen saturation levels were low. Thanks to further intervention by our cardiologist, Emma's surgery date was moved ten days closer.

Surrendering a child for surgery is always a difficult thing to do, but we'd been given such slim chances of a full recovery and such a grim prognosis that we felt like we were saying goodbye. Once Emma's internal line was placed, the surgeon came in to talk with us. "I wouldn't be doing this if I didn't know she'd die soon without the surgery. But we'll do the best we can. I'll see you soon."

Thankfully, the initial updates were hopeful, although we knew Emma wasn't yet out of the woods. Finally, after sitting for hours on the edge of our seats, we saw the surgeon come through the door. "I have good news," he said. "Her pulmonary pressures are half what we thought we'd see. We did a full repair. You can see her in about an hour." He shook his head. "It's unexplainable."

"Oh, I have an explanation," I said, my heart soaring. "LOTS of prayer."

Emma continued on the fast track to recovery—so fast, in fact, that we brought her home after only four days, without any need for pulmonary medication. At just two weeks post-op, she got herself up into a "tripod sit" several times and was beginning to roll around again. Her smiles were back full force and her cries were louder than ever (a good thing!).

Now, ten months later, Emma is sitting, crawling, and has new braces to help her stand! Emma has a sparkle in her eye and a desire to live. In fact, she started school eight weeks after her heart surgery, something no one was ever sure she'd do. She's beginning to use sign language and verbalizations to communicate, she's gaining weight, and she's grown several inches in length since coming home. Emma has also decided that she likes her glasses and enjoys seeing what's going on in the world around her.

That world, of course, includes three very active and loving siblings. Kristopher recently started preschool, and loves coming home to play with "his friends." He helps Emma when she drops her bottle and makes sure Micah doesn't steamroll her in the playroom. Brianna is learning to walk, uses sign language, and is beginning to mimic many sounds and motions. Her heart is functioning very well, and she only needs annual exams with the cardiologist. Micah is now pulling to a stand, and has doubled his weight since coming home. He wears tiny little professor glasses and has a smile to share with everyone.

Will Emma ever walk? Will she ever talk? Will she ever be toilet trained or take food other than in a bottle? I can't answer these questions right now, but if the past few months are any indication of her ability to persevere, I think one day we'll set her wheelchair aside and go for a walk on the beach while we talk about the waves and the seagulls and throw them bits of bread from our sandwiches.

● ● ●

Meredith lives in Florida and is happily married to Michael. Three of their four children have Down syndrome and each is a unique blessing. Meredith volunteers with Reece's Rainbow Down Syndrome Adoption Ministry as the Ukraine Family Coordinator. She maintains a family blog at http://cornishadoptionjourney.blogspot.com. For more information about sponsoring or adopting a child with Down syndrome, visit www.reecesrainbow.org.

Kristin Enkvetchakul and Matthew Haag

55.
They Changed the World

By Kristin Enkvetchakul

GROWING UP, I was taught that I had a lot of people to be grateful to, and a lot to be grateful for in this life. My parents and teachers taught me that I should be grateful to veterans of our armed forces for preserving the freedom I enjoyed. I was taught to appreciate the civil servants of our country who kept me safe—the police and firefighters—and the ones who helped me learn—the teachers and librarians. I learned to appreciate and be grateful for my parents, family, and friends.

It was only when I was well into my thirties, however, that I became aware of a whole other group of people to whom I, and the world, owe much. I "discovered" this amazing group of people in early October of 2007, when my brother Bill and his wife, Ria's, first child was born. The arrival of this precious little bundle was not unexpected. That he came in a Down syndrome package *was* unexpected.

The kind physician at the hospital who confirmed the diagnosis told Bill and Ria to expect a sense of loss, a mourning period, as they adjusted. He said this was healthy, and encouraged them to work through it without guilt. He assured them that their sense of loss over not having the baby they expected to have would give way to embracing the baby they *did* have: a baby with untold promise, a baby who would surprise them with an abundance of love. Bill and Ria named their baby Matthew, as it means "Gift from God."

The doctor also told Bill and Ria about the state program called First Steps, an early intervention program for babies who were likely to have developmental delays. Being people who quickly moved from "Why us?" to "It is us, what do we need to do?" they decided to join the program immediately. In the days that followed, they were flooded with advice from positive, supportive professionals who gave them introductory information about what First Steps could offer their child.

Through First Steps, a battery of wonderful professionals visits Matthew at his home every month, working with him and teaching his parents ways to help him maximize his potential, whatever that potential may be. At nine months old, he has a physical therapist, a developmental therapist, an occupational therapist, a speech therapist, and a coordinator to help facilitate it all.

The existence of this incredible program is owed to the previous generation or two of parents of children with Down syndrome. In a world where children with Down syndrome were regarded as burdens, these parents said, "They are not burdens—they are our children!" To a world that locked children with Down syndrome away, these parents said, "No—our children will not be hidden!" In a world where children with Down syndrome were pitied, these parents said, "They are not to be pitied; they are to be loved!"

These parents saw potential in their children, and sought ways to unlock it. Because of them, legislation was passed, laws changed, and programs developed. Because of them, my small nephew has been born into a more welcoming world.

I wonder, if I had been one of those parents a few decades ago, would I have had the courage to stand up against the social standards of the time and change the world? Would I have had the courage to make silent history, so that others after me would have it easier? I would like to think I would have, but not having been in those circumstances, I can't say for certain.

I am certain, however, that Bill and Ria would have. Already they are quietly championing their son, watching with pride as he works toward his goals, being behind him, in front of him, and beside him, all at the same time. Matthew meets his challenges with earnest determination and an infectious smile that leaves a wake of melted hearts everywhere he goes.

They say love can move mountains. I don't know about mountains, but I now know that love can change the world. A courageous group of parents has proven that. Without Matthew, I never would have realized it.

● ● ●

Kristin is a self-taught chef of traditional Asian cuisine and is the author of Introduction to Asian Cooking. *She lives in the Midwest with her husband and their two children. She is proud to not only be Matthew's aunt but also his godmother, and is thrilled that her children have the fortune to call Matthew not only "cousin," but also "friend." For updates on Matthew, visit his mother's blog at http://billandria. blogspot.com. Kristin would like to thank her mother, Margie, for encouraging her efforts with this essay.*

Kristen Mueller Adams

56.
Finding Faith

By Kristen Mueller Adams

IN THE SUMMER of 2001 I accepted a teaching position at a school for children with Down syndrome, which served as a laboratory school on the campus of the local university. I would be the lead teacher in the toddler class for children ages eighteen months to three years. Having taught special education for six years, I had worked with children of a wide variety of ages and abilities and was excited about entering the field of early childhood education. I eagerly purchased bulletin board supplies, new books, and toys in an effort to create a stimulating and inviting classroom for my new students.

The day before school started, I was in the classroom preparing for the first week of lessons. I thought I was prepared for anything. I would soon learn how wrong I was. Taking a break from the daunting task of organizing my classroom, I went to the front office to hand in some forms for human resources. As I turned the corner, I came face to face with Faith. At first glance, Faith appeared frail, quiet, and somewhat helpless. Her mom explained that Faith was recovering from leukemia, had required heart surgery shortly after birth and had spent much of her first two years in the hospital. Now in remission and relatively stable, Faith would attend our school and be in my class.

Sitting in her stroller, Faith warily surveyed her surroundings with eyes that were remarkably bright considering her physical condition. Her hair was just beginning to grow back after several rounds of chemotherapy and was a soft, light brown fuzz. She sat slumped over, her muscles too weak to support her body. Her complexion was pale; I could see tiny blue veins beneath her transparent skin and a deep crack in her bottom lip that had been unable to heal due to a suppressed immune system.

Faith clung tightly to a red-and-white polka-dot cup, which her mother identified as Faith's comfort object. When she began to fuss as her mother filled out enrollment papers, I knelt down to comfort her. When I began speaking to her, however, she flung her cup on the floor. I retrieved the cup, handed it back to her, and tried again to distract her while her mother completed the enrollment process. Faith stopped crying, looked at me intently, and once again threw the cup. This time, when I went to retrieve it, she pulled herself forward in the stroller to watch me. When I again handed her the cup, I saw the briefest smile flash across her lips and knew this child possessed a remarkable spirit.

I spent the rest of that day and much of the evening wondering how I would teach Faith: Where would I start? Faith was nonverbal, unable to sit independently, much less stand or walk, and was exhausted by the slightest physical exertion. Although I had consulted several books about educating young children with Down syndrome, I realized that I had not taken into account the numerous modifications I would need to make in order to provide a quality education for a student like Faith. For that matter, how was I going to teach an entire class of children whose needs might be far beyond my capabilities? Although I felt I had a broad range of experience working with children who have special needs, I did not have experience in an early childhood classroom.

I suddenly felt inadequate as I looked over lesson plans that were clearly inappropriate for Faith and felt panicked at the thought that I would soon face a classroom of children with needs far different from what I had anticipated. I was overwhelmed by the prospect of twelve sets of parents handing their children over to me the next morning; I feared I would not meet their expectations. I lay awake that night wondering if I had made the right decision when I accepted this position. I was so afraid of disappointing parents who were putting a great deal of trust in me as an educator and wondered what I would expect if I had a child with special needs. I knew I had a lot to learn, but eventually decided that I would simply approach my students as I would any group of children—with high expectations, an open mind, and a lot of love.

As I muddled my way through that first semester, I learned a great deal about teaching young children with Down syndrome through my graduate classes, and I found myself spending hours at home researching methods for teaching various skills. But I learned even more valuable lessons from the students themselves. I watched individual students struggle to use utensils, manipulate a toy, and take their first steps. Regardless of how many attempts a task required, my students worked through frustration and continued to try. They approached each day with a joy and eagerness that became an inspiration to me. I learned about determination, wonder, patience, and perseverance in a way I had not experienced before.

And from Faith, I learned to appreciate life. Although in remission from her leukemia, she continued to require chemotherapy and had to endure painful medical tests. Having spent so much time in the hospital, her muscles were atrophied and she tired easily. Yet when she arrived for school, she was excited to see her friends and eager to try new things. At Halloween I bought miniature pumpkins for each child and let them scoop out the seeds and pulp. The activity was more difficult than I had anticipated, but Faith loved it and worked to get out every last seed. When the spoon I had provided didn't work well, she set it down and began using her hands. She was excited by materials in the sensory table such as beans, sand, and water. Eventually, this center became a motivation for her to stand and exercise her leg muscles. Faith tired easily, but had a spirit and drive that helped her push through therapies, lessons, and even her treatments.

I spent time at the hospital each time Faith was admitted and got to know a family that had experienced a great deal of heartache. Her parents had left their home and the family farm in west Texas and moved to Ft. Worth in order to be near the children's hospital for Faith. Although their extended family could offer emotional support through phone calls and letters, Faith's parents were alone in a new city and faced with the overwhelming task of helping their daughter survive a brutal illness. During several of my trips to the hospital, Faith slept and her parents took turns sitting by her. These moments allowed me the opportunity to get to know her parents as individuals. Often the room was dimly lit and we talked in whispers; I learned about the journey they had taken from heartbreak and disappointment to acceptance, to celebration of the child they so appropriately had named Faith. They loved Faith with deep devotion and had a fierce determination to provide the highest quality of life for her. It was easy to see where she had gotten her strong spirit.

In time, Faith's health strengthened, the family welcomed a new baby and eventually moved back to west Texas in February of 2002. I wondered how and when our paths would cross again, and I was grateful to receive frequent updates from the family over the months that followed. The following August, Faith was scheduled for heart surgery on the same day I delivered my second child. Although risky, the procedure would greatly improve Faith's quality of life. Without the surgery, Faith would constantly struggle to get enough oxygen throughout her body and would be restricted to minimal physical activity. Her parents wanted Faith to be able to run and play and to fully express the zest she had for living. There was no question in their minds that the surgery was a necessity. Although preoccupied by the birth of my son, I thought about Faith and her family throughout that day. I prayed that the surgery would go smoothly and would be a success. I asked God to spare her family further disappointments and felt confident that Faith could endure anything. That evening as I fell asleep, I was sure that all had gone well and that Faith was already on the road to recovery.

But three days after the surgery, I received a phone call from our school's director explaining that while the surgery had gone well, Faith had experienced a massive stroke and was not expected to survive. The news came as a shock to everyone, including the doctors. Faith had come through the heart surgery without any complications and had been recovering without incident when she and her family were dealt an awful blow. Just as everyone had begun to breathe a sigh of relief, Faith began slipping away.

The next day I arrived at the children's hospital just a short drive from my home to say good-bye to Faith. As I entered her room, I was shocked by the scene. The heart monitor offered the only sound, an eerie, steady beeping, and the once vibrant child I remembered was entangled in a mass of tubes and wires. Her face was swollen due to medications and framed by thin, wispy hair that had begun to grow back. She lay motionless and barely resembled the Faith I knew. I leaned over to kiss her and was unable to hold back my tears any longer. I was angry at a God who had seemingly played a cruel joke on us all—allowing us to know and love such a special child, to see her through great adversity, only to watch her slip away. I firmly believe that throughout our lives doors are opened and we choose what direction our lives will take. I questioned why I'd been given the opportunity to teach in that classroom, why I had come to love this child so deeply and why her family had to lose her. Having lost faith, I was unwilling to pray and unable to hope. I returned home to await the final phone call.

The phone rang after less than forty-eight hours. It was Faith's mother informing me that she had made a full recovery. I struggled to comprehend what I was hearing. I was struck with the paralyzing fear that this glimmer of hope was only prolonging the inevitable. But Faith's mom recounted a miraculous turn of events: Just before her life support was to be turned off, all of Faith's vitals were checked one last time. Where there had been no brain activity, now there was some. The doctors explained to Faith's parents that she would likely be blind and might never be able to walk, and cautioned them not to hope for a full recovery. Although only a faint glimmer of hope, it was all her parents needed.

In less than two days, Faith was sitting up in bed tossing a ball to anyone who would play. I remember walking into her room and being greeted with a "Hi!" as a ball flew at me—she always had a strong right arm! I had been so afraid of this encounter—afraid that Faith would no longer embody the spirit I had come to love. As I approached her room I realized my heart was racing and I struggled to catch my breath. Yet when I reached the doorway and caught the ball she'd thrown, it was as if the events of the past few days' had never occurred. Her left arm was slightly limp, but she sat erect and was alert and even energetic. Her bright eyes eagerly engaged visitors in the room. As I left the hospital that day, tears streamed down my face as I finally let go of the grief I had been containing in anticipation of Faith's passing. In place of the grief was a joy only a miracle can bring. Faith's life had been extended, which was wondrous to me. But even more wondrous was my realization that her life was miraculous, beautiful, and worthy of faith no matter how long she might live.

Faith has gone on to recover fully from her ordeal and is enjoying life with her family in west Texas. The last time I saw her, she had dark brown hair down to her shoulders and barely resembled the child I had known. She doesn't remember much about me or her experiences at our school, but I will never forget. As a result of my time with Faith and her family, I have learned that we never really know how much time we have with loved ones, and that it's important to cherish every smile and to celebrate the smallest successes. I have learned to enjoy today because you never know what tomorrow will bring. I have learned that laughter and love are a powerful combination. I have learned that great wisdom comes in the most unlikely of packages, and that miracles do happen. And I have learned to never, ever lose faith.

• • •

Kristen graduated from Texas Christian University in 2003 with a M.Ed. in special education. She currently teaches at the KinderFrogs School, an early intervention program for children with Down syndrome. Kristen lives in Ft. Worth with her husband, James, and their four children. She plans to pursue a doctoral degree in educational leadership with a focus in early intervention.

Max and Katharina Gebert

57.

Follow Your Dreams

By Katharina Gebert

SIXTEEN YEARS AGO my brother Max was born in Germany. Just minutes after Max's birth, a doctor pulled my father aside and told him Max had Down syndrome. The doctor lacked the courage to deliver the diagnosis to my mother, and asked my dad to do it. During an initial consultation the following day, the pediatrician opened the conversation by telling my parents that their son would never be able to finish high school, and would only be able to speak and walk (or do anything, for that matter) with significant difficulty. My parents were sure their dreams of relocating to America and having a large family were now impossible. They would have too much work on their hands with Max, and the move to America could possibly cause unwanted stress on him.

When talking to yet another doctor, my parents sadly related their sense of loss regarding the future of their family life. But this time the doctor had encouraging words to offer. "Don't give up your dreams because of your son," he said gently. "Wherever you are happy, Max will be too."

My parents took his advice to heart. Over the next two years they welcomed my older sister and me into the family. When I was two and a half, my father was offered a job in Princeton, New Jersey, and he jumped at the chance to move the family to the States. He believed this would bring opportunities for all of us, especially Max, who was then almost five. The doctor's encouraging words made my parents realize that Max was not a setback. He could do anything my parents, and everyone around him, supported him in doing. My parents had heard of all the wonderful opportunities in America, not only for Max, but for all of us, and decided to take the risk. A few months after we arrived, my little sister was born, and the large family my parents had desired was complete.

Thanks to their courage in following their dreams, I have many rich childhood memories of playing games, running around the yard, and going swimming with my brother and two sisters. Max was always part of the action. And rather than being a detriment to our relationship, his disability has given me lots of opportunities to feel close to him. Since he was held back in school twice, from fifth grade onward we were in the same grade. We went to different schools, but nonetheless when people heard we were in the same grade they'd often comment, "Oh! You must be twins!" In church classes, which were arranged by grade level, I would always be with Max. In some ways it was difficult for me, since I felt responsible for any mistakes he made. More often than not, the teachers would come up to me and say, "Can you help us? Your brother is being stubborn again."

Although there are 100 things that annoy me about my brother, there are 150 reasons why I love him so much. Our shared experiences have allowed us to build a special relationship. My mother will frequently ask me to come along while buying clothes for Max, so I can tell her which clothes guys in my grade are wearing. Max will frequently come home with exciting news as to what book his class is reading in school, or what material they are covering. Very often, although he might be learning a simplified version, we are doing the same thing. This makes him feel included, and gives us fun things to talk and share about. This year, for the first time ever, Max and I are in the same school. This is a big change for both of us, because he normally does not see any of his siblings in school, and I have never attended the same school with him. It gives him so much joy to see me in the halls, and get to say hi, which he never had the chance of doing before.

Because of the closeness Max and I share, I can easily persuade him to do things that others in my family cannot. For example, when my siblings and I were younger, and wanted to play a round of "house," we often wanted Max to be the father in the family. Since this was not always a very appealing game for Max, I would simply persuade him to do so with ice cream, or a round of foosball later on that day. After some contemplation, this would convince him, and we would be able to play. Even when Max is in one of his all-too-common stubborn phases, it is so easy to simply talk to him, and convince him that whatever must be done is not that bad after all. For example, if he doesn't want to get started with his homework, I always tell him I have to do my homework too, and that it's not just him. Max can be stubborn at times, but diverting him from the problem at hand or persuading him with simple rewards always works—for me, at least!

Thanks to that one doctor in Germany who told my parents to follow their hopes and dreams, and thanks to my parents for following his counsel, our family has been rewarded in innumerable ways. We're all living happily in the States. Without Max, my parents would have moved back to Germany after my father had worked here for two years. Max opened their eyes to the immense opportunities available to us all, and my sisters and I are enjoying many opportunities we may not have had in Germany. Max is receiving the best education possible for him, here in Princeton, and because of that education, his cognitive abilities are quite high. Just recently he demonstrated the Pythagorean Theorem for us on the chalkboard. Our jaws dropped and my mom began to cry. She said she wished those other doctors in Germany could see Max right then.

●　●　●

Katharina lives with her family in Princeton, New Jersey, where she is a freshman at her local high school. Her interests are shopping, playing the violin and tennis, and photography. She likes to travel to Europe, where her extended family still lives.

Tom and Bryan Lambke

58.
Going for the Gold

By Tom Lambke

I WAS TWENTY-SIX years old when I became a father. My wife, Karen, and I had been married over four years and we were excited to be starting our family. Like most fathers, I was hoping for a boy to share my love of sports, but also hoping for him to have ten fingers and ten toes. As I watched the doctor deliver our son, I noticed our baby's eyes looked different. They seemed to have a slight almond shape. I immediately realized our son may have Down syndrome. Among many other questions racing through my brain, I wondered, "Who will I play baseball with?" I could not have possibly predicted that our son, Bryan, would grow up to be a young man who enjoys playing *every* sport, except baseball!

Yes, Bryan was born with Down syndrome, and Karen and I really had no clue what to do. The year was 1981, and as of yet there was no Internet. The library only had a couple of books about Down syndrome, both written by doctors in a way that was not useful to us. So we decided to do what we thought was best for Bryan: raise him as if he was a "normal" baby. By the end of our first year together, I still had many unanswered questions about Down syndrome. To make matters worse, Bryan needed heart surgery, and I was worried about the possible outcome. But on the day of his procedure, just before the doctors wheeled him away, he looked up at me and said his first word: *dada*. I knew then we had a fighter and that everything would be fine.

As Bryan got older, his interest in sports became obvious to us. He enjoyed running and throwing the ball around. So when he turned eight, we got him started in Special Olympics. He ran the 50 meter dash and 200 meter relay run and did the softball throw. When we took Bry to his first practice, I was the one who was nervous. We had no idea how well he would take to competitive sports and having coaches tell him what to do. But once again, he proved to be a resilient young man and adjusted well to his new friends and mentors. In the nineteen years he has been participating now, he has also competed in basketball, bowling, swimming, dragon boat racing, kayaking, and Challenger baseball. He has excelled at each except baseball, and has won numerous medals and ribbons.

By far his most treasured medal is the gold medal won at the 2003 Special Olympics Summer World Games in Ireland. In the summer of Bryan's twenty-first year, he and I were chosen to represent our country on the world stage as a Unified bowling team. Getting picked to compete as one of 7,000 athletes from 162 countries at such a huge event was an incredible honor, and we wanted to do well. For seven months, he and I each bowled a total of fifteen games *each week*, courtesy of our local bowling center. By the time we left for Ireland, we were as ready as we could be!

After five days of practice in Belfast, we were bussed to Dublin and treated to a spectacularly colorful and loud opening ceremony, held in Croke Park. The 80,000 spectators, including Karen and our daughter, Shauna, were witnesses to a kaleidoscope of color and sound as we were entertained by hundreds of performers, and we were all left open-mouthed in awe. Stars such as Colin Farrell, Pierce Brosnan, Jon Bon Jovi, Arnold Schwarzenegger, and Muhammad Ali led the parade of countries into the stadium where over one hundred Riverdancers, the band U2, Nelson Mandela, and many others helped turn the night magical.

After earning only a fourth place ribbon in our first competition, we were given another chance two days later. This time we successfully earned gold medals by trusting the skills we had learned at practice. The rest of the trip was a blur of watching other competitions, sight-seeing, and shopping. For me, at least, this was a life-changing, incredible experience that led to my writing a book: *SPIRIT, COURAGE and RESOLVE: A Special Olympics Athlete's Road to Gold*. The book takes the reader from Bryan's birth to our fifteen days in Ireland.

Since that amazing experience in Ireland, Bryan and I have worked together to pursue a different kind of gold: Down syndrome awareness. He and I decided to write a second book together, about Down syndrome. *I JUST AM: A Story of Down Syndrome Awareness and Tolerance* contains pictures and easy-to-read text that explains how Bryan feels about his disability. We also included a section on facts about Down syndrome and language guidelines. Our goal was to use this book to do school presentations and educate the public about disabilities and Down syndrome awareness. Bryan may not talk as much as me, but he does a great job answering any questions the students have. We are extremely proud that both books have been sold in all fifty states and twelve countries. We are honored that *I JUST AM* can be found on the desk of Eunice Kennedy Shriver. We are blessed that it has been translated into Romanian and French. But it is even more satisfying when we are told how beneficial our books and talks are to people. We really feel like we are touching lives and making a difference.

This past year we were honored to witness Bryan's induction into the City of Chandler Sports Hall of Fame for his numerous accomplishments in Special Olympics. His bronze plaque commemorating his achievements is on display in the Chandler Museum along with his gold medal. It is rather thrilling to take visitors there and show off our son and his display.

But of all the things that make me proud to be Bryan's father, what I treasure most is how he has changed me as a person. I grew up an ignorant, punk kid who called people retards if they looked "different." Now I am a paraprofessional in special education in Bryan's old classroom. Thanks to him and our three-legged German shepherd, Ozzie, I am now an advocate for people and animals with disabilities, and in the process I have discovered a new side of myself. Bryan has helped me to face life's challenges positively. He has helped me to see those who are different, differently.

It has now been twenty-seven years since Bryan was born. I wonder what my response would have been that day if someone had told me he would grow up to be an international gold medal winner. I am so grateful we have been able to work as a team to pursue and achieve his goals. But while Bryan's accomplishments in sports are remarkable in many ways, I believe the joy and inspiration he brings me, our family, and others is his greatest victory.

● ● ●

Tom is a paraprofessional in special education at Corona del Sol High School in Chandler, Arizona, and also works as a baseball and softball umpire. His daughter Shauna is a paraprofessional in special education at a local high school as well. Along with his wife, Karen, he is the founder and former president of Recreation and Athletics for the Disabled (RAD). RAD is a nonprofit group in Chandler that financially assists individuals with disabilities to participate in recreational activities. Tom and Bryan will be speaking at the World Down Syndrome Congress in Ireland in 2009. Learn more about Tom's publications at www.spiritcourageresolve.com and www.ijustam.org.

Patricia Sprague, Tabitha Thompson, and her cat named Jefferson

59.

Letters in the Sand

By Patricia Sprague

IT WOULD BE impossible to home school Tabitha. There's no cur-riculum labeled "For a child with Down syndrome." Besides, I'm not specialized in teaching a mentally challenged child....

Such were my thoughts when my daughter Tabitha reached school age. I felt strongly inspired to teach her at home, and I had successfully home schooled her older sister the previous year, but given my lack of experience and materials in special education I felt inadequate at best. So I ignored the promptings to home school, and enrolled Tabitha in public school.

Prior to classroom placement, Tabitha had extensive testing in the areas of communication, socialization, motor skills, adaptive behavior, and daily living skills. I received the test results at the first IEP meeting. Each of the tests gave Tabitha's developmental age in that skill area. Her highest was three years, eleven months; her lowest was one year, eleven months. I'll never forget the pain that gripped my heart as I read over the numbers. I couldn't believe they were accurate. For a moment I considered speaking up, but I felt intimidated as I looked around at the professionals and experts at the table, including teachers, speech-language pathologists, a social worker, a psychologist, and the principal.

It was determined that Tabitha would attend an inclusive class for part of the day, and a special education class for the rest of the day. I immediately signed up as an aide in the inclusive classroom, hoping to enhance her school experience in any way I could. As I served in the classroom, many things about the learning environment troubled me. For example, I noticed the time constraints the teachers had to place on the different activities, for the sake of maintaining a schedule. Tabitha was always lagging behind. One day during music time, the children took turns saying their names in a microphone. Tabitha consistently had trouble pronouncing her name and usually would not say it. This time, when her turn came she hung her head and did not say a word. I vowed to approach the speech specialist and insist that we teach Tabitha to sign and spell her name. But deep down inside I knew it was I, not the speech specialist, who needed to teach Tabitha. I still didn't feel ready, though, and kept pushing those thoughts back into the recesses of my mind. But the impressions surfaced again and again: I needed to teach Tabitha at home.

Halfway through Tabitha's second year in public school, I decided I could no longer ignore what my heart was telling me. Finally, I began to prepare for home schooling. I earnestly searched the Internet for curriculum ideas, special-needs forums, and home school sites. I developed a schedule with plenty of time for activities, lessons, and writing. I created custom worksheets for Tabitha, and also found K- 5 workbooks in stores. I purchased alphabet and number flashcards, puzzle cards, and music tapes. My dear husband made us a huge flannel board and I glued small pieces of sandpaper on the backs of alphabet and phonic cards and they stuck right on the board. I was ready for our shared learning experience to begin.

Our early days included many successes. Tabitha sat at a cute wooden desk that a friend had given us. All her books and pencils and crayons fit inside under the lid. Tabitha had lots of fun with the flannel board letters, and she especially loved the Bible story cards that had puzzles on the back and a corresponding coloring page. Of course there were challenges, too. Our first lesson in manuscript printing was exasperating. I had found a printing book that suggested using capital letters, starting with the letter F. I gave Tabitha a small pencil and she tried her best to copy that straight line. It was difficult for her to put enough pressure on the pencil to make the line show up. She was at the point of tears. But when we replaced the pencil with a marker, which doesn't require as much pressure to make a mark, there were sparkly eyes, hugs, and a big, toothy smile of accomplishment. Later, I discovered a "Learn to Write ABC's and 123's" vinyl book that used erasable markers. Tabitha kept busy wiping her letters off over and over again and smiling to herself.

I found home schooling Tabitha to be a tough yet gratifying job. On many days, it was a struggle to keep her motivated, and her frequent sinus and ear infections often made her miserable and not a very pleasant person to teach. Those situations required imagination and flexibility on my part. But our experience overall was a positive one. Our days were full with lessons at home, including educational computer and video games that Tabitha taught herself to play. We had a home school group each Friday, and a speech class two times a week at the public school. Tabitha also helped me deliver meals once a month for Meals on Wheels, and these were precious times of visual and hands-on instruction for Tabitha to learn to help others.

When Tabitha was nine a new, experimental Christian school accepted her as a student, and I was thrilled. She was the only person in the school with special needs. The curriculum included a series of videotaped lessons to teach the children in each grade level. In Tabitha's grade, the teacher in the video was actually leading a real Kindergarten class where the students answered questions, sang songs, played games, and much more. Subjects included Bible Study, Skills Development, Phonics, Numbers, Activity Time (Science or Art), Oral Language Enrichment, and Reading.

When the Christian school closed the next year, I decided to use the same video program with Tabitha at home. My philosophy became, if you don't get it the first time, do it over until you do get it. When Tabitha knew all her letters and sounds, when she could write them all without help, when she could count many items in sequence, when she could sound out three-letter words, we would move on.

We continued to supplement our activities with speech therapy, Meals on Wheels volunteering, and our weekly home school group meeting. These meetings created many wonderful memories. On a particular Friday afternoon, one mother talked about her Indian heritage. We played games, ate buffalo and deer jerky (well, at least tried to eat it), and drew pictures on paper bags. Tabitha drew a cloud, some grass, and a tree. We all shared our pictures and imagined an Indian name for each of us. When I asked Tabitha what she had drawn, she said, "croud and a twee." The names immediately popped into my mind: *Singing Cloud* for Tabitha, and for myself, *Sitting Tree*. Tabitha often sang (very loudly) in the car, the store, or whenever she felt like singing. To me, *Singing Cloud* represented Tabitha's freedom to be herself, and not be tied down to a specific curriculum in the public school system. Sitting Tree symbolized that I would always be there to watch out for her and to be a strong advocate in her life.

Frustration. Endurance. Repetition. Patience. Joy. These words describe my home schooling experience. I wish I could recount all the highs and lows, the thoughts and feelings, the figurative major and minor heart attacks, the countless clothing changes (I've told my husband we should own stock in pull-ups and wipes), the joys and the sorrows, but alas my editor would surely be getting her cutting shears out. Tabitha has humbled me and kept me on my knees. She has made me laugh at the thousand different facial expressions she makes. She has exasperated me to the point of anger, followed by very quick prayers for immediate help. She has strengthened my relationship with the God who created her and inspired me to teach her at home.

I'll try to sum up all of this in a sweet remembrance of a special moment with Tabitha. One early November day, when the leaves were brilliant colors, the sun warm, and the air a bit cool, I took Tabitha to the park to enjoy the swings, slides, and sand. Tabitha has always loved sand. I usually kept the sand toys in the car, but I had forgotten them that day, so I showed Tabitha how to draw letters in the sand with a stick. She took the stick from me and said, "I'll show you." She wrote very clearly the letters: M O M. Then she said, "See…MOM."

Tears came quickly to my eyes as she looked at me with her sparkly eyes and her big, toothy grin. I hugged her, remembering our diligent handwriting practice and all the other learning experiences we'd shared. In that moment, all the challenges and frustrations of home schooling vanished completely, leaving only the joy of Tabitha's love letters in the sand.

For with God, nothing shall be impossible. (Luke 1:37)

● ● ●

Patty lives in Vandalia, Illinois, with her husband, Randy. Together they share in loving six children and eleven grandchildren. Tabitha (1995) enjoys home school, challenger baseball, church youth group, visiting her older siblings and nieces and nephews, and playing with "Jefferson," her feisty cat. Patty has written a book, No Tears for Tabitha *(Publish America, 2006), detailing the challenges and struggles before, during, and after Tabitha's birth. Please e-mail her at newfaith1981@yahoo.com.*

Susanne, her mother, and Bill, 1980

60.

BILL

By Susanne Pelikan

FRIDAY, DECEMBER 21ST was my grandfather's birthday and the day that my Uncle Bill's heart stopped beating. This was a bittersweet time for my family. Bitter, because it had been a very tough year for us—Bill had been recovering from a difficult surgery and had been doing well. Sweet, despite Bill's recent health issues, because this was an unwelcome yet simple passing. He was surrounded by friends and caregivers who knew and cared for him deeply, and those of us who couldn't be there find comfort in knowing that he had such good and loving people around him. As a family we were sad to see him go, but happy that he found peace.

When I think of my Uncle Bill, I always picture big square block letters that spell **BILL,** for that's how he wrote his name. The style signifies him very well: Simple yet bold, no hidden meanings, nothing fancy to bring about some dressed-up conclusion. When I was young, I had no idea how much his life would affect mine. As a little girl, I just saw him as this different kind of uncle who was fun to play with. When I was four or five, I was amazed that an adult would play such great games of cowboys and Indians. We would lie on the floor of my grandmother's house and line the little toy characters up just so. I didn't always understand what Bill was trying to say but I definitely enjoyed the game. Elvis Presley was his passion. He had an impressive album collection and played along on his Mickey Mouse Club guitar. Of course he knew all the words—or at least he thought he did!

In my teen years, Uncle Bill taught me that it takes all kinds of people to make up the world. My relationship with him inspired me to volunteer as a swimming assistant at my high school. This experience opened my little teenage world to a whole new variety of people who faced challenges far greater than my typical teenage problems. Those kids taught me that it was okay to be yourself, have fun, and not care that others might think you are different.

I saw a news clip recently where a woman was describing her son with Down syndrome. She was proud of her son and saw rich meaning in his life. Yes, his disability had brought challenges to his development. However, because of these challenges she had enrolled him in a swimming program as a baby, and as a young adult, he went on to the international Special Olympics as a competitive swimmer. His life was rich; he was loved, he had friends, he had a job, and he had accomplished something with his unique abilities and talents. She pointed out that he had achieved all that any of us can hope for in life.

Her words have reminded me that my Uncle Bill also lived a great life. He was deeply loved by his family. He gave love freely and generously, and taught many people about the true meaning of love. He had many friends, including friends of the family, teachers, and those who lived with him in his group home. He mourned the loss of friends when they passed away or moved out of his life. He was proud of the work he did, and genuinely enjoyed being employed at his local workshop.

But his influence didn't stop there. Simply by living so long, Bill showed the world something unexpected. In the 1940s, when he was born, the life expectancy for individuals with Down syndrome was less than eighteen years old. Bill lived to be sixty-two! When Bill was born, the term "Down syndrome" didn't exist—my mother grew up calling her brother a "mongoloid." At that time, most children with an extra chromosome were institutionalized, because it was believed that they were profoundly retarded, wouldn't accomplish anything, and would require great care. My grandmother and grandfather fought hard to keep their son in their home. They fought for educational opportunities, understanding, and support. Together with Bill, they opened a door of opportunity for others and showed the world that with the proper tools, people with mental and physical disabilities can achieve great things.

Bill's biggest legacy can be seen right here in my home, as our little Jake starts his life's journey with the challenge and opportunity of Down syndrome. When Jake was born in April of 2007 with an unexpected diagnosis, we were devastated at first. But I realized that, thanks to Bill, I was better prepared than some parents. When I heard "Down syndrome," I knew a face and loving personality to attach to those words. I knew that I would love and cherish this child just like my other children. And as I learned about all the resources and

Susanne and her son Jake, 2009

help that were available to Jake and our family, my goals and expectations for him surpassed any that my grandmother could have dreamed of. Imagine a world where people with Down syndrome earn high school diplomas and attend college classes. I think of this every time I open the door to one of the many people who come to help us achieve our best.

Thank you, BILL.

●　　●　　●

Originally from the east coast, Susanne and her husband Jim have lived in Southeastern Wisconsin for the past seven years. Susanne is a stay-at-home mom to four children, including Jake (2007), who was diagnosed with Down syndrome at birth. The family affectionately calls him their surprise that keeps on surprising. Susanne hopes to one day continue her career as a landscape architect.

Bill Irish was born and raised in Northern Indiana. He moved to group homes as an adult and passed away in 2007. His mother, Esther Irish, was a founding member of the ARC of Indiana.

THE GIFT OF JOY

Dr. Joann Richichi, Alexander Chianese, Dr. Anthony Chianese

61.

An Enlightening Snow Day

By Alexander Chianese

SNOW DAY. I knew it the minute I woke up and saw the blanket of white outside my bedroom window. School was closed, as the mixture of ice and snow made driving conditions hazardous. It was March, for goodness sakes—about time we finally had a snow day! As the wind blew outside my window and the hail tapped gently against the pane, I drummed my fingers on my desktop, my mind wandering to what could be in store for me today. It was Tuesday— Mom's day to work in the operating room. Maybe I could watch one of her surgeries.

Ever since childhood I've enjoyed joining my mother at work. After school most of the kids scattered off the bus eager to get home in order to dispel some of their pent-up energy by playing with friends or climbing trees. I would return home with anticipation and excitement about the possibility that my mom might once again take me to work. I took pleasure in following my mother around the hospital whenever I had the chance because I enjoyed the way she interacted with her patients and how they in turn showed their appreciation for her efforts and dedication. Plus, whenever I showed up, I was pampered by many a nurse. Better yet, on rare and special occasions I was able to witness a surgery, or best of all, a birth.

While gazing out of my bedroom window watching the precipitation form a blanket of snow, I couldn't help but hope that some adventure or experience awaited my participation. My hopes were fulfilled by a phone call. When I picked up the phone, my mom's voice was full of joy and excitement. She said, "Alex, get Dad to take you to the hospital quickly. My patient is in labor and she would like you to witness the birth of her child. It's her fourth child so she should deliver pretty soon." Before I could respond, the phone's dial tone sounded. I ran to find my father, who was shoveling the driveway, and asked for a ride to the hospital. As he navigated the slippery roads, I thought of how amazing it was that this patient, whom I'd met during prior office consultations, recalled that I wanted to become a physician and, despite the pains of her contractions, had invited me into the delivery room so that I could share in her memorable experience.

During the ride to the hospital I thought about my future. As a tenth grader, I was already making plans for college and medical school. Ever since I could remember, I'd had the desire to become a physician. Some might assume that both my parents, my mom (an obstetrician/gynecologist) and my dad (a general practitioner), unduly influenced this desire. But my parents never pushed me in any direction. They just wanted me to be content with my career choices. They never needed to say, "My son, the doctor" because they were just happy loving me for who I was and not for the title I might achieve in the future. As we approached the hospital that blustery

March morning, I didn't realize that I would soon have an even more clear understanding of their love for me.

After arriving, I went straight to the Labor and Delivery Unit, a familiar place for me. I was greeted by the OB-GYN resident on call that morning. She said, "Your mother is finishing up another case in the operating room. In the meantime she would like me to introduce you to her patient. By the way, this patient's baby has Down syndrome and will be born retarded." She wasn't deliberately being insensitive; rather, she was trying to prepare me for what was to come.

I wasn't sure what to say in response. "I'm sorry to hear that," I finally replied, wondering why my mom did not convey this slight detail over the phone that morning, and worried about how the baby's mother might react to the diagnosis. "Does the patient know?"

"Of course she knows," the resident replied. "She knew all along and still decided to proceed with the pregnancy." At that moment, a large and burdensome weight was lifted from my shoulders.

As I walked to the patient's room, I wondered how different this birth would be from the dozens of other births I had witnessed over the years. I also thought of how I would introduce myself and wondered if it was appropriate to say that I was sorry about the diagnosis. I found myself trying to grasp why a couple with three healthy daughters would elect to have a fourth child with a disability. While waiting to be introduced to the patient, I couldn't help but wonder why the patient and her husband chose not to use prenatal technology to their advantage in order to prevent what most individuals would consider a tragic birth. At the time, their decision not to invest in prenatal testing made me feel sorry for the family and the hardships they would have to endure in the future. But when I arrived at the delivery room, I realized that to feel sorry was an inappropriate emotion. The family was so elated about the impending birth that their anticipation and joy were nearly palpable.

When I finally entered the delivery room all I could think to say was, "Hi, I'm Alex. Thank you so much for this opportunity." The parents greeted me with open arms and sparkling smiles. The mother asked, "Do you remember watching a video when you were a young boy of your mother delivering a baby?"

"Yes," I said. "I do remember. I think that was the only time I saw my mother deliver a baby on video."

"That was my first child," the mother said. She looked at me and smiled, her warm eyes filled with joy and excitement for the upcoming arrival. And there I was, almost eight years later, watching another one of her children coming into the world.

Down the hallway I could hear my mom's voice. She had finished her case in the O.R. and was approaching the delivery room. The room was already packed with a team of medical staff—residents, interns, medical students, and nurses, all for the arrival of the baby. I greeted my mom with a big hug and a kiss of appreciation. Mom told me about the long and strenuous delivery she'd just attended, and when she saw her long-time patient and friend sprawled out on the delivery room table, she assured her, "Not to worry, your delivery will be quick since you've already had three other children." The patient sighed with relief and chatted with my mom about past deliveries. I thought there would be tension and anxiety in the room, but everyone was joking and laughing, led by the banter between my mom and her patient.

My mom was right—things progressed quickly from that point. The mother didn't push very long before everyone was scurrying about getting things ready for the birth. Her husband scrambled to get the camera ready. My mom barely had her gown on before that special baby came into the world. The delivery process certainly involved a lot of teamwork. The nurses were rooting for the patient to "push harder" while my mother frequently encouraged the patient's every effort by saying, "You can do it. Your baby is almost here." The patient squeezed her husband's trembling hand as he struggled to capture the delivery with the video camera in his free hand. The delivery seemed almost magical as the newborn baby created an entirely different aura throughout the room. The shouting from the medical staff came to an abrupt silence as everyone gazed at the fragile child.

One glance at her baby girl, and the mother cried with happiness. She said, "She's beautiful. Her name will be Gabriella." I immediately walked up to Gabriella and caressed her small, smooth feet.

Everything about the delivery process appeared completely natural, "a delivery for the books," as my mother called it. There were no complications and most importantly, no disappointments. When I asked my mother why she hadn't told me about the baby's diagnosis, she responded, "There was no need to tell you because it wasn't going to change the delivery process. The delivery of a child with Down syndrome is just the same as any other child."

But aside from the obvious similarities between the birth of a so-called normal baby and a baby with Down syndrome, there was one difference. The parents of the other babies whose births I had witnessed were all expecting a typical child, perhaps one who would grace their lives with a future of achievement in competitive sports, creative arts, and academics. However, Gabriella's parents did not know what their child might achieve. At the time, I wasn't aware that people with Down syndrome have not only cognitive impairments, but can also have a variety of possible medical issues, such as intestinal and cardiac problems. This couple was well versed on those potential issues, and even knew that the baby definitely had a heart defect, yet they embraced their baby with warmth, love, and tenderness, which was truly miraculous for me to witness.

As I watched the parents welcome their new baby with joy, I saw reflected in their faces my parents' own unconditional love and support. I understood why my parents didn't push me with my studies and why they just wanted me to be happy with who I was, not with who I may become. When my mother embraced the new baby girl and her parents, I understood why my parents became doctors despite the challenges they face. And on that enlightening snow day, as I posed for a family picture that included me, my mom, Gabriella, and her parents, I understood beyond reason the meaning of love: The joy of sharing part of yourself with someone else.

●　●　●

Alex is a sophomore undergraduate student at Drew University, where he is currently enrolled in the pre-medicine track. He has many interests outside of the academic curriculum, such as painting and drawing, play-

ing the violin, and working as a part-time patient escort in the hospital.
Alex is very grateful for his experiences with his mother in the hospital,
where he continues to witness the practice of medicine in action.

Caitlin and Zoey Needham

62.
Through Rose-Colored Glasses

By Caitlin Needham

MY MOTHER IS as blind as a bat. She literally could not function without her contacts or her glasses. I've seen some pictures of her in her childhood, and let me tell you, she wore some nice, thick glasses. My dad's eyes are pretty much the same. He has recently bought a pair of reading glasses (from what I understand, this is some rite of passage in middle to late adulthood). My sister Jessica has worn glasses since fifth grade, and she too cannot see a thing without glasses or contacts. But my sister Taylor has perfect vision. My brothers Jake and Joe, we have yet to find out.

Then there's me.

I have 20/20 vision. Nothing medically wrong with my sight. But as of the last year and a half, I have begun "wearing" a type of glasses. I guess you could say they're rose-colored glasses. Typically, that phrase carries a negative connotation: ignorance, denial, feigned optimism, perhaps even foolishness. But is this really so? Or is seeing the world with a soft pinkish glow actually a gift of sorts?

I would support the latter.

My littlest sister, Zoey, came into my life at a time of grayness. By gray I mean that I was going through the motions of life, skating by, taking all for granted. My existence up to that point was a self-centered one that revolved around my schedule and my agenda only. My days were filled with a monotonous routine of school, an after-school job, and socializing with friends as I saw fit. There was no color. Even the warmest, sunniest days seemed dull. I found it much easier to remain apathetic in so many areas of my life, rushing around and trying to do what was best for only myself.

But everything changed the day I met Zoey. Though she made a relatively smooth entrance into the world, her tiny heart strained and pumped, trying to oxygenate her fragile body, compromised by an atrioventricular canal defect. Instead of taking her home with us, her home became the NICU at Children's Hospital Los Angeles. Underneath a tangle of tubes and wires, her ferocious spirit battled for life, giving me a run for my money in the courage zone. As I gazed at her, she wordlessly told me, "Slow down. Stop and look around for a minute."

So I did. And that's when Zoey handed me a pair of glasses with rose-colored lenses.

My new glasses felt a little funny. The discomfort stemmed from somewhere deep inside myself, in a place that knew that my priorities needed to be reordered. I wanted to step outside of myself and begin to take steps toward looking forward instead of backward. I wanted to be the glass-half-full type, not someone who dwelled on setbacks, adversity, or doubt. So even though I'd never really worn glasses like these before, and I wasn't even sure they fit correctly, I gave them a shot.

It was amazing: When I put on the glasses, everything took on color. The senseless seemed more manageable, and hope overtook discouragement. With my newfound faith and optimism, everything seemed a little brighter, a little more vibrant. Sometimes doubts would surface—was I really cut out to wear these glasses? But as I persisted in a new way of seeing the world, the twinges of doubt became fewer and farther between. More often than not, I felt warmth and joy shining through the usual gray of my life.

But new challenges surfaced as time passed. I struggled to balance my increasingly busy schedule, and I began to worry about my future and about Zoey. Her medical setbacks seemed overwhelming and daunting. Zoey had arrived with a few unexpected tagalongs—namely, transient myleoproliferative disorder (a type of leukemia), feeding issues, and a middle cerebral artery infarction, more commonly known as a stroke.

Each diagnosis was devastating enough on its own, but when all these issues teamed up at once, there seemed to be nothing we could do but wait and try to make sense of the senseless. Percentages and statistics intimidated my courage. The glasses seemed powerless to soften life's harsh truths. There were times I chose to take them off. There were times I threw them across the room, there were even times I contemplated stepping on them. When Zoey developed infantile spasms, a devastating form of epilepsy, it seemed that she would never be cut a break. She seized throughout the day, fogged in an epileptic haze. But Zoey never gave up, so I didn't either. And through rose-colored glasses, I came to see the stark contrast of all that is worthwhile and meaningful and all that is void and purposeless.

How did such a little baby know about these glasses? How did she know to give them to me? The amazing thing is, Zoey has a pair herself.

She was born wearing them.

The blueprints for her glasses were located on her third 21st chromosome, and they genetically formed right into her very being. In every cell of her body she contains the secret to living a beautiful life: optimism, perseverance, and joy. Zoey is a world-class hugger and snuggler. She willingly thrusts herself into the arms of strangers.

She waves to anyone and everyone who passes by. She dances and wiggles when she hears the beat of a drum. She is a professional kiss-blower, offering not one kiss, but twenty to the privileged recipient. She tolerates multiple interruptions for g-tube feedings and medications a day, though she'd rather be rolling around the house to keep up with her brothers. Unlike nearly every other two-year-old, Zoey is most content sitting on the lap of her mommy or daddy, reading books, poised and ready to turn the pages. She endures endless blood draws, checkups, invasive diagnostic procedures, and toxic chemicals being pumped in her veins so that she might overcome her latest medical enemy, AML, acute myelogenous leukemia.

The day Zoey was diagnosed with leukemia, I went through a gamut of emotions. I felt despair and anger. I wished I had been diagnosed with cancer instead of my precious sister. I felt numb. I felt invincible and resolute that Zoey would overcome such a terrible disease. I felt weary. I felt strong because I wanted to provide strength. Highs followed lows and vice versa. And, though I felt a little silly saying it, I was heartbroken to think of Zoey's little head, bald from chemotherapy. I couldn't imagine her without her auburn curls. I dismissed the thought, telling myself, "It will grow back. She can be bald for a while and have a lifetime to grow back her hair."

When chemotherapy commenced, I prepared myself to see Zoey with a new hairdo, or lack thereof. Rounds one and two came and passed, and her curls were intact. Every time I would go to visit Zoey or see her between rounds at home, I prepared myself to see her hair thinning and disappearing, but that day never came. Now, as she completes her sixth and final round of chemo, Zoey's hair is as long, thick, curly, and wild as ever. Between the smiles and the curls, she looks perfectly healthy. Her reddish brown waves and curls shimmer in the sunlight. Ringlets dangle down her neck in flawless spirals. She is a work of art. She is a warrior in every sense of the word, pressing on and fighting the good fight without flinching. A cancer patient, a stroke survivor, an open heart surgery alumna, an epileptic who hasn't seized in a year, a sister, a daughter, an inspiration.

Zoey's rose-colored glasses are not a mark of her ignorance or her foolishness; they are a symbol of her ability to persevere in an unfair world. She didn't have to buy these glasses, shop around for them, or try them on for size, they just came perfectly tailor made for her. For me, wearing glasses like Zoey's hasn't come so naturally, but I am learning. Down syndrome is beyond human control. But many other things are not. I have been empowered with the power to choose. I can choose an optimistic attitude. I can choose to take the time to appreciate joy amidst pain. I can choose to push on during the times when giving up seems like an easier option. I can choose to rejoice in the unimaginable promise of my life and Zoey's life. I can choose to embrace this ephemeral existence for all it's worth. I can choose to share my point of view with others.

And from my point of view, life is looking pretty rosy these days.

● ● ●

The second oldest of six children, Caitlin currently resides in La Jolla, California and works for a nonprofit organization assisting adults with developmental disabilities. She plans on pursuing a career in special education. Caitlin and Zoey's mother keeps a blog chronicling their family and their journey with Down syndrome called "Little Wonders" at www.littlewonders-heather.blogspot.com.

Lynne Goldklang and Hannah Greenstein

63.
From Hannah to Broadway

By Lynne Goldklang

"WHO WILL BUY this wonderful morning...?"

I watch the young people singing, dancing, and acting their hearts out as they recreate a glorious moment from the musical *Oliver,* dressed in the ragged clothes of street orphans from long ago. Vendors appear on the stage hawking their wares—flowers, milk, fruit, sweets. One of the young orphans has been rescued from homelessness and celebrates the new day with a rousing dance. Others join in and the stage is filled with vibrant young people. The audience is clapping, cheering, and crying. The actors are teens and young adults with Down syndrome and other disabilities, part of a troupe of about thirty players started thirteen years ago by Mary Rings, an actress and teacher with two grown sons, the youngest with Down syndrome. And thanks to my granddaughter Hannah, I get to be part of the action.

Hannah made her entrance into this world on Valentine's Day of 2006. My daughter Carol's pregnancy had been normal until the last trimester, when the baby suddenly stopped growing. The decision was made to induce labor a month early. I was at Carol's home watching over her two older children when the ring of the telephone jolted me out of restless sleep, just before dawn.

"Mom," came Carol's exhausted voice, "our little girl was just born. She's okay. Only, I need to tell you something...." She paused for a few seconds as I held my breath.

"Mom, please don't be sad, but she has Down syndrome."

I must have been in a trance, because I felt the fervent command: "Don't be sad" enter my subconscious and root there like a strong tree. Still, I had mixed emotions. In the place where sorrow might have been was fear: fear for the baby's health and future well being; fear for my daughter, son-in-law, and their two trusting children who were waiting to see their new sister. Yet I also felt joy at the birth of this tiny infant, who was immediately attached to tubes and taken to the neonatal unit of the small hospital where she was born.

When Hannah came home after a few weeks of hospital care, my mixed emotions continued, especially as I began to research information about Down syndrome to supplement the information the family was already receiving. I thought Down syndrome meant some mental retardation and awkwardness of movement. I had no idea that every system of the body was involved and that serious problems could occur at any age. In the early months when I would visit Hannah, I felt confident that her future would be bright because she just seemed like any other baby, only happier. Life seemed "normal." But when I came back home and resumed my reading, the fears returned in full force. I was overwhelmed by the stories that were often uplifting but also told of serious medical, social, and school challenges. The accounts of major illnesses kept me up at night with worry.

I wanted some reassurance that the babies and children I was read-ing about could make it to adulthood with lives of quality. I wanted to hold a positive picture in my mind of Hannah all grown up and tak-ing her place in the community. So I began to search everywhere for faces with those lovely almond eyes, especially in adult populations. Where were the teens and grown-ups with Down syndrome?

Then I saw a flyer for a play at the local college featuring the Born To Act Players. I looked carefully at the picture in the flyer and saw lots of beaming faces of teenagers and young adults with Down syndrome. Not long afterward, I found myself in a crowded theater watching a performance that would change my life and give me hope for Hannah, as well as all the Hannahs who are still babies and toddlers.

The performance was an Improv show featuring musical num-bers and comedic skits. The opening act was interpretive dance. At least twenty-five people participated onstage in their simple black tee shirts with *Born to Act Players* printed on the front. Many of the troupe danced with grace and fluidity to the beat of the music, while others made up for any lack of coordination with their enthusi-asm and heart. In the acts that followed, the players performed lots of lively theater games, including take-offs on *The Dating Game.* They spontaneously invented scenes from first and last lines suggested by the audience. Some of the skits were as funny as anything you would see on *Saturday Night Live.* I quickly forgot that I was watching young people with disabilities and gave myself over fully to the experience of being influenced and entertained. As the performance evolved, I real-ized that I was seeing talent, passion, and ability—not disability.

When the performance ended, I wanted to hug everyone just as their proud families and friends were doing. My heart was overflow-ing with gratitude, optimism, and awareness. From the time I'd sat down in the theater with a pounding heart, to the final curtain call, my knowledge of what is possible for anyone with Down syndrome expanded way beyond my expectations. I realized that the performers whose talents I'd just enjoyed were pioneers who came to that stage the hard way—born in an era just a few years beyond the time when ba-bies with Down syndrome were usually taken away to an institution.

Surely their parents had fought for every bit of progress they achieved, from adequate schooling to enrichment programs to acceptance in the community. I felt real hope for my granddaughter and her generation, born in a more enlightened time with so many opportunities.

When I got home, I went to the troupe's website for more information. I was surprised by the variety of productions they had performed, including scenes from Shakespeare. I contacted the director and asked if I could help, thinking maybe they needed a grandma to run errands or lend support. The welcoming voice of Mary

Mary Rings (director) and her son Casey Powell

Rings reached out to me immediately, inviting me to come to the next rehearsal and become one of the troupe's assistants.

Soon my life expanded to include spending every Saturday morning with the most engaging, hard-working group of young people. I will always remember how nervous I was the first day and how I was soon wrapped in hugs and words of encouragement. It's a challenge for me to keep up with these talented actors, but they accept me lovingly in spite of my limitations.

The assistants do everything the players do, including acting in the performances. Several of the assistants are professional actors; a few have siblings with Down syndrome. We help players who need a boost and assist with many behind-the-scenes tasks when it is production time. A popular activity is to form small groups for improvisations with assistants as leaders. The "kids" are so much more spontaneous than I am, so I must really focus to help them turn their terrific ideas into skits. One Saturday, Hannah and her family came to a class rehearsal, and they were embraced as if they were celebrities. Seeing little Hannah among all the grown-up "Hannahs" was a sight that brought me full circle.

Hannah will soon turn three. She is now walking, running, and even dancing. So far, none of my fears for her have been realized. She had a hole in her heart that miraculously began to close just as surgery was to be scheduled. She has ear tubes and wears glasses but is basically healthy, happy, and making steady progress on her own timetable. I'm flooded with gratitude toward that enchanting child for leading me into new worlds that have calmed my fears and opened my mind to new hopes and possibilities. I am thankful to my daughter Carol for asking me not to be sad on that Valentine's Day a few years ago when Hannah graced our world with her presence. As a psychotherapist I respect painful feelings, but sorrow is not the pathway I'm on as Hannah's grandmother. Sorrow is not in my heart as I spend time with the amazing Born to Act Players and their families. Tears sometimes come, but they are tears of joy.

● ● ●

Lynne is a psychotherapist, speaker, and coauthor of Count It as a Vegetable and Move On, *a book about weight management. She's the adoring grandma of five including Hannah, the youngest. She is passionate about the Born to Act Players (www.borntoactplayers.com) and is a supporter of DS Action, a group that includes Hannah's parents and others who raise funds for the first Down syndrome clinic in Southern California (www.dsaction.com).*

Laura Riddle and her niece, Elise Friou

64.

Two Blanks

By Laura Riddle

"THERE ARE TWO blanks left in the baby book," my sister said casually over a basket of chips at our favorite Tex-Mex spot. *"Baby's First Word* and *Baby's First Steps."*

As she spoke, "Baby"—my niece Elise—looked up at her mom and began using sign language to communicate requests. I couldn't take my eyes off Elise as she showed us *more* and *cracker* and *please*. It was a scene I couldn't have imagined seventeen months before, when she was born with Down syndrome.

We were told early on that Elise would probably walk and talk, but that we might have to wait years. And here was this little ball of energy sitting in a highchair and teaching me, definitely a pleasant surprise.

Elise learns new signs as quickly as they flash on her sign language DVDs and TV shows. Her parents reinforce them for her. And though she has a great team of therapists, she's the one teaching them new words. She's teaching us, too. The grandparents, the one-year-old cousin, and other family members are learning to sign and enjoying it. We call my sister, ask what new signs Elise knows, and try to learn them over the phone—perhaps not the easiest way to go about it. We look the signs up online if we can't picture them. The latest one was "monkey." My son and I guessed the sign would be underarm scratching—and we were right.

Elise's signing brings some humorous moments, and some beautiful, poetic ones, too. Now that she has a baby brother, she has begun signing *all done brother* when he cries, but *more brother* when she wants to spend time with him—and it really doesn't get sweeter than that. Recently she staged her first toddler protest: It was naptime and she kept signing *more* when the sign language DVD ended. Denied another viewing, she sat on her tiny velvet chair and pounded her arms on the armrest.

I refuse to make predictions about her physical milestones as well, because Elise defies them. My sister called me one day when my niece was four weeks old, asking when babies typically roll from tummy to back, as Elise had just done. (Two to three months, I told her.) None of us could believe what we were hearing. "Check out my 'developmentally delayed' baby!" my sister wrote with the video proof she e-mailed to family and friends.

That's the wonderful thing about Elise: She likes to follow the beat of her own drum—sometimes literally. Music really got Elise moving. When she got musical instruments for her first birthday, she took to them as if she had been playing her whole life. (Meanwhile, my daughter, who is two months younger and was at the same party, sat nearby trying to eat one of the drumsticks.) When Elise was fourteen months old, she observed her peers crawling around music class week after week. One day, she heard the same songs from class playing at home and began to crawl. The funny thing was, when the music stopped, she did, too, in a musical-chairs kind of way. But before long, she realized she didn't need the musical cue to take off.

These days Elise's physical therapist has her using a walker, and she's gaining confidence all the time. She's shaky enough that she needs a hand ready to catch her in case she falls forward, but she pushes the hand away. She can taste her freedom. First steps or not, she's moving forward in life.

Those two blanks in Elise's baby book remain. But when I see her scooting around the wood floor and smiling at her reflection in a new part of the house, like the sliding glass door in the kitchen or the freestanding mirror in her parents' room, I wonder how someone would capture that kind of progress. These joys just can't be conveyed with words or numbers. Baby books have a tendency to pin you down with rigid lines that dictate expectations. Elise has the opposite effect, urging us to "lighten up a little, close that baby book, and just watch me grow."

It's not that we don't want to hear Elise's first spoken word. Our chatty family is looking forward to her 10,000th, too. But for now, sign language has given Elise a voice, and I beam with pride every time she signs *aunt*. Elise has enriched my life, reminding me that communication transcends words. Her bright smiles speak volumes to me. It's not always about the bigger lessons, either. I love just spending time with her and watching her laugh and play with my children.

I will celebrate with my sister when she completes the suede-covered baby book that I helped her choose before Elise was born, but I'm not waiting until then. I celebrate Elise every day.

● ● ●

Laura is a mother of three and a newspaper editor in Dallas. Just before Elise's second birthday, she started taking her first steps. Then came her first word: "Mama."

Connie Szarek and granddaughter Rylie Volz

65.

Perfect

By Connie Szarek

TO ME THERE is only one thing more exciting than becoming a mother, and that is becoming a grandmother! My first granddaughter was three years old, and she had brought so much joy to my life. Now my daughter was telling me that another little angel was on the way. With joyful anticipation, I imagined how good it would feel to hold a tiny, newborn infant again and breathe in that sweet, powdery, baby smell. My daughter was young and healthy, and so we had no warning and no reason at all to suspect that our new little darling would be anything but perfect.

The big day finally arrived. I was at home anxiously awaiting news when Vince, my son-in-law, called me and said, "Mom, you have another granddaughter!" Overjoyed and relieved, I began making those "proud grandma" phone calls, letting my family and friends know that Rylie had arrived.

Then my daughter Valerie called, sounding both tired and somewhat upset. "Mom," she said. "Some of the baby's toes are stuck together, and she's having some trouble breathing. They only let me hold her for a minute before they took her away, and they haven't brought her back yet."

I tried my best to assure her that the webbed toes were a relatively minor problem, and that newborns sometimes need a little help with breathing in the beginning. "She'll be fine," I said.

But after a short while, Valerie called again. This time she was crying hard, and her trembling voice was filled with panic. "Mom, they're saying that they think she has Down syndrome. I can't believe it! She seems fine to us. They say she has to have a blood test, and then we'll know for sure."

Down syndrome. That sounded terrifying to me. My knowledge was limited to childhood memories of children with disabilities being teased and called awful names. I had once seen a TV show in which one of the actors who had Down syndrome was portrayed in a very positive light. But that was TV; real life wasn't always so easy. I had never known or even talked to a single person with Down syndrome in my entire life. My joy over my new granddaughter started slipping away as fear took over, but I wasn't ready to give in yet. "They could be wrong," I told Valerie. "Let's just wait for the test results. They're probably wrong."

I drove to the hospital, my arms aching to hold Rylie. Although there were numerous wires and tubes connected to her tiny body, the nurses kindly let me hold her for a while, and I fell immediately in love with her. She had little rosebud lips and light brown hair that was a bit unruly sticking out from under her pink knitted cap. She kept sticking her tongue out, which we thought was so cute, not knowing at the time that this could be one of the characteristic signs of Down syndrome. We waited three agonizingly long days, holding onto hope, and then the results of the test came back confirming that Rylie did indeed have Down syndrome.

This was unknown territory, and I was worried. Would Rylie be able to walk, to talk, or to interact with us at all? Would she play and be happy? Would children make fun of her? Would her life be meaningful? And what about Karlie, who was so excited about having a baby sister? Would she ever be able to have a close sister relationship with Rylie? My expectations started out low. But from the earliest days, she seemed to be winking at us and saying "Don't worry, I'm gonna work real hard, you'll see!" And she did. If I'd known then what I know now, I wouldn't have worried one bit.

I didn't know Rylie would be so strong. The doctors said she would be floppy, due to poor muscle tone. But at two days old, in the hospital's Neonatal Intensive Care Unit, Rylie arched her back and lifted her head. At home a few weeks later, while lying on her stomach, Rylie pushed up on her tiny foot, swung her little arm up high, and rolled over onto her back. Really! We have the video to prove it.

I didn't know Rylie would be so smart. When she was less than a year old, Rylie began to learn sign language to help with communication, amazing me with the complicated movements of her tiny hands and fingers. We still laugh about her first visit to Santa Claus. She had had enough of him and wanted to get off of his lap. She signed "Done!"

I didn't know Rylie would be so entertaining. Whenever she appears, hilarity ensues. She bounces into my kitchen exclaiming, "Look Mom-Mom! My new pants! And look! My hair!" as she pulls her pigtails out to each side of her head as far as they can go, making sure that I take notice of her pretty new hair ribbons. At her recent preschool graduation program, Rylie amazed us all with her flawless, enthusiastic performance. Her gorgeous brown eyes sparkled, and her smile reached from ear to ear as she proudly sang and danced her part. She alone is able to keep her baby sister from crying by putting on a show just for her. Wearing a glittery, pink princess dress, a fuzzy green hat on her head, and with a guitar in her hands, she belts out a song and baby Cesalie is instantly transformed from screaming baby to captive audience, singing and clapping along.

I didn't know Rylie would be so stubborn! For better or worse, her self-confidence and independence is evident in everything she does. If her shoes are on the wrong feet, she doesn't care—all that matters is that she put them on all by herself. It's no problem that her French fries are smothered in so much ketchup that you can barely see them—she did it by herself. And when her big sister isn't around, Rylie has been known to sneak into her room to listen to her MP3 player. *No* has always been one of her favorite words. (Thankfully, a grandmother can laugh at some of the things that parents find trying, a cute little defiant face being one of them.)

I didn't know Rylie would be so vibrant. Her charisma and her magnetism affect everyone around her. As a toddler, she made all the men in our family feel so special. They always got the big hellos and the bulk of her hugs and kisses. When her grandfather and I would visit, Rylie would give me a little wave (and I do mean little—barely a flip of her wrist) and a half-hearted "hi." Then she would bound over to my husband with arms outstretched, yelling, "Hi Pop-Pop!" And when I came to visit alone, she would greet me with, "Where's Pop-Pop?" But one day when we walked in and I, of course, was expecting the usual stingy wave, Rylie smiled and said, "Hi Mom-Mom." And of course, my heart melted.

I didn't know Rylie would be so personable. Recently, we were a bit apprehensive about how Rylie's new classmates would treat her since she is one of only two children with special needs in an inclusive kindergarten class. One day her teacher took a picture during the lunch break and gave it to Rylie to take home. There she was, eating her lunch and chatting away, the center of attention, surrounded by friends. As for Rylie's relationship with her big sister, I didn't know that these two little girls would love each other so much. Today, I watch them together—laughing, playing, fighting, and developing a very special bond that I know will grow deeper as they grow older— and I'm comforted and blessed.

A verse in the Bible aptly describes what Rylie has done for me: "I thank my God upon every remembrance of you" (Philipians 1:3). When I picture my granddaughter's sunny smile, when I recall her excited chatter, when I think of all the times she's made me laugh until I cried, and when I realize all of the amazing things she has accomplished (ordinary milestones as well as her own unique talents), then my joy overflows and I do thank God. Rylie really is that perfect baby we were waiting for; I just didn't know it then.

But I do now.

● ● ●

Connie lives on the east coast where she works in the field of law enforcement administration. She is passionate about cooking and baking, and also spends many happy hours tending to her flower garden. She and her husband of thirty-eight years have raised three children together and are now enjoying the many blessings of having three adorable granddaughters. You can read more about her granddaughter Rylie and her family at www.karyces.blogspot.com.

Jacob Nehrbass and Sarah Grace Nehrbass

66.

My Sister Sarah

By Jacob Nehrbass

MY SISTER SARAH has Down syndrome.
She spreads love and joy through our lives.
She is older than me, she is smaller than me,
    and she has a cute little smile.
She has a giggle like a thousand laughs.

When I was little, me and Sarah had schemes up our sleeves.
She taught me how to climb out of my crib.
We would mess up our room together.

We'd chase each other around the house, tickle each other,
    and tackle each other.
We give each other lots of "high fives" and
    wrestle each other to the ground.
She puts up a pretty good fight, and she is strong, quick, and fast.

Now we giggle and laugh, giggle and laugh,
    and sometimes dance around.
Sometimes she gets into my things and breaks all my stuff.
She threw a pillow at my cereal and it got on dad's shoes.
I took the blame.
But that's okay.

She gets sick a lot.
But she loves to eat chicken soup and salads.
When I am sad she makes me happy by smiling and giving me a hug.
When she is sad I am nice to her too.
She tells me what to do, and I sometimes listen.
I tell her what to do, and she sometimes listens.

Sarah is afraid of dogs.
She jumped into my arms once so I could protect her.

Sarah has always just been Sarah.
She is different than other kids.
She doesn't talk the same.
Sometimes we use sign language together.
If my friends make fun of her, I tell them to back off.
I tell them that she is the best gift of all to me.

I am so proud of her.
She has learned how to dance, ride horses, and swim.
We love to sing together.
We have fun together.
She is so silly, and she laughs at me.

I hope someday that Sarah will learn how to read and write.
Most important I am glad she is my sister.
I can't imagine having anyone else as my sister.
I love my sister, Sarah.

●　　●　　●

Jacob (1997) and his older sister, Sarah (1994), live in Hopkins, Min-
nesota, with their parents. Their father, a Lutheran Pastor/ballroom
teacher, and their mother, a choreographer/writer, own a local dance
studio. Jacob attends St. Peter's Lutheran School and loves to tap dance,
bike, play piano and drums, build LEGOS, and read. He and his sister
have an amazing relationship and enjoy swimming, dancing through
the house, sledding, and popcorn/movie nights together.

Andreca Burton and Taylor Freeman

67.
Taylor Made for Me

By Andreca Burton

MY NIECE TAYLOR makes beautiful memories.

I remember riding to the hospital the night my sister went into labor. It was raining, and my brother-in-law drove so slowly, I thought I would scream. I just wanted to get to the hospital so I could finally meet my niece or nephew (my sister wanted to be surprised by the sex of the baby). After arriving, my sister slept during all her contractions and only woke up when it was time to push. "It's a girl!" the doctor announced, and I heard the sweetest, most gentle cry from my niece.

I remember walking to her and staring at her in amazement. She was so pretty, her hair so thick and black, her skin a light gold, her little lips pink, her hands and feet so tiny. She looked into my eyes, and I cried because I had never seen someone so beautiful. After being weighed, she kept sticking out her tongue and sucking her lips—she was ready to eat. Into my sister's arms she went for breastfeeding, and afterward the nurses took her to the nursery and gave her a bath. Everywhere Taylor went I was sure to follow, and when I finally went home that night, I couldn't sleep.

I remember arriving at the hospital the next morning and hearing from my sister that the doctors wanted to run tests on the baby. They thought she might have trisomy 21. "It won't matter," I told my sister. "It won't change the way we love her." I took Taylor into my arms and held her close. She was like a little ray of sunshine streaming into my soul. I leaned close and whispered in her ear, "You can do anything you want to do."

I remember watching Taylor lift her head for the first time. At the time I was caring for her during the day while her parents worked, and going to college at night. She absolutely hated lying down on her belly, as the physical therapist wanted her to do, but I knew how important it was for her to practice. So I would place her on her stomach throughout the day to get her used to the position. One day, completely unexpectedly, she lifted her head straight off the carpet. The PT and I started clapping, and I gave her extra kisses and hugs all day long.

I remember Taylor's second birthday. She had her party at Chuck E. Cheese. She wasn't afraid of Chuck E. like her cousins are; she would give him handshakes and high fives. She enjoyed her pizza and Sprite, and then she was ready to play all the games. On that day and on every subsequent visit, Taylor was very generous to the other children; she would go around putting money in her game console as well as the other children's games. I laugh every time I think about her feeding the tickets to the ticket machine—she loves the crunching noise the machine makes.

I remember Taylor receiving a trampoline for Christmas, something she'd wanted very much. When she saw her gift she smiled wide, gave her granny a great big hug, and said "I got trampoline!" After climbing on she would jump, fall over, and then laugh. She loves it when I jump with her because I can bounce her high, so high. But every time I see her, she lifts me higher still, filling me with joy, happiness, and the deepest love.

Yes, my niece Taylor makes me the most beautiful memories.

● ● ●

Andreca lives in Hartwell, Georgia. She is currently working on her master's degree in Counseling and will be graduating in October 2009. She enjoys spending her spare time with family and friends, especially with her niece Taylor.

Jenni and Kate enjoying the conference together in Boston

68.

The Best Day

By Jenni Von Tobel

WHEN I RECEIVED a phone call at work asking if I knew of any families who would be willing to host a twenty-two-year-old woman with Down syndrome so that she could attend college classes, I thought to myself, *That would be a cool thing to do.* So when I sent out an email to families that I thought might be interested, I copied my husband, Paul, on the email. He called me immediately.

"This is a no brainer," he said excitedly. "Let's do it!"

"Really?" I asked, a bit surprised but excited too.

"Yeah, I mapquested the distance from her college to where I work and it's only a few miles. "

"Okay," I said, my mind racing to keep up with him. "I can call the family back and get the details."

"Great!" He paused. "This is the kind of thing we love to do. What a great opportunity for this college student. And for us!"

When the doorbell rang a week later, I opened the door to greet a young woman with short blonde hair and a big smile. "You must be Kate," I said, and she smiled and nodded. A few minutes later, she was sitting in our living room impressing us with her desire to continue attending college. She was going to be a sophomore and couldn't wait for the spring semester to start. Her family lived several hours from the college, which is why they sought host families to house Kate while she attended school. As we listened to Kate speak about her goals and dreams, Paul and I strongly felt that we should be her host family. We wanted to make a difference in her life. Little did we know how much of a difference she would make in ours!

People are often curious about why my husband and I have dedicated our lives to advocating, supporting, and loving individuals with special needs, particularly Down syndrome. Neither of us have family members with Down syndrome, but both of us have always been drawn to these individuals. In fact, we first met each other through a woman with Down syndrome at work, and when the time is right, we hope to adopt a child with special needs. With over fourteen years of experience in the field of special needs, I'd become well acquainted with individuals with Down syndrome, but Kate's influence on us was deeper than I anticipated.

"I had the best day of my life!" This was Kate's response every evening when I asked her how her day was. She might go on to tell me that she was bullied at school or that she got a C on a test, or that she got in a fight with her sister, but even so she proclaimed it had been the best day of her life. The first few times this happened, I simply smiled at her and thought her positive outlook was sweet. But as I got to know Kate and watched her deal with everyday challenges, I became more and more impressed by the depth of her joy. It naturally exuded from her, typically in the form of song. She would sing in the morning, in the car, doing homework, in the evening. She filled the whole house with music and lightened the mood as Paul and I did our everyday chores. (Her goal is to be on *American Idol* and with her incredible voice, it is seriously a possibility!)

Shortly into her stay with us, Kate's father became sick. It was hard for Kate, as her family was hours away, yet she remained strong and showed Paul and I a faith that humbled our own. One evening, though, when Kate and I were chatting as she helped me make spaghetti for dinner, she told me that her father had had another heart attack. As her eyes filled with tears, she shared that she was scared for his life and that it was very hard being this far away from her family. A little later, as we enjoyed some ice cream together, I asked her if today really had been the best day of her life even though she had so many difficult things to handle. She looked at me as though it was an odd question to ask and replied, "Yes, it's the best day of my life because I am living it right now."

I mulled over her reply for a few days, wondering if it really could be that simple. As I continued to watch Kate excel at school, deal with the ups and downs of her father's health, and sing through every situation she encountered, I realized that she truly understood the way to have true joy. Not the jump-up-and-down, laugh-out-loud kind of joy, but the kind that comes from knowing today is a gift—one that needs to be lived to the fullest.

After six months, Kate's time with us drew to a close. "All right, Kate," I called up the stairs on her last day, "do you have everything packed?"

"Yep! I'm ready to go!" She had her backpack on and a smile spread across her face. But slowly her smile turned into a pout. "I'm really gonna miss you both."

"I know, we'll miss you too. But we'll see you in a few weeks at Paul's training conference."

"Yeah! I can't wait to sing at it! And then I'll see you in Boston at the National Down Syndrome Conference in a few months!"

We said our goodbyes, which felt much more like see-you-laters since we knew that this friendship would continue long after she moved out of our home. It was a bittersweet day, but we all knew it was also the best day—because we were living it right then.

● ● ●

Jenni has over fourteen years experience working with children and adults with special needs. Currently, she is the Executive Director for GiGi's Playhouse Inc., Down syndrome awareness centers (www.gigisplayhouse.org). She is also the Production Director for Special Gifts Theatre, directing plays put on by children who have special needs (www.specialgiftstheatre.com). Jenni and her husband, Paul, run the Disability Ministry at their church and plan to continue opening their home for adult foster care and/or special needs adoption. She dedicates her story to Diane Murawski and JJ Johnson.

Karen and Sydney Bigger

69.
The Big Win

By Karen L. Bigger

MARCH 4TH, 2001. Race day. NASCAR was in town, and my husband, John, and I had tickets for the big race.

Around six o'clock in the morning the telephone rang; our older son Joel was calling to tell us his baby girl had finally arrived. "Kelley and I talked it over and decided that you all should just go ahead and go to the race," he said. I had a fleeting thought that this was a strange remark. Of course we would go to the race—this was to be my first time attending a Winston Cup race, and our younger son,

Ryan, had paid almost $100 per ticket for himself, his dad, and me. Of *course* we would go to the race!

The racetrack was bursting with carnival-like atmosphere. The exquisitely painted cars roared with supercharged power and the robust fans echoed that roar with exuberance. Ryan bought a little teddy bear with "I LOVE NASCAR" printed on its little T-shirt for the new baby. The day was beautiful, despite an earlier threat of rain, the cars were fast, and we were soon to meet our very first new grandchild. Could anything possibly be any better?

After the sounds of deafening engines and screeching tires slowly faded and the victorious driver made his way to victory lane, it was finally time to go and meet our new granddaughter.

We found our way to the hospital without too much trouble, and paused by the information desk to inquire about Kelley's room number. Before the receptionist could respond, Kelley and Joel came walking down the hallway. A sense of urgency belied Joel's stoic attempt at a calm exterior. "The baby has Down syndrome," he said. "And she was born with a serious heart defect."

Those last two words horrified me. Of course I knew what Down syndrome was and what some of the implications could be, but I didn't care one bit if my little grand baby had an extra chromosome. I just worried about her health. Since I myself had experienced the loss of a child years before, only twelve hours after he was born, the only thing that mattered to me was having a sweet baby to take home and hold onto and cherish and love. But a heart defect. The perfect little girl we had dreamed of had a *heart defect*. Joel reassured me that the problem would be rectified with surgery, but I was still extremely concerned.

Since Sydney had been transferred to Children's Hospital shortly after birth, I informed Kelley that we'd have to leave soon because we were anxious to meet our granddaughter. "You don't have to," she said, with a touch of melancholy in her voice. My heart broke for her as she struggled with the idea that her baby might not be worthy of our full affection and interest.

I wanted to reassure her and make everything better, but I realized that her grief was her own and that she'd deal with it in her own time. So I simply answered, "Of course we have to—she's our grand-daughter. But more importantly, we *want* to."

Joel had chosen to stay with Kelley, rather than follow the ambulance to Children's Hospital, because he knew that Sydney was in good hands and he felt that his wife truly needed him by her side right then. He walked over and gave me a huge hug. "It'll be okay," I said gently.

He replied, "I guess you guys are old pros at this kind of thing, huh?" He was referring to the fact that our younger son had been di-agnosed with neuroblastoma, a rare form of cancer, when he was only two. For a brief moment Joel was my little boy again, and I put aside my own fears to embrace him with all the power a protective mother feels for her child. When he stepped back I saw a new strength and determination in his face as he reassumed the role of father.

But as we made our way across town to Children's Hospital, I sat in silent fear, my thoughts racing as fast as the NASCAR automobiles had raced only a couple of hours earlier. What if Sydney had taken a turn for the worse? What if she didn't make it? My heart was breaking as each new tragic scenario tormented my mind. Would she be tiny and fragile looking, possibly hooked up to numerous wires and moni-tors? Would it be painfully apparent that she was near death?

After we finally reached the NICU, had our ID's made, and donned our hospital garb, the door to the nursery was opened. Ly-ing in an incubator just a few feet away, amid several tiny preemies, was the most beautiful child I had ever seen. The rest of the world blurred into nonexistence as I stared into the ebony eyes of this gor-geous, healthy-looking, eight-pound-plus baby girl, looking huge in comparison to the other babies in the room. Her hair was as dark as her eyes, which squinted in apparent but adorable anger as I stroked her silky little arm. I asked her nurse how she was doing and she as-sured me that she was doing well. She then added, "She shows signs of Down syndrome."

"I know," I replied calmly. I embraced that diagnosis because it was a part of this precious little child who had suddenly become the most important person in my life. I couldn't tell if I loved Sydney so fiercely in spite of the diagnosis, or because of it. Most amazingly, my fears for her heart defect became much less pronounced as I sensed a certain strength in her being, much like the strength I'd seen in her Daddy's eyes only a few minutes earlier.

In the following days, as Sydney remained in the NICU, I found myself unable to stay away from her bedside. Each morning I would tell myself that I wouldn't go to visit that day, but before the day was over I would be there, touching her, talking to her, and reassuring myself that she was just as healthy as she had been the day before. Then one day, the nurse said the magical words, "Would you like to hold her?" I was ecstatic! The nurse laid her in my arms and, if it was at all possible, I loved her even more as her warm little body snuggled contentedly in my lap for the first time.

Soon after Sydney was released from the hospital, seemingly in good health but with orders to see a cardiologist, her mom had to return to work and my tiny granddaughter became my constant companion during the day, five days a week. The cardiologist diagnosed her with a large ventricular septal defect (VSD) and a couple of other minor heart problems that would be addressed during surgery. He advised us to keep an eye on her and let her gain weight, and said he'd schedule her surgery as soon as her breathing became labored. I delighted in holding her for hours at a time and rocking her to sleep, then diligently watching over her as she slept. Her sweet beauty constantly held my attention and I took many photographs to lock my time with her in my memory. I even painted her portrait as a surprise for Kelley and Joel.

Just a couple short months after Sydney was born, the time for her heart surgery was upon us. I wrestled back and forth between the idea that I desperately wanted to be with her during her surgery and recovery and the fact that I just couldn't bear to see her lying in the hospital, hurting and sick. As a mom, I'd spent many hours in PICU at UCLA Medical Center with Ryan after his cancer surgery and then during his subsequent radiation therapy and numerous checkups. That was my duty as a parent and I gladly accepted it, but now I was the Grandma. Did I have to relive that very difficult time in my life with my beloved granddaughter?

I reluctantly explained to Kelley and Joel about the feelings I was having and they totally understood; in fact, they may even have been a little relieved. This was a time for their family to endure together and for me to stay at home and wait for happy reports of Sydney's successful surgery and relatively uneventful recovery. Of course, that was easier said than done. On the day of the surgery, I stayed very close to the phone, enduring increasing worry and dread as time passed between each call, then releasing sighs of relief as bits of good news arrived.

Within a few weeks, Sydney was back in my arms with a nicely repaired heart, and nothing to show for her traumatic journey but a scar on her chest. We picked up where we left off, with Sydney in my care during her mother's working hours. That arrangement continued until Sydney was old enough to begin school, and she still loves to come to "Cowma's" house whenever she can. We have definitely bonded for life.

Sydney is now eight years old. She and her little sister, Olivia, both have their own rooms at my house, complete with brightly colored decor, dozens of stuffed animals, and numerous toys, books, and games. Sydney especially loves putting together jigsaw puzzles and finding objects in "look and find" books with Grandpa and me looking on. Another of her favorite pastimes is playing baseball in the living room with me as the pitcher and her as the batter. She's becoming quite the little hitter, although my pitching needs definite improvement. I've set up her favorite game sites on my computer and she delights in logging on by herself and sharing her computer skills with me by proudly announcing each new accomplishment. My favorite times are when she snuggles into my lap, looks at me adoringly, and with a big smile says, "Cowma, I'm your Punkins."

How ironic that I worried so about Sydney's heart defect when her strong little heart knows how to love as well or better than anyone on this earth. She has so beautifully grown into the perfect little girl I longed for on the day of her birth. Strangely, as big a NASCAR fan as I am, I have no recollection of which car and driver first took the checkered flag that day she came into the world. But I know our family was a big winner.

•   •   •

Karen lives in Las Vegas, Nevada, with her husband and two dogs. She has two grown sons and two granddaughters: Sydney and her little sister, Olivia. She enjoys reading, painting, and spending time with family. Sydney now plays "real" baseball with Challenger Little League, a league formed especially for children with disabilities, and is becoming quite a star.

Karen and Matthew Dorsey

70.

When the Ordinary Is Extraordinary

By Karen Olsen Dorsey

MATTHEW PLACED HIS chair in the center of the room facing his audience. He sat down and cleared his throat making sure that everyone was focused on him. He held up the book and showed the cover to his audience. Then he began to read.

"*Too Many Dogs* by Lori Haskins."

He opened the book to the first page and slowly panned the room making sure that everyone could see the illustrations just like his teacher did at school.

"Big dog…Bigger dog…Biggest dog of all." He read each word clearly and made sure he showed the pictures on each page.

As he read, Matthew's growing excitement was apparent. This was his favorite book, and he knew how the story would turn out. He wanted his audience to enjoy it as much as he did. As he turned each page, his blue eyes sparkled.

"Howly dog…Growly dog." Matthew enunciated clearly and slowly. His speech therapist would be so proud of him!

"Doggies, please get OUT!" He shouted the last word because he knew that capital letters meant that he needed to give that word special emphasis.

He continued reading until the last page. Pausing for dramatic effect, Matthew read the very last word, "WOOF!"

He stood up and took a bow. The audience clapped. Matthew took another bow and received high-fives from his brother, mom, and dad. Once again, he had exceeded our expectations. Once again, we were celebrating.

While other families celebrate the special moments in their lives, they may not celebrate the ordinary moments. But we do. It all started when Matthew was born with Down syndrome. His pediatrician told us to love him and have high expectations for him, and we did. We got him the extra help that he needed, worked with him continuously, and watched him accomplish one goal after another, rejoicing each time. Matthew's older brother, Peter, loved to celebrate his brother's accomplishments, so we took his cue and began celebrating each of *his* accomplishments also. Before long, our children were celebrating what they considered to be *our* accomplishments. I would bake a cake and receive applause. Their father would play a game with them and receive high-fives.

I often think how different our lives might have been if we had not had Matthew. We would probably have taken many things for granted. Peter was our first child, and we were doting parents. We were so proud that he reached many of his milestones early and walked when he was just nine and a half months old. Looking back I now realize that we never doubted that he would reach a milestone.

We expected it to happen. We encouraged him and praised him, but most things just came easily for Peter.

When Matthew first arrived I had no idea what he would be able to accomplish. I did not know any children with special needs and knew very little about Down syndrome. I was afraid that Matthew would not be able to do the things that Peter did so naturally. When he rolled over ahead of schedule, I was surprised and relieved. When he smiled every time his big brother talked to him, I knew that they were real smiles. My heart filled with joy, and I allowed myself to have hope.

While a few things came easily for Matthew, he had to work hard to accomplish most of his goals. Praise seemed to encourage him to try again and again, especially when the physical therapist worked with him. He would often take a long nap after those strenuous workouts. I was in awe of his amazing attitude and determination. Since praise was a motivating factor for him, I became his cheerleader. His therapists became his cheerleaders too as they were captivated by this child who was so eager to please them and driven by simple praise. The line between ordinary and extraordinary began to blur.

What would be considered ordinary in most households became extraordinary in our home because of the time and effort that went into reaching each goal. Because of this, celebrating the ordinary became a way of life for our family. When other children visited our home, we didn't even think about it. They received high-fives and praise too. The look of joy and amazement on their faces reminded us that we were unique, but it also showed us that all children respond to praise. When Matthew started attending a regular preschool, he loved being with the other children. He often gave another child a high-five or told them, "Good job!" This positive approach helped him to make friends and be accepted and continues to be a part of who he is today.

Will we tone down the praise and celebrating as Matthew gets older? I guess we'll have to see. There are still many challenges ahead for Matthew, and for now we are content to live in the present moment and continue celebrating each accomplishment. But I doubt that we will ever take things for granted when it comes to Matthew.

Even though he is now ten years old and can run, jump, and climb with ease, I still remember the hours of effort that made these things possible. Just this summer at a local park, I watched Matthew play hopscotch, a skill I thought he would never master. He then skipped over to the slide, which he climbed with confidence and then swiftly slid down running off to find another adventure. *When did he master these skills*, I wondered?

As Matthew has gotten older, he has had so many goals to work on at one time that it often becomes overwhelming for me. Some things become priorities and others are put on the back-burner. We've learned that it does take a village to raise a child, especially a child with special needs. Teachers, therapists, paraprofessionals, aides, and peers have all helped Matthew along the way. When we watch Matthew and see the new skills he continues to develop, we also celebrate the many special people who have been a part of Matthew's life.

Our family has had the opportunity to celebrate a few extraordinary moments over the years. After three years in seminary, my husband was ordained as a Presbyterian Minister. That was a big moment for our family. We were surprised and delighted when Peter won the Bus Safety Poster Contest for the state of Pennsylvania. Our family got to go to Harrisburg, where Peter was presented with a trophy and honored with a tour of the capitol, a special luncheon, and an awards ceremony. He was interviewed by our local newspaper and even got his picture in the paper. Both of our boys have gotten straight A's on their report cards and won various contests over the years. They have been involved in Christmas pageants and concerts.

But despite the specialness of such moments, in our family, the ordinary moments are the most extraordinary. Like each night at dinner, when Matthew insists that we all hold hands while we say grace. When it's Matthew's turn to share one thing that he is thankful for that day, he can rarely confine himself to just one.

"Thank you for Mom, Dad, Peter, and Zoe, and my parakeets, Goldie and Gloria. Thank you for Grandma and Grandpa. Thank you for my cousins James, Jesse, Harley, Brittany, Eric, and their dog, Bella Boo. Thanks for Alexander and Cameron, Bryan, and baby Jackson.

"Thanks for my best friend, Tyler K. who plays with me at recess and wants to come over and play at my house, and for Anna who wants to marry me someday.

"Thanks for gym, which is my favorite class. Thanks for lunch. Today was hotdog day. I love hotdogs!

"Thanks for my horse, Boo. I was suppose to say 'Ride On' but I said 'Run' so we got to trot, and it was fun. Oh and thanks for SpongeBob!"

Sometimes we have to hurry him up because his list is so long, and our dinner is getting cold. But always, our hearts are warmed by Matthew's appreciation of the small joys that make life worthwhile, and we are thankful that our family celebrates the ordinary moments because it is these moments that make our lives extraordinary.

● ● ●

Karen lives in Pittsburgh, Pennsylvania, with her husband, Doug, and two sons, Peter (1993) and Matthew (1998). She is a stay-at-home mom and advocate for Matthew. She is currently the President of the Parent Networking Group, a support group for parents of children with special needs within her school district. This group promotes best practices in special education, provides an opportunity to network, and helps parents gain knowledge and keep current on relevant legislation through educational programs.

Emily and Elizabeth Pinto

71.
Elizabeth Joy

By Emily Pinto

I'D WANTED A younger sibling for as long as I could remember. When birthdays and holidays rolled around, I didn't ask for a Nintendo, a new bike, or other items that could be found on a store shelf. I wanted a little sister—someone who would love all the things I love, someone who would try to emulate her "cool big sister" the same way I had with my older sister, Micki. However, instead of complying with my wishes, my parents patiently explained why another child was just not possible. They hoped this rationale would silence my persistent requests. Unfortunately for them, an eight year-old is rarely rational. An eight year-old can't grasp conversations about "multiple miscarriages" and "the significance of being over forty years old." Disregarding these finer points, I just asked more frequently and eventually took it over my parents' heads, often praying that God would intervene and bless me with a little sister.

My prayers were answered on May 15, 1999. "This is your new sister, Elizabeth Joy," my mom whispered from her hospital bed. Knowing wholeheartedly that God's intervention had brought this addition to our family, I smiled at the tiny baby. Minutes ago, on the way to the hospital, my dad had explained that my sister was born with Down syndrome and, as a result, would take a little longer to learn and develop than "typical" kids. I wasn't sure what to make of the explanation at the time. But as I took the sleeping baby into my own arms, I was able to understand what Down syndrome truly means: Not much. Elizabeth Joy was still my baby sister, what I had wanted for so long. She was, quite appropriately, a perfect bundle of joy. And to a ten-year-old, that means everything.

Nearly a decade later, my sister still means everything to me. At the young age of nine, she reminds me every day about an important life lesson: happiness is simple, as simple as surrounding ourselves with people and things that make us happy and then basking in their presence. For Lizzy, happiness is as simple as jumping into a pile of freshly raked leaves, blowing bubbles high into the air, or having the special treat of a hot dog for dinner. Happiness is as simple as having someone to snuggle with when falling asleep at night. Lizzy constantly radiates her joy of life into my family with her spontaneous "I love you" hugs, contagious silliness, and enthusiastic good-bye kisses. I feel infinitely blessed that Lizzy was sent to my family to help us experience that joy every day. It's the glue that keeps my family together and the magic that, without fail, always brings a smile to our faces.

And that's just in a typical day.

When my family celebrates someone's birthday, Lizzy celebrates *everyone's* birthday—hugging and proclaiming "happy birthday" to each person in the room. Each vacation, holiday, and event, no matter how seemingly insignificant, is enthusiastically talked about weeks and even months before its occurrence. I love taking Lizzy on outings because there is never a dull moment when she is around—she can make a game out of anything and is never at a loss for words. In fact, it makes me laugh every time I remember Lizzy's speech delays when she was very young. She didn't start speaking in full sentences until she was four, and she hasn't stopped talking since. (I like to call those first four years the "quiet years.")

Lizzy may be making up for lost time with her constant chatter, but I don't mind. The clever things that come out of her mouth never fail to delight me and I love witnessing the progress she's making with her speech therapists. I realize that communication plays a key role in my sister's ability to connect with others and spread her joy. I am currently studying to become a speech pathologist because I know I will be fulfilled doing for others what speech therapists have done for Lizzy.

One of the most powerful ways my sister spreads her joy is through music. Whether partaking in a *High School Musical* karaoke duet, dancing to the radio, or "performing" for our family (Lizzy singing to my piano accompaniment), the happiness that comes from feeding our passion for music is mutual and something we enjoy each and every day. Music is also the one thing that enables Lizzy to lose her inhibitions and shyness. As lively as she is in the presence of people she knows, Lizzy is not one to welcome an audience of strangers. However, once music starts playing, she will forget herself and dance—whether she is on stage at a dance recital, at mass, or simply in a supermarket aisle.

Today it is easy to see my sister's positive influence on our family. I am unspeakably grateful that my parents had the grace nine years ago to see the joy my sister would bring despite the dim outlook from skeptical doctors. When Lizzy was diagnosed shortly after her birth, the medical professionals expressed their sympathies regarding an outcome that was different than they had hoped. They did not realize that this difference was something to be celebrated rather than grieved over. Yes, my sister is "different": she exudes more joy in one day than most people experience in one lifetime. And that joy is contagious. With unguarded joy, Lizzy has taught me to embrace life, always try my best, and when all else fails, dance.

● ● ●

Emily Pinto is a sophomore at Temple University, where she is studying speech pathology. She divides her time between Philadelphia and her home in south Jersey, where she lives with her parents and two sisters. Emily enjoys going home to spend time with her family and friends, especially her favorite little sister and best friend, Lizzy. Emily's hobbies include writing, photography, and spending time at the Jersey Shore.

Sarah Catherine Buzby and Madonna Dries Christensen

72.
A Child Shall Lead Me

By Madonna Dries Christensen

"WE'RE HAVING A baby," a happy couple announces.

"Wonderful. Do you want a boy or a girl?"

"It doesn't matter," they say, "as long as it's healthy."

That sentiment is well-meaning, but when a baby arrives with health problems, will the parents love him or her any less?

In 2004, my daughter and her husband were living in South Africa when their second child was prenatally diagnosed with Down syndrome. When they informed family and friends, they added,

"This baby is still a gift, just in different wrapping." We all eagerly awaited the new addition.

With an immense geographical distance between us, I could not gauge the extent of their feelings, but surely their minds eddied through a storm of emotions, fears, and questions. Still, I felt confident they could handle whatever came their way. This child, who would require open heart surgery, was in the best parental and professional hands.

My daughter went into pre-term labor at thirty-six weeks. With medication, they were able to control contractions for a week before she returned to the hospital, where Sarah was delivered by C-section. Due to difficulty breathing and eating, she remained in NICU for three weeks. At home, lacking the strength to breast- or bottle-feed, she took formula and medication through a tube and was attached to an oxygen monitor. Pride and admiration spilled over when I watched my daughter change the tube with speed and precision, causing Sarah the least amount of trauma. Soon we all relaxed and began treating her like any newborn. After three months, her cardiologist said the time had come to repair Sarah's heart. Family and friends formed a prayer circle that wrapped itself around the world via the Internet. The surgery went well, and Sarah's walnut-sized heart began functioning properly.

When Sarah was five months old, the family returned home to Virginia. My son-in-law, whose civilian job had taken them to Africa, had been mobilized with the Army Reserve to Afghanistan. Sarah was immediately enrolled in early intervention programs and she plunged into life full speed ahead. She wiggled across the floor when laid on her tummy. One could hardly hold onto her when changing her diaper. She crawled at eleven months, spoke her first word at fourteen months, and walked at eighteen months. At twenty-eight months, she shouldered a pink backpack and climbed aboard a bus to the public school's special needs class.

Unaware that she might always need to try harder, Sarah has a healthy enthusiasm for learning that moves at a pace that's right for her. Her first communication was signing, but she's now verbal. At age five, she knows the basic colors and recognizes almost any animal and imitates its sound. She counts to five alone and to ten with help. Her big sister is her favorite teacher. She sings the ABC rhyme and likes to dance and perform. She "reads" books aloud, adding "the end," on the last page. She cheers herself and others for a job well done. She has chores: feeding the dogs and carrying dishes from table to sink. Her teacher, assistant principal, and therapists agree that she's very bright. They and her parents have high expectations for her.

Sarah's upbeat personality brightens a room. Children gravitate toward her (her mother privately calls her Queen Sarah). She captivates adults with her disarming smile, her blue eyes, her corn silk blonde hair, and her sunny disposition. Well, sunny *most* of the time. Belying the myth that people with Down syndrome are always cheerful, she has a solid command of the word "no." She exerts a strong will, independence, and spunk. She knows right from wrong and sometimes gives herself a time-out. When she has a conflict with another child and tells Mommy, "I'm sorry," Mommy tells her, "Don't tell *me* you're sorry." She goes to the person with whom she tangled and makes amends.

Sarah's energy propels me to stay fit, mentally, physically, and emotionally. When my grandchildren ask me to play, I'm ready for Hide and Seek, brisk walks along the creek, fun at the playground, and romping with "Happy Horse." For mental exercise, we choose Bingo, Candy Land Castle, Sequence, jigsaw puzzles, flashcards, and books. Having children snuggle on my lap while I read aloud is as luxurious as life gets. I've also learned to slow down; to be more patient when waiting in line or when an automated telephone voice puts me on hold. If the interim music is too loud and not to my taste, I remember that all birds sing, not just those with pleasant voices. *Different* voices have a right to be heard, too.

Before Sarah, I paid scant attention to people with Down syndrome. Now I recognize beauty in their distinctive features, the mischief in their eyes; the honesty of their smiles and laughter. I chat with the young man who bags my groceries and talk about reading with the teenaged girl who shelves books at the library. I understand that people with Down syndrome want to be, and can be, productive members of society. My husband and I attend Special Olympics and cheer each athlete's performance. We participate in Buddy Walks to promote awareness of Down syndrome and raise funds for education and research, as well as in Barnes and Noble's Down Syndrome Awareness Day. Confident of Sarah's capabilities, we contribute to her college fund.

An old adage claims that children with special needs are given to special people. With no disrespect to those who believe this, I do not. I do believe that those who choose to love and nourish these children become more understanding and nurturing as a result. I admire my daughter and son-in-law's calmness and steady hands as they make decisions regarding Sarah's future, and use those skills to guide their other children. Through their example and by watching Sarah's progress, I've learned to value the lives of people of all ages, with and without visible problems. At seventy-plus, I'm blessed with being led by a healthy child who knows how to live each day to the fullest.

● ● ●

Madonna and her husband live in Sarasota, Florida, beside Worlud Pond (governed by an impressive 'gator). Their daughter and husband and three children live too far away, in Virginia. Madonna is the author of Swinging Sisters *and* Masquerade: The Swindler Who Conned J. Edgar Hoover; *the editor of* Doorways Memoirs; *and Contributing Editor to* Yesterday's Magazette *and* The Perspiring Writer. *Stop by Worlud Pond at www.madonnadrieschristensen.com.*

Lisa and Lily Huckleberry and Sophia Ross

73.

Unexpected Joy

By Lisa Huckleberry

IT'S AN ORDINARY Friday morning at home. After Lily and Sophia finish their midmorning snack, we head downstairs to play "babies." In the basement we have a great play area set up with music equipment, a slide, a child-sized kitchen, and a nursery for baby dolls. Three-year-old Sophia pretends to put her baby to sleep in the crib, while four-year-old Lily feeds her baby something "nummy." The girls are only seven months apart, and I'm often asked if they're twins. For the sake of convenience I usually answer, "No, they're friends." But they're actually much more than friends. Although Lily

and Sophia aren't related in any way, and their parents aren't married
or anything close, they live together like sisters. They share a home
and even a bedroom. The situation is quite unusual, yet wonderful:
I'm a single mom to Lily and a live-in nanny for Sophia. As I watch
the girls play, I reflect on the amazing chain of events beginning four
years ago which brought us together.

October, 2004. I hyperventilated as the nurses rushed me down
the hall to the operating room and the anesthesiologist covered my
face with the mask. A few hours before, my labor had been induced at
thirty-five weeks gestation, and I didn't know if my daughter would
be alive when I awoke from the emergency C-section. I'd found out
prenatally that she would be born with Down syndrome, and also a
heart condition that would require open heart surgery. The Non-Im-
mune Hydrops she'd developed in my last trimester gave her a 50/50
chance of surviving birth. I had already accepted her diagnosis of
Down syndrome and had weathered the grief it can entail. As a result
I had an incredibly deep bond with this baby girl, and the thought of
losing her was more than I could bear.

When I awoke from the anesthetic I felt groggy and miserable,
but all I cared about was my daughter. "Is she alive? Is she alive?" I
kept asking. And she was! That feisty little girl of mine was in critical
condition, but she was alive. She surprised all of the doctors by how
quickly she got better. In November 2004, after Lily had spent nearly
six weeks in the NICU, I was able to bring her home.

In May of 2005, another little girl with Down syndrome was
lovingly carried home from the hospital. Her name is Sophia Anna,
the daughter of Scott and Anne. I met Anne through an online support group for families with children who have Down syndrome. We
discovered we lived fairly close together, and made plans to get our
girls together someday soon. Sophia was born with the same heart
condition Lily had, and Scott and Anne ended up choosing the same
surgeon who had performed Lily's heart surgery the previous month.
Of course, Anne was scared about the heart surgery and had lots of
questions about how the procedure might impact Sophia and the rest
of the family. We emailed frequently as the surgery date approached,
with full intentions of meeting up one day after everything settled

down for both of us. Unfortunately, our visit never came to be. Not long after Sophia's surgery, Anne was diagnosed with leukemia and passed away suddenly, in February 2006. She left behind her husband, their eight-year-old daughter, Adrianna, and Sophia, who was just eight months old at the time. I was heartbroken for her family and all those who loved her so.

At the funeral viewing I met Anne's husband, Scott, and Anne's best friend, Michele. Michele had heard much about Lily and me through Anne's descriptions, and she and I felt an immediate bond of friendship. Before parting ways we exchanged email addresses, and afterward we contacted each other regularly. Sometimes Michele would write to give me updates on Scott and the girls. Although they were experiencing incredible grief, they also were trying to move forward the best they could. Michele filled me in on the new things Sophia was doing and said she was the happiest little girl in the world. Through our quick "hello" emails as well as our longer, more detailed exchanges, we kept in touch throughout the year following Anne's death.

In June of 2007, I was having some struggles in my personal and professional life. A difficult situation at work and resulting financial problems were causing me a lot of stress. It was then that Michele emailed me with a crazy idea. At the same time I was having these problems with my job, Scott was also having a rough time finding a decent nanny. Michele thought it might work out for *me* to be the nanny! Scott was looking for live-in help, which would solve my money troubles, and as a bonus Lily would have a full-time playmate. I thought the idea was a little wild—moving in and taking care of Anne's daughters. But I did want to help the family. And since I was having such turmoil at my job, this possibility almost seemed like the answer to all of my problems.

A few weeks later Scott had emailed me about the job. I still wasn't completely sure it was a good idea. It was hard enough being the mother of one child, and if I took the position I would have to handle three, including two with special needs. After much thought, and with mixed feelings, I finally picked up the phone. That began a month-long process during which Scott and I got to know each other. For several weeks we met every weekend, just to make sure we were both 100 percent committed to the plan, as it would be such a huge transition for all of us. In September, Lily and I moved in and began our new life with Sophia and her family.

Nearly one year later, Lily and I continue to enjoy sharing a home with Sophia, Adrianna, and Scott. While we certainly aren't a typical family unit, we have in many ways become like family to each other. At the end of our busy days, we sit down at the table to share dinner together, and while we do many things separately with our individual families, there are many times we all just hang out together. As unique as our situation is, I feel we live a fairly normal life. I feel everyone has tried to make the most of a situation nobody had control over, and in many ways have benefited greatly from being together. I feel especially blessed to share my life with three amazing girls.

All three girls love each other one second and are picking on each other the next, just as if they were real sisters. And Lily and Sophia provide me with ample entertainment all day, every day! While Lily and Sophia both have the same extra chromosome, they are really quite different from one another. Sophia is the lover of the two and will give you the best hugs you have ever had. At the same time, she is one tiny little fireball who is tougher than most adults I know. Sophia loves people, and loves to dance and sing. She has shoulder-length brown hair, twinkling blue eyes, and beautiful olive skin. This petite little girl brightens up any room with her smile, and will strike up a conversation with anyone because she has a lot to tell the world!

Lily is my sassy and spirited little redhead. She has long strawberry blonde hair, eyes of ocean blue, and fair skin with a few freckles. She's fairly tall for having Down syndrome. She has been well known for her mean looks and silly faces since she was a few months old, and while she can be loving and sweet when she wants to be, it's definitely on her own terms. Lily is caring and gentle with me, but she often greets others with a scowl and takes her time to warm up. She can be cold one second and blowing kisses the next. I believe it was all that feistiness and sass that kept her alive when the doctors told me she might not live.

Both Sophia and Lily have powerful, unique personalities, but add these two little girls together, and you get a force to be reckoned with! They are partners in crime and know how to play up the charm in a moment's notice. Together, they've been known to cause tons of smiles and infectious laughter in even the grumpiest of people. They have taught me to cherish the simple things in life, such as butterfly kisses and rubbing noses. They've shown me the importance of personal boundaries and respect for the fact that we all love differently. They continually remind me that not all great things happen "on time," and that greatness is not just measured in milestones achieved at whatever age doctors deem appropriate. I watch them in amazement as they persevere to learn new things, never giving up, but with incredible determination forging forward and trying again until they get it right.

It's nearly noon—time for me to start making lunch, and for the "junior" moms to feed their dolls again. Just a typical day, and yet it's full of so many blessings. I still mourn Anne's death—it surely makes no sense why someone so young should be taken away from those who needed and loved her most. I imagine it will always be the one thing that will never make sense. But as I watch Lily and Sophie tuck their "babies" in for a nap, kissing them ever so gently on the forehead, there is one thing that does make sense: The magical beauty of unexpected joy.

Dedicated to Lily and Sophia, for making this all possible, and Adrianna, for sharing your life with me and brightening my days, and in memory of Anne, who will always be loved and missed forever.

● ● ●

Lisa lives in the Midwest and is the mother of Dustin, an adult son, and Lily, a young daughter prenatally diagnosed with Down syndrome in 2004. Lisa enjoys playing the piano, writing, reading, and spending time with her family along with the two amazing girls she cares for. Lisa currently maintains a personal blog at http://mymagicalmiracle.blogspot.com.

Back row, left to right: Cynthia Cobb, Patrick, Katie, Brian.
Front row, left to right: Jessica, Kelley, Sarah, Molly.

74.

The Greatest Reward

By Cynthia Cobb

TEN ADOLESCENTS AND young adults with Down syndrome sat at the front of the room, facing the audience. It was easy to see from their excited faces that they were eager to be part of this parent network meeting for Down Syndrome Indiana. They had all prepared. It was their chance to have a voice. As a speech and language therapist for children with Down syndrome, I was quite interested to hear what my students would contribute. As the panel moderator, I could see the confidence in their faces as they beamed at me. This place and time remains a joyful milestone for me.

For twenty-five years, young people like these had enriched my life with their laughter, honesty, and kindness. On a daily basis, I have been privileged to witness an inner and outer beauty that has made me grateful for my occupation. What I have seen start out as Old MacDonald animal sounds has given way over time to singing and dancing to the chorus from Disney's *High School Musical.* As each student's command of language has increased, so has their worldly knowledge. Now, instead of identifying their country as Old Country Buffet, my students have learned the names of all fifty states. Children who once were challenged by reading their own name are now reading an adaptation of *Romeo and Juliet* for their high school English class. Their hard work, combined with training, expanded their communication skills and their world.

As the panel discussion began, I experienced with everyone else there how much bigger their worlds had truly become as a result of their years of perseverance. Each student shared with pride his or her experiences as a self-advocate. They adeptly fielded questions and talked about topics ranging from their jobs and education to experiences with family and friends, as well as their personal interests. Their responses were strictly off-the-cuff and spontaneous. Kelley read a letter from her high school strength and conditioning teacher, who recognized Kelley as "both a privilege and a pleasure" to have in class who made him "look forward to each day." Katie S. spoke about her recent accomplishments of receiving a Childhood Development Associate certificate from Ivy Tech Community College and getting a job as a teacher's aide in a preschool. Brian talked about winning the Volvo for Life Friendship Award with his best buddy Brad. He added, though, that the most important thing he had won was a friend.

It was heartwarming to listen to them speak, but not surprising. Over the years, I'd noticed many of my students' unique appreciation for life's rewards, both great and small, and this night they were continuing to help others develop the same life-rewards attitude. As the panel discussion continued, Molly proudly announced that she recently won "tons" of medals for state and national Special Olympics swimming. Jessica shared that she's a happy young woman with a good job and loving family, but made it clear she works at staying busy socially. Patrick stated he wants to improve his computer skills, as he hopes to become a "businessman" and take over his dad's business. Katie C. talked about her work at Community Hospital and the importance of focusing on "ability and not disability." Sarah made the audience laugh when she shared that her favorite foods are prepared by her father, as her mother rarely cooks.

The enthusiastic applause as the panel discussion ended provided the very much deserved validation my students had merited. They smiled radiantly at the praise. Needless to say, I was extremely proud of them and every good thing they had worked so diligently to achieve. Over the course of two hours, the audience had been treated to laughter and tears as they witnessed, firsthand, the wit and perseverance of these inspiring self-advocates. For all the rewards they had cherished in their lives, helping them develop and improve communication skills so they could share the richness of their accomplishments with others was my greatest reward of all. They are my joy.

● ● ●

Cynthia, a speech-language pathologist (www.spscarmel.com), lives in Carmel, Indiana, with her husband, Steve. She has served on the DSI Board of Directors, speaks at conventions and parent support meetings, supports the Buddy Walk, and hosts student socials. She has over twenty-five years of experience working with individuals with Down syndrome.

Travis and Christena Gunther

75.

My Favorite Brother, His Name Is Travis

By Christena Gunther

WHEN MY ONLY brother was born a month premature in 1987, I was heartbroken. Not because he had Down syndrome (that was something unusual since it was a nice big word that meant he, and therefore I, was special), but because he was a boy. My three-year-old heart was set on having a baby sister whom I could teach about fashion and *Sesame Street,* and could be named my all-time favorite name: Jennifer. One of my earliest memories is trying to persuade my parents to change my brother's name from Travis to Jennifer, but they gently convinced me that Travis was a better name for a boy. Although disappointed, I rallied my strength and became determined to accept my brother's gender and love him anyway. It turned out that loving him didn't require much effort on my part.

Once Travis learned to talk he started singing, and he hasn't really stopped since. His greatest ballad, "The Best Sister/Brother Song," is one we wrote together more than fifteen years ago. Intended to be sung by Travis and me in unison, the lyrics may vary, but go something like this:

My favorite sister
Her name is Christena
She's the cutest button (tap sister's nose)
In the world
Because she's my sister.

(Repeat several times, getting more dramatic each time. If necessary, insert funny names, such as Jennifer, to lighten the mood.)

Now that we're both adults, Travis and I talk almost every day on the phone despite our nearly 1,000-mile separation. Living in New York City can be discouraging at times, especially in the dreary winter, and hearing his jubilant voice on my cell phone as I navigate the crowded sidewalks warms my heart and brings joyful tears to my eyes. When I'm unable to answer, he leaves me messages—often the "Best Sister Song" sung with some improvisational twists, or other songs he has spontaneously composed that express his love and/or compliment my beauty, intellect, popularity, and hair. I have several of these messages saved to listen to if I need to hear his happy voice at any moment.

Travis shares his uplifting talents with others as well. With his finely tuned hug radar, he senses when someone requires cheering up, and intuitively reaches out to him or her—although this radar does not extend to strangers or newly formed acquaintances, since he takes the "no talking to strangers" rule very seriously. After the untimely death of Bud, a close friend, neighbor, and employer (Travis faithfully retrieved the mail for their family every day), Travis reached out in love to Bud's family. After several bear hugs and silent, soulful moments, Travis instinctively and solemnly counseled them to "remember the good times and not to think of the bad because he's in heaven now." He shared memories of eating ice cream sandwiches with Bud on balmy summer evenings, and reminded them of the time Bud had kissed his cheek, causing extreme embarrassment. He recalled Bud's laughter at his wife, Hazel's, funny jokes. Bud's daughter later told me how moved she was by Travis's support and encouragement.

Singing and hugging aren't Travis's only gifts, either. For more than half of his life, he has been drawing, painting, and creating art in his office (where he has a placard that reads "Travis Gunther, The Boss"). Some of this art is for the "art factory" he hopes to build in a blighted part of the city where he lives, but much of it he creates to give to others. Many of his pieces begin as sheets from legal pads, on which he draws small squares with smiling faces inside of them, adding bright colors to each square.

Travis sends these pieces to friends and family members to brighten our days, and when visiting sometimes brings two boxes full of drawings for my husband and me (he certainly is prolific). One of the pieces that garnered much attention (and even an award from VSA arts) was a portrait featuring his muse. This painted collage depicted a Medusa-like girl with long and wild brown hair that closely resembles how I look in the morning. In fact, it's titled *Sister Waking Up*. This piece in particular showcases Travis's genuine artistic ability, but just as importantly, it makes people smile. On several occasions Travis has seriously stared at me with his bright blue eyes and said he wants his art to bring happiness to people who are sad because it is his "commission in life." He consistently fulfills that commission with his talent and humor.

I never did get that baby sister I wanted, but in hindsight I'm relieved. Growing up with Travis has been the greatest gift a big sister could ask for, and I cannot fathom my life without my best friend and biggest supporter. While we've certainly had our disagreements (there was that time he threw my toothbrush out of our second-story bathroom window, but perhaps it was provoked), Travis exudes joy with every breath he takes. In my bleakest moments when I cannot bear to talk to anyone else, I call Travis, who will share his love for life with such ease—completely without judgment or question—and sing me songs to enliven and refresh my spirit.

I am going to go call him right now.

● ● ●

Christena's only brother, Travis, was born with Down syndrome in 1987. She has her B.A. in Art History and French from the University of Wisconsin-Madison, and her M.A. in Visual Arts Administration from New York University. Christena and her husband live in New York City, where she strives to make a major art museum accessible to visitors with disabilities. Christena and Travis are big supporters of VSA arts. Visit www.vsarts.org for more information.

Hannah Walker, Sandra Walker, Jessica Walker

76.
A Precious Gift

By Sandra Walker

TODAY I AM feeling sorry for myself. It is one of those days at the end of a long summer when we all need to get out of the house. But where to go? What to do? The beach is nearby, but shoving that wheelchair through the sand and then hoisting Jessica over the logs is more than my back can bear today. The local theater is offering free family movies this morning…but would Hannah be able to handle the volume? Somehow that extra chromosome translates into extra sensitivity where noise is concerned. My mind flashes back to a dear friend's observation, "It's not just our kids who are disabled; it's our whole family." Yes, today *I* feel disabled.

But Hannah is feeling fine, and she wakes up today like every other day, with the same burning question on her mind, "Where are we going today, Mom?"

We decide on the library. Ah, the library...computers, books, music, movies...what more could a child ask for? And our library boasts an added feature: a nearby pond stocked with fish that is home to about a dozen amiable ducks. Hannah hits the doors of the library with purpose. Head down, feet flying, stay-out-of-my-way-I'm-headed-for-the-computers purpose. Jessica and I take a detour to the book drop and the reserved books shelf. When we find Hannah in the children's section, she is in tears. The only computer not occupied is out of service. The world is coming to an end. Yes, today *I* feel disabled.

We check out the reserved books I have in my hand and then check out of the library as quickly as possible. I remind Hannah that the ducks are waiting for us and suddenly the world is in motion again, spinning on a simple, familiar pleasure. She grabs the bread from the van and places it on Jessica's lap. "Here, Jessa, you carry the bread." Then she grabs the handles of Jessica's wheelchair with her chubby little hands and heads off across the parking lot with purpose. Head down, feet flying, stay-out-of-my-way-I'm-headed-for-the-pond purpose.

Without warning, she stops. She has spotted them: a group of women with all their earthly belongings sitting on the lawn next to the pond. She alters her course before I realize what she is doing. I try and grab the reins of the wheelchair to steer her away, but I am too late.

"Oh, hi!" she yells, as though these strangers are long-lost friends. Hannah greets everyone she meets in this manner. Furrowed brows, turned heads, muted voices mean nothing to her. If need be, she can carry on a conversation with herself indefinitely, and eventually she always finds someone willing to chitchat.

But there is no hesitation from these new friends. They wave and welcome Hannah with mutual unhesitating fervor, surprised to have been approached at all.

"I'm Hannah and this is my sister, Jessica." She gracefully extends both of her hands toward her sister as though she were introducing the First Lady. "Smile, Jessa." Jessica always obliges this request and the beauty of that smile is worth the thousands of words she has locked up inside her.

"And this is Mom," Hannah continues without missing a beat.

"Hi," is all I can get out before she's on to the next important subject.

Hannah plops herself down next to one woman's bags. She is on her usual fact-finding mission. Favorite colors, birthdates, and pet's names usually top the list of Hannah's must-know items. The women's responses come with some hesitation. It has been a while since anyone asked them about favorite colors. It has been a while since anyone even sat down to talk with them.

I lean against the wheelchair and watch my daughter with amazement. Those clear blue eyes, that contagious laughter, the innocent heart overflowing with love and acceptance...these are the priceless gifts Hannah offers free of charge to anyone who will but accept them.

Then, just as suddenly as she came, she is ready to go. "The ducks are waiting for me," she announces importantly as she gets to her feet.

One woman reaches into her bag and pulls out a loaf of bread. She hands it to Hannah. "Would you like this?"

I open my mouth to protest, realizing that a loaf of bread represents several meals for this woman. But fortunately, my daughter is quicker than I am with a response. She snatches the bread out of her new friend's hand and presses it close to her heart. "I LOVE bread," she replies sincerely. A smile breaks across the woman's face and the creases that have dominated her face for so long seem to melt away with the morning sunshine. Her whole body relaxes and she nods her head over and over as if to affirm what has taken place in these few short minutes. I sense it's been a long time since this woman has been able to give a gift to anyone—much less such a precious gift to such a precious child.

With a quick wave, my daughter is off, running up the path to talk with some more friends, the ducks. She is completely unaware of the magnitude of what transpired today—the gifts that were given and received. But I snatch a glance back at the women still stationed on the grass and I know they understand.

Yes, today *I* was disabled. I was blind, but my eyes have been opened by a simple act of unpretentious kindness. I was lame, but my feet have been borne along a path of compassion that few will ever discover. My heart was broken, but my daughter has bound it together with the cords of love.

● ● ●

Sandra and her husband, James, live in the Seattle area. They have three children: James (1994), Jessica (1995), and Hannah (1998). Before having children, Sandra was an elementary school teacher for nine years. Now, as a stay-at-home mom of three children—two with special needs—she spends a lot of time advocating for each of them. She also enjoys writing, singing, watching her son play the drums, dancing with her daughters, and playing with the crabs at the beach.

Kathryn Lynard Soper with her son, Thomas

About the Editor

● ● ●

KATHRYN LYNARD SOPER is the mother of seven children. Her youngest, Thomas, born in 2005, was diagnosed with Down syndrome at birth. She's the author of a memoir about Thomas, **The Year My Son and I Were Born**, and the editor of two other anthologies, **Gifts** and **The Mother in Me**. She is president of The Segullah Group, Inc., a nonprofit organization that produces personal writings, and editor-in-chief of *Segullah*, a literary journal by and for Latter-day Saint (Mormon) women. Kathryn lives with her husband, Reed, and their children in the mountain west.